ENCYCLOPEDIA OF
BRITISH
HISTORY

ENCYCLOPEDIA OF
BRITISH
HISTORY

PHILIP STEELE

MILES KELLY
PUBLISHING

This edition first published in 2003
(originally published in larger format, 2001)
by Miles Kelly Publishing Ltd
Bardfield Centre, Great Bardfield, Essex CM7 4SL

Copyright © Miles Kelly Publishing Ltd 2001

24681097531

PROJECT MANAGER:
Kate Miles

DESIGNER:
John Christopher/White Design

PICTURE RESEARCH:
Ruth Boardman

REFERENCING:
Liberty Newton

PRODUCTION:
Estela Godoy

COLOUR REPRODUCTION:
DPI Colour

British Library Cataloguing-in-Publication Data
A catalogue record for this book is available
from the British Library

ISBN 1-84236-360-3

Printed in Singapore

www.mileskelly.net
info@mileskelly.net

CONTENTS

INTRODUCTION

THIS BOOK helps you to travel back in time. You can find out how people used to live long ago, about the way they worked and played, and the kind of societies in which they lived. It is the story of you, your parents, their parents and countless generations before them.

New technologies may speed up social and economic change. Charles Babbage's mechanical calculating machine preceded the electronic computer by a hundred years.

TIME TRAVEL

A period of 1,000 years may be hard to imagine. Perhaps it is easier to imagine your grandmother living to be a hundred years old. Ten of her lives going back in a row would take you to the days before the Normans invaded the British Isles. Another ten would take you back to the days when Celtic chieftains rode into battle on chariots. Another twenty would take you back to the age when the great pillars were being raised at Stonehenge.

MANY PEOPLES, MANY STORIES

The islands of Great Britain and Ireland have never been home to a single people. There has been invasion and settlement over many thousands of years and the modern population is a mixture of English, Irish, Welsh, Scots, Jews, Roma, Asians, Africans, Caribbeans, as well as peoples from all over Europe. When did their ancestors arrive in the British Isles and why? What kind of nations have they built up?

HOW HISTORY IS MADE

In this book you can see how England, Scotland, Wales and Ireland came into being, how the United Kingdom and the Republic of Ireland were formed, how parliaments limited the power of kings and queens, how ordinary people won the right to vote in elections or work for a fair wage.

These stories are often exciting, dramatic tales, as are the power struggles between royal families or nations. Individuals can play a crucial part in history, but the real driving force which sweeps them along is economics – the way in which people use the environment and organize work

Palaeontologists search rocks for the fossilized remains of prehistoric plants and animals.

and reward. Social organization depends on economics and can be changed by people campaigning or grouping together to form or oppose government. That is called politics. It is the story of Roman Britain, of England in the Middle Ages, of the Civil War, of the rise and fall of the British empire. It is the story of Britain and Ireland today.

LESSONS TO BE LEARNED

History is more than just a series of battles, tales or dates to be learned. By studying the way in which human society has developed in the past, we can understand the real forces that shape our society today and can plan for the future, too.

Study of the past might help us to avoid future conflict or war. It might help us to understand why populations rise and fall, or learn lessons about caring for the environment. An understanding of history is the key to social change.

FINDING OUT

How do we know what really happened long ago? Since people began to keep records of events, we have written documents – letters, accounts, agreements, newspapers and history books. These are very useful, but we must always remember that the people who win a battle will tell a different account of it than the loser, and that writers do not always tell the truth. Other evidence may be set in stone. In the British Isles there are still many ancient buildings and monuments, and these reveal a great deal about life long ago.

Archaeologists excavate ancient sites. They examine human remains, and can often tell from these what food was eaten, what work people did, what illnesses they suffered from and even what the climate was like at that time. Modern science allows us to date material with ever greater accuracy. The past may be a lost world, but we are forever learning more about it.

HOW TO USE THIS BOOK

This book is divided into seven chapters, each dealing with a different historical period in Britain and Ireland. At the beginning of each chapter you can see what was happening in other parts of the world at the same time. Along the top of each page runs a timeline of events.

At the end of the book you will find a list of places to visit and another list of useful websites.

The glossary explains some of the more difficult words to be found in the book. Look in the index if you are searching for a particular subject.

Travel back 4,000 years with a visit to Stonehenge, in Wiltshire, England.

1

THE ANCIENT ISLANDS

500,000BC–700BC

THE WORLD AT A GLANCE

ELSEWHERE IN EUROPE

c12,000 BC
Cave paintings in France and northern Spain

c7200 BC
Dugout canoes are being made in the Netherlands

c6500 BC
Farming reaches the Balkan peninsula from Asia

c3200 BC
Wheeled vehicles in use in Eastern Europe

c2300 BC
Start of the European Bronze Age

c1900 BC
Rise of Minoan civilization on the island of Crete, palaces and script

c1400 BC
Rise of Mycenaean civilization in southern Greece, walled citadels

c900 BC
Rise of Etruscan civilization in northern Italy, fine statues

ASIA

10,500 BC
Pottery being made in southern Japan

c8350 BC
Foundation of Jericho, the world's oldest known walled city

c6400 BC
The wheel is invented in Mesopotamia, in the Middle East

c6250 BC
Town of Çatal Hüyük is founded, southern Turkey

c3,250 BC
Writing is invented in Mesopotamia

c2500 BC
Rise of civilization in Indus valley, at Mohenjo-Daro and Harappa

c2300 BC
Sargon of Akkad founds first Asian empire

c1500 BC
Shang emperors rule China, slaves, bronze weapons, silk

AFRICA

c12,000 BC
Grindstones used for making flour from wild seeds

c8500 BC
Start of rock art in the Sahara region, which was still fertile

c7500 BC
Decorated pottery being made in the Sahara region

c6000 BC
Start of farming in the Nile valley, Egypt

c4000 BC
Sailing boats being used in Egypt

2530 BC
The Great Pyramid is raised at Giza in Egypt

1325 BC
Egypt's young ruler, Tutankhamun, is buried in the Valley of the Kings

c1000 BC
Growth of the kingdom of Kush, in southern Nubia

"The earliest history of Britain and Ireland is written in stone, bone, wood and clay…"

beaker pottery

NORTH AMERICA

c18,000 BC
One of several possible dates for the first peopling of the Americas

c16,800 BC
Possible date of tools found at Cactus Hill site in Virginia

c5000 BC
Maize is being grown in Mexico

c2300 BC
Earliest pottery in Central America

c2000 BC
A wave of Inuit migrations through the Arctic region

c1200 BC
Olmec civilization in Central America, carved stone and temples

c1000 BC
Rise of Adena culture in eastern woodlands of USA, burial mounds

c800 BC
Zapotec civilization in Mexico, first writing in the Americas

SOUTH AMERICA

c12,500 BC
Possible date for human occupation of Monte Verde, Chile

c8600 BC
Beans, gourds and peppers are grown in Peru

c3500 BC
Llamas are being used as pack animals, to transport goods

c3200 BC
Maize is first grown in South America

c3200 BC
Dead bodies made into mummies, Chile

c2800 BC
Villages built in the Amazon river basin

c2500 BC
Cloth is woven using looms, irrigation of fields

c1500 BC
The first metal-working in Peru

c900 BC
Rise of Chavín civilization in the Andes, stone temples

OCEANIA

c50,000 BC
Aborigines settle in Australia, migrating from Southeast Asia

c28,500 BC
Humans settle the land now known as New Guinea

c10,000 BC
New wave of Aboriginal settlement in Australia, tame dogs

c7000 BC
Taro root is grown as a food crop in New Guinea

c5000 BC
Rising sea levels, New Guinea and Tasmania become islands

c1500 BC
Ancestors of the Polynesians start to migrate eastwards across the Pacific Ocean by canoe

c1000 BC
Stone settlements built in southeastern Australia

c1000 BC
Polynesian ancestors reach Tonga and Samoa

❋ c500,000 BC
Homo erectus living in
western Europe

❋ c250,000 BC
Neanderthal people living in
western Europe

❋ c70,000 BC
Start of the last great Ice Age.
Britain is frozen north of the
Thames valley

❋ c59,000 BC
A warmer period, called an
interglacial interrupts the
Ice Age

❋ c37,000 BC
Another interglacial period
affects northern Europe

THE LONELY HUNTERS

THE British Isles are a group of small islands lying in shallow waters off the northwestern coast of Europe. The two largest islands are called Great Britain and Ireland. Today these lands are green, with a moist and mild climate. Fifteen thousand years ago, they were in the grip of Arctic weather conditions. Great Britain was roamed by reindeer and bears and by prehistoric hunters. It was still part of the European mainland and the River Thames flowed into the Rhine. There were no villages or towns and humans were very few and far between. The population of the whole world in 15,000 BC was probably about the same as that of Scotland today.

THE OLD STONE AGE

The earliest period of settlement in Britain is called the Palaeolithic ('Old Stone') Age. Tools and weapons were made of chipped and flaked stone, bone and wood.

Flints were used to make knives, axes and spearheads.

Flint scrapers could be used to scrape the flesh off the hides of wild animals.

Herds of woolly mammoth were hunted during the Ice Age in northern Europe and Asia. They were a kind of elephant which had adapted to cold weather conditions.

THE 'RED LADY' OF PAVILAND

In 1823 a man called William Buckland discovered a skeleton in a cave on the Gower peninsula in South Wales. He thought it was that of a Roman lady. Because it was covered in red ochre (a type of earth) the find became known as the 'Red Lady' of Paviland. Modern scientists now know that the skeleton was actually that of a young man who had been alive in about 24,000 BC.

 The Paviland burial was carried out with great care. The pouring of red ochre on to the body tells us that people at this time carried out funeral ceremonies and must have believed in gods or spirits.

During the Old Stone Age, people became more and more skilled at making weapons of stone, bone and wood.

THE FIRST INHABITANTS

We do not know when the first human-like creature known as *Homo erectus* ('upright man') first appeared in the British Isles, but most European remains date from 500,000–200,000 years ago. Some finds from this period may be very early ancestors of humans. At times the hunters were driven away from Britain by severe Ice Ages. However during warmer periods called interglacials ('between the ice'), they returned.

IN THE BEGINNING

We find out about human-like creatures and early ancestors of humans by studying the remains of fossilized bones and stone tools.

✳ **c350,000 years ago**
Site: Boxgrove, Sussex, England
Type: *Homo erectus* or very early human

✳ **c250,000 years ago**
Site: Swanscombe, Kent, England
Type: human ancestor

✳ **c230,000 years ago**
Site: Pontnewydd cave, northeast Wales
Type: Neanderthal

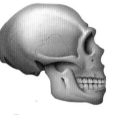

Neanderthal people were living in Britain by 250,000 years ago. They were short and stocky. They had probably died out by about 30,000 years ago. Some may have intermarried with true humans.

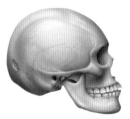

True humans – people just like us – did not appear in Europe until about 35,000 years ago. They lived by hunting and by gathering shellfish, berries and roots. The scientific name for a true human is Homo sapiens ('wise man').

LIFE IN THE OLD STONE AGE

Between about 35,000 and 8500 BC, the peoples of western Europe learned to produce fine tools and weapons. They were nomadic hunters and used every part of the animals they killed – meat for food, skins to make clothes and cloaks, gut to make thread, bone to make needles and other tools, fat to make grease and lamp fuel. They took shelter in caves or made tents of hide and timber. They made marvellous paintings of wild animals on the walls of caves and studied the stars.

12

❋ c8500 BC
Start of the Middle Stone Age
in the British Isles

❋ c8300 BC
Melting of the last glaciers
in Britain

❋ c8000 BC
New waves of hunters cross
into Britain from the European
mainland

❋ c7600 BC
Star Carr in Yorkshire has a
population of about 250

❋ c7600 BC
A wooden paddle from Star
Carr, first evidence of boats in
Britain

THE RISING SEA

ALONG the western coasts of Wales, Cornwall, the Scilly Isles and Brittany, there are ancient folk tales of lands lost beneath the sea. It could be that these are distant memories of real floods, for between 8000 and 3000 BC sea levels rose rapidly. As the climate warmed, the water expanded, spilling over coastal plains and filling channels. By about 6500 BC the strip of land joining England to mainland Europe had been swallowed up by the sea for the last time.

THE RIDDLE OF THE SNAKES

Why are there no snakes in Ireland? An old tale claims that snakes were banished by a miracle carried out by St Patrick, the Christian saint. In fact, snakes entered Britain when it was still linked to France by a strip of land. However Ireland was already an island at that time, and snakes could not swim across the Irish Sea.

THE MIDDLE STONE AGE

New forests of birch, hazel and pine soon blanketed the warmer British Isles. As it became still warmer, oak, ash and elm spread far and wide. The human population increased and spread northwards through Britain. Hunters now crossed by boat from Scotland into Ireland. Tools and weapons were still of stone, bone or wood, but were made with much greater precision. This period is known as the Mesolithic ('Middle Stone') Age.

After the mammoths had gone, people learned how to hunt smaller animals such as deer. Hunters camped on high ground to spy out the dense forests, or by lakes and shores which offered a good supply of fresh fish.

❀ c7600 BC
Skull of dog at Star Carr, first evidence of tame animals in Britain

❀ c6500 BC
Rising sea levels make Great Britain an island

❀ c6000 BC
Settlements on the east coast of Ireland

❀ c5000 BC
Oak forest, spreading north since 11,000 BC, now covers most of Europe

❀ c3000 BC
Climate stops becoming warmer; end of coastal flooding

13

STAR CARR SETTLERS

A typical encampment from about 7600 BC has been found at Star Carr in Yorkshire, England. It was built in birch forest beside a lake and boggy land along the River Derwent. The settlement was home to about 250 people, with a territory of about 25 square kilometres. The people of Star Carr killed red deer, boar, elk and big wild cattle called aurochs. They paddled canoes and wore head-dresses made of deer antlers.

HUNTING WITH DOGS

Middle Stone Age hunters used harpoons, fish hooks, bows and arrows. Many weapons were fitted with tiny, razor-sharp flints called microliths. The hunters tamed dogs and used them for chasing red deer.

Rising sea levels made Great Britain an island. This would affect its history in many ways for the next 8500 years.

✸ c9000 BC
Farming begins in southwest
Asia and spreads westwards

✸ c5000 BC
Farming skills reach parts of
western Europe

✸ c4500 BC
Start of the New Stone Age
in the British Isles

✸ c4000 BC
Farming spreads through the
British Isles

✸ c3840 BC
A timber trackway is laid
down across marshy land
in Somerset, England

THE FIRST FARMERS

The first wheat crops needed improving, to produce better yields of grain. Farmers did this by only choosing seed from the very best plants.

The first sheep in Britain were tough and wiry creatures, rather like today's Soay breed.

FEW discoveries changed the way people lived more than farming. In southwest Asia, grain crops were being grown and sheep were being raised as early as 9000 BC. Farming soon spread into North Africa and westwards across Europe. It was first brought to southern Britain by invaders and traders from the European mainland, about 6000 years ago. They brought with them seed for planting and livestock.

A SETTLED LIFE

People no longer had to live as nomads, hunting for their food. They could settle in one place, building permanent villages and storing up grain for future use. They could exchange any extra produce for other goods. In the Old Stone Age, every man, woman and child had been a food producer. Now, a surplus of food allowed some people to specialise as traders, craft workers, labourers – or rulers.

❀ c3500 BC
Simple wooden ploughs being used in the south of England

❀ c3200 BC
New Stone Age settlement at Skara Brae, Orkney

❀ c3000 BC
Grimes Graves flint mines, Norfolk, England

❀ c3000 BC
New Stone Age peoples invade Ireland

❀ c2500 BC
Horses are used in the British Isles

15

THE NEW STONE AGE

Farming spread throughout the British Isles from about 4000 BC. Field patterns from about 3000 BC can be seen today at Céide Fields, above high cliffs near Ballycastle, on the west coast of Ireland. They have been excavated from layers of peat bog. The arrival of farming marks the beginning of the period known as the Neolithic ('New Stone') Age.

SKARA BRAE

In 1850 a severe storm battered the coast of Orkney, an island off the north coast of Scotland. When it was over, the ruins of a New Stone Age settlement were revealed in the shifting sands. Skara Brae had been inhabited from about 3200 to 2300 BC. Its people were fishermen or herders of sheep and cattle, for crops would not have grown well on this bleak and windy shore. The houses were built with stone blocks, the roofs made of turf and the bones of whales. The houses were linked by covered passages.

By about 4000 BC, flints were being mined underground. Over 360 mine shafts have been found at the Grimes Graves flint mine in Norfolk, England. It dates back to 3000 BC

Down the shaft
Miners climbed down timber ladders or ropes.

Flint beds
Flints are balls of hard stone found in layers of chalk

Cutting tools
Miners used picks made of deer antlers to dig out flints

Baskets of flint
Flints were carried to the surface to be chipped and flaked

MAKING THINGS

New Stone Age peoples were skilled craft workers. They produced baskets, jewellery and, from about 2500 BC, pottery. Wood was used to make farm tools. Stone was used to make hand mills called querns, for grinding grain into flour. Stone was also polished and ground to make axes for clearing the forest. In stony areas, axe-heads were produced at factory sites and exported right across the British Isles – from Northern Ireland to the southeast of England, from Cornwall to the northeast of England.

New Stone Age living rooms can be seen at Skara Brae. There are wall alcoves, dressers, stone beds and a central, smoky hearth.

The people at Skara Brae used herbs and wild plants as medicine. Centaury was used to heal wounds and treat snakebites. Henbane made the patient drowsy and relieved aches and pains.

centaury

henbane

✲ c3500 BC
A henge is in use at Llandygai,
North Wales

✲ c3500 BC
Gathering places (known as
'causewayed camps') built in
southern England

✲ c3300 BC
The first stone circles are
erected in the British Isles.

✲ c2700 BC
Silbury Hill, an artificial mound,
is built near Avebury, Wiltshire,
southern England

✲ c2600 BC
Massive stone circles and
ditches are raised at Avebury

STONES OF MYSTERY

I N THE years between about 3200 and 1500 BC, massive pillars of stone or timber were raised in the British Isles and other parts of northwestern Europe. Some were placed on their own, others were arranged in long avenues. They are called standing stones and may have been used to mark tribal borders or ceremonial routes. Some pillars were arranged within oval, ditched enclosures called henges. These seem to have been observatories, used to mark the appearance of the Sun at midsummer or midwinter, or to track movements of the stars. They must have been sacred places where religious rituals were carried out.

Stonehenge towers over the grasslands of Salisbury Plain in southern England. It was built in several stages and was in use from about 3200 to 1100 BC.

PEOPLE OF THE MEGALITHS

Archaeologists call the monuments of this period megaliths ('great stones'). The builders of Stonehenge must have been very organised, with a large workforce. They were powerful and wealthy, trading across a large area of northwestern Europe. They had advanced technology and a knowledge of astronomy.

Over 1,000 stone circles and over 80 henges are known to us today in the British Isles alone. Below are the Stones of Callanish, on the island of Lewis in the Outer Hebrides, Scotland.

❀ c2250 BC
85 stones transported to
Stonehenge from southwest
Wales

❀ c2000 BC
Main phase of building at
Stonehenge, England

❀ c2000 BC
Henge at Cairnpapple,
Lothian, Scotland

❀ c1800 BC
Stones of Callanish, Outer
Hebrides, Scotland

❀ c1500 BC
End of megalithic building in
the British Isles

17

Megaliths could weigh as
much as 26 tonnes. They
were quarried by being
being cracked with stakes,
fire, water and hammers.

The base of each pillar
was placed over a post-
hole. Ropes and timber
scaffolding were then
used to raise the pillar
to an upright position.

Massive stones like this
one would have been
transported on
wooden sleds and
timber rollers hauled
by ropes. These were
pulled by perhaps as
many as 1,000 men.

*The builders of Stonehenge
transported some massive
blocks of stone all the way from
the Preseli mountains of southwest
Wales, a distance of over 215 km.*

IN LATER AGES

The megaliths were held in awe
long after the people who had
built them had passed into
history. Peoples such as the Celts
regarded the stones as sacred. In
the Middle Ages, however,
Christians believed them to be
the work of the devil. By the
1700s, many sites had been
raided by farmers to build
houses and walls. In the 1800s
archaeologists revived interest in
the sites. In recent years many
people have dreamed up far-
fetched theories about the
mysterious stones.

*The village of Avebury in
Wiltshire, England, is built amidst
a circle of nearly 100 stones which
date back to about 2600 BC.*

18

🏵 **c3700 BC**
First phase of Wayland's Smithy long barrow, Oxfordshire, England

🏵 **c3600 BC**
West Kennet long barrow, Wiltshire, southern England

🏵 **c3200 BC**
Passage grave at Newgrange, Boyne valley, Ireland

🏵 **c3000 BC**
Belas Knap long barrow, Gloucestershire, England

🏵 **c2500 BC**
Barclodiad y Gawres passage grave, North Wales

THE BUILDERS of henges and stone circles also used the great stones we call megaliths to build burial chambers. All over the British Isles, these stone slabs have survived long after the simple huts of their builders have disappeared.

PLACES OF THE DEAD

DEATH IN THE NEW STONE AGE

During the New Stone Age, bodies were often placed in burial chambers once they were already skeletons, or else cremated. Some burial sites could hold the remains of up to 50 bodies. Most burial chambers were covered by great mounds of earth. These may have served to mark the ancestral lands of the chieftain's family, or perhaps they acted as a platform for religious ceremonies. One can imagine a priest standing on top of the burial mound at sunrise, calling up the spirits of the dead. Below, the people shivered as they waited for the sunrise.

🔽 *Megalithic burial chambers like Chun Quoit in Cornwall were built from upright slabs supporting a heavy cap- stone. Many were covered with mounds of soil. Over the ages, most have been stripped bare by wind and rain.*

NEWGRANGE

The Brú Na Bóinne area of eastern Ireland includes three megalithic tombs – Dowth, Newgrange and Knowth. The Newgrange tomb was built in about 3200 BC and is made up of a huge mound over a passage grave. A slit in the roof allows the rising sun to creep into the gloomy burial chamber at midwinter. Many of the stones are decorated with swirling spiral patterns. Later peoples believed that the Newgrange site must have been made by the gods.

🔘 *Megalithic tombs such as Newgrange are older than the pyramids of Egypt.*

DESIGNS FOR THE DEAD

New Stone Age people were often buried under narrow mounds called long barrows. Some of these were just made of earth, but others covered megalithic burial chambers. Some megalithic tombs are called passage graves. Here the chamber is reached by an underground passage, beneath a rounded hump of earth. After 2200 BC new peoples arrived in the British Isles and built round barrows for single burials.

Long Barrow

Long barrow exposed

Passage grave

🔵 *The passage grave of Bryn Celli Ddu on the island of Anglesey, was built on the site of an older henge.*

⚫ *West Kennet long barrow in Wiltshire, England, was in constant use from about 3600 BC to 2500 BC. The barrow was used to bury at least 46 adults and children.*

A MAGIC POTION

At Barclodiad y Gawres, an Irish-style passage grave on Anglesey, in North Wales, archaeologists found cremated bodies. A magic potion had been used to put out a fire. It included the bones of mice, snakes, toads and eels as well as seaweed and limpet shells.

Toad

Seaweed

East-West
Long barrows were lined up east to west, to face the sunrise

Burial chambers
Five burial chambers were built from upright slabs and cap-stones

The passage
A central passage led to the burial chambers. Its entrance was sealed by massive stones.

The mound
The mound was made of chalk rubble, soil and turf. It was about 100 metres long.

✵ c6000 BC
Copper being worked in
southwest Asia and southeast
Europe

✵ c3000 BC
Bronze made from tin and
copper in Asia and southeast
Europe

✵ c2500 BC
Copper working reaches
British Isles from southeast
and southwest Europe

✵ c2200 BC
Early 'beaker' burials
in British Isles

✵ c1700 BC
Bronze first appears
in British Isles

THE MAGIC OF METAL

THE BUILDING of great stone monuments outlasted the New Stone Age, for builders of the later megalithic monuments and the round barrows knew the secret of working metals. Copper was being worked in southeast Europe and western Asia by about 6000 BC. Within about 3000 years, smiths in these regions had worked out how to make alloys (mixtures of metals). The most useful alloy was bronze, a combination of tin and copper. Bronze-working skills had reached the British Isles by about 1700 BC, but it was many more years before they became widespread. Bronze tools and weapons were sharper than those made of stone and harder than those made of copper.

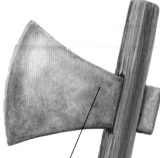

Blade
This blade has been fitted to the handle in the simplest way possible – by being forced through a slit in the handle

Haft
The axe handle would have been made of hard wood. Only metal parts survive for the archaeologist to find.

Bronze axes were so precious that they were often only used in ceremonies. Some were used in battle, but stone axes continued in everyday use for a long time.

INTO THE FURNACE

Metal workers had to heat the mined rocks until the ore melted. This process is called smelting. The smelted metals were then mixed, with just under 1 part of tin to 9 parts of copper, and placed in a pot called a crucible. Blow pipes or simple bellows were used to make the fire burn hotter and hotter.

Molten bronze would be poured into moulds, perhaps made of sandstone. The inside of the mould was smeared with soot and grease, to give a smooth finish. When the bronze had cooled and hardened, the mould could be knocked away.

Open mould
Simple one-piece moulds like this could be used to make axes, daggers and other simple shapes. This sandstone mould is seen sideways on.

Mould
Viewed from above, the axe-shape cut into the mould can be clearly seen. Molten bronze was poured into the hollow.

ORES AND MINES

The British Isles were rich in ores (rocks containing raw metals). Ireland had gold and copper, Cornwall had tin and exported it far and wide. Copper was also to be found in western and northern Britain. Mining became an industry in these areas and Scotland and Ireland became major centres of bronze manufacture.

❋ c1600 BC
Wealth and power in the
Stonehenge region

❋ c1600 BC
Manufacture of bronze in
Scotland and Ireland

❋ c1400 BC
Decline of the 'Wessex'
culture of central southern
England.

❋ c700 BC
Bronze workshop finds,
Heathery Burn cave, Durham,
England

❋ c600 BC
End of the Bronze Age in the
British Isles

21

WEAPONS AND ORNAMENTS

Bronze was used to make spearheads,
daggers, swords and axes. The designs varied
over the ages. Axes were joined to the
wooden hafts (handles) in various ways –
wedged through a hole, mounted in a metal
socket, inset and bound or fitted over a
projecting strip of wood. Rings, jewellery,
tweezers, cauldrons and harnesses for horses
have also been found. Most Bronze Age
objects have been found in the graves of
chieftains, for gold, bronze and copper were
used to show off the wealth and power of
their owners.

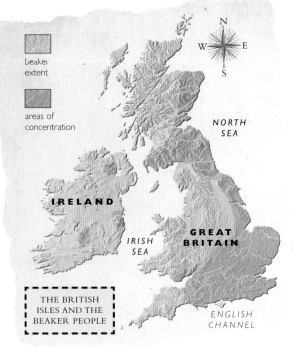

beaker
extent

areas of
concentration

NORTH
SEA

IRELAND

IRISH
SEA

GREAT
BRITAIN

THE BRITISH
ISLES AND THE
BEAKER PEOPLE

ENGLISH
CHANNEL

The technology and
customs of the Beaker
People may have originated in
Spain, a region rich in metals,
before spreading through Europe.
Beaker sites are found in both
Great Britain and Ireland.

Bronze needed to
reach a temperature
of about 900°C before it
could be poured into
moulds and left to cool and
harden. It was then
hammered and polished.

WHO WERE
THE BEAKER PEOPLE?

At about the time that metals
first appeared in the British
Isles, there was a change in the
way in which people were
buried. Personal possessions
were now often placed in single
graves, along with pottery
containers called beakers. These
burial customs spread to the
British Isles from mainland
Europe. It is possible that new
invaders or traders arrived by
sea at this time, and that it was
they who introduced the skills
of metal working. By this
period of history there was a
Europe-wide
network of
trading routes
by land and sea.

Beaker

2

CELTS AND ROMANS

700BC–AD446

THE WORLD AT A GLANCE

ELSEWHERE IN EUROPE

c700 BC
Rise of Celtic civilization in Central Europe

509 BC
Rome expels kings and becomes a republic

432 BC
The Parthenon temple is built in Athens, golden age for Greece

52 BC
Romans finally defeat the Gauls (Celtic tribes living in France)

27 BC
Rome becomes an empire under the rule of Augustus

AD 9
Germanic tribes under Arminius (Hermann) defeat the Romans

AD 285
The Roman empire splits into two halves, east and west

AD 410
Visigoth warriors sack the city of Rome

ASIA

c660 BC
Jimmu, legendary first emperor of Japan

c563 BC
Birth of religious teacher Gautama Siddhartha (the Buddha) in Nepal

550 BC
Cyrus the Great founds the Persian empire

334 BC
Alexander the Great begins the Greek invasion of Western Asia

322 BC
The Mauryan empire is founded in India

221 BC
Chinese empire unites under Qin Shi Huangdi

cAD 30
Possible date for the crucifixion of Jesus Christ in Jerusalem

AD 132
Jews rebel against Roman rule and are scattered into exile

AFRICA

600 BC
Meroë in Nubia (Sudan) becomes a powerful city

c500 BC
Bantu-speaking peoples start to spread out from West Africa

c450 BC
Rise of Nok civilisation in Nigeria, iron working, terracotta heads

c400 BC
Phoenician city of Carthage, North Africa, at height of power

331 BC
Greeks found city of Alexandria, Egypt

AD 44
Romans now rule North Africa from Egypt to Morocco

AD 50
Kingdom of Axum, in Ethiopia, rises to power

AD 429
The Vandals, a Germanic people, found kingdom in North Africa

"Iron swords are drawn — for the tribe or for the empire?"

wild boar

NORTH AMERICA

c500 BC
Picture writing (hieroglyphs) at Monte Albán, Mexico

c310 BC
Chiefdoms in America's eastern woodlands - the Hopewell culture

c100 BC
The Hohokam people of the American South irrigate their crops

cAD 1
North Pacific coastal villages, carving and building in cedarwood

cAD 1
Villages being built in the American Southwest

cAD 1
Possible date for first Arawak settlement of the Caribbean islands

cAD 50
The city of Teotihuacán is built in Mexico, massive pyramids

cAD 300
Height of the Maya civilization in Mexico, great cities

SOUTH AMERICA

c700 BC
Rise of the Parácas civilization in Peru

c400 BC
The great temples of Chavín de Huantar, Peru

c200 BC
Rise of the Nazca civilization in Peru

c200 BC
Nazca people scratch ceremonial lines across the desert, Peru

c200 BC
Decline of the Chavín civilization

cAD 1
The Moche people of northern Peru, gold working and pottery

cAD 100
Growth of the city of Tiwanaku, near Lake Titicaca

cAD 400
Powerful chiefdom on Marajó island at mouth of the River Amazon

OCEANIA

c700 BC
Pacific trade in obsidian, a black stone used to make weapons.

c300 BC
Polynesian settlement of Ellice Islands (Tuvalu)

c200 BC
Later burials at Aboriginal site of Roonka Flat, Australia

c200 BC
Polynesians reach the Marquesas Islands

cAD 1
Large increase in the Aboriginal population of Australia

cAD 150
Egyptian geographer Ptolemy suggests 'unknown southern land' - perhaps Australia

cAD 400
Polynesians reach Easter Island, in the eastern South Pacific

cAD 400
Polynesians reach the Hawaiian Islands, in the Central Pacific

MASTERS · OF · IRON

THE CELTIC
PEOPLES
1ST CENTURY BC

**ALBION
OR ALBU
(GREAT BRITAIN)**

Caledonians

Votadini
Selgovae
Novantae

Venicontes
Robogdi
Erdini Darini
Nagnatae Volunti
Auteni Eblanii
GAELS Cauci
Gangani Manapi
Usdiae Coriondi *IRISH*
Iverni Brigantes *SEA*
Vellabori

Brigantes
Parisi

BRITONS

Deceangli Cornovii Coritani
Ordovices
Iceni
Catuvellauni Trinovantes
Demetae Dobunni
Silures
Durotriges Atrebates Cantiaci

*NORTH
SEA*

**IERNE
OR ÉRIU
(IRELAND)**

Dumnonii *ENGLISH
CHANNEL*

The British Celts, like the Gaels, formed many different tribes. Some were new invaders from the European mainland, others were native peoples who took up the Celtic way of life.

Copper and bronze continued to be used for making all sorts of tools, weapons and jewellery, but soon a new metal was being worked in Europe. It was iron – so hard and tough that for centuries it was believed to be magical. Iron working was first mastered in western Asia, between 2000 and 1500 BC. By about 600 BC smiths were hammering out glowing bars of iron in the British Isles, too.

THE ANCIENT CELTS

One group of Europeans became expert at working the new metal, iron. The ancient Greeks called them 'Celts'. Their ancestry may have been the same as that of the Beaker People. The Celtic homeland was in Central Europe, southern Germany and the Alps, but after about 700 BC their influence spread across a vast area of Europe, from Turkey to Spain, from northern Italy through France to the British Isles. They raided and looted, they settled and farmed new lands. Trading and travel led to their way of life being adopted by other peoples, too. Northwest Europe was dominated by three main Celtic groups. Gauls lived in what is now France. Britons lived in Great Britain and Gaels lived in Ireland.

The Celts were brilliant metal workers who often decorated their work with birds, animals and interlacing patterns. Bronze mirrors like these were used after 100 BC by the Belgae, Celtic tribes who had settled in southern England.

∞ c350 BC	∞ c250 BC	∞ c150 BC	∞ c150 BC	∞ c100 BC	25
Celtic settlement of north and south of England, and Ireland	New waves of Celtic settlement in England, Scotland and Ireland	Fifteen Celtic tribes ('Belgae') invade England from Gaul	Celtic way of life at its greatest extent in Europe.	Celts increasingly under attack in mainland Europe	

CELTIC SOCIETY

The ancient Celts never saw themselves as one people and were rarely united. Celtic tribes were ruled by kings and by queens, too, for women held considerable power. Warriors came from noble families and prided themselves on being brave, heroic fighters and skilled hunters. They loved feasting and drinking. Both British and Gaelic tribes fought endlessly amongst themselves, quarrelling and raiding each others' cattle. The poorer members of the tribe were farmers, toiling on the land, raising animals and cutting the hay. They served as charioteers and fort-builders. Prisoners of war and lawbreakers were treated as slaves.

The ancient Celts were famed for their love of gold and jewellery. Nobles wore splendid brooches, rings, armbands and torcs (ornate metal collars).

This 2000 year-old iron chain was once fixed around the necks of slaves. It was found in a Welsh lake called Llyn Cerrig Bach, along with swords, spears, daggers, shields and chariots. They may have been thrown into the lake as offerings to the gods.

This ancient white horse design is carved into the chalk at Uffington, Oxfordshire, England. Its date is uncertain. By the Iron Age horses had become very important. The Celts mostly rode small, stocky ponies, but probably bred larger, more powerful horses too.

CELTIC LANGUAGES

Most of the languages spoken today in lands from Western Europe to northern India share a common origin. They are called Indo-European. Some languages still spoken in modern times came down to us from the ancient Celts. The language of the Britons turned into Welsh, Cornish and Breton (spoken in Brittany, France). The language of the Gaels gave us Irish, Scottish Gaelic and Manx (spoken on the Isle of Man). In Britain, no fewer than six rivers are called Avon. Why? It is simply a Celtic word for 'river'.

⊙⊘ c600 BC
First settlement at Colchester,
Essex England

⊙⊘ c450 BC
A flourishing of Celtic arts and
crafts across Europe.

⊙⊘ c325 BC
First documented reference to
the name British ('Pretanic')
Isles

⊙⊘ c300 BC
According to legend, a
hospital is founded in
Armagh, Ireland

⊙⊘ c200 BC
Fortified mountain settlement
of Tre'r Ceiri, Llŷn peninsula,
Wales

FORTS HAD been built in the British Isles before the Iron Age. They were large enclosures protected by earthworks and walls, and were sited on hilltops and headlands. They often enclosed dwellings which were occupied in peacetime as well as war. New enclosures were raised by the Celts. Within Tre'r Ceiri hillfort, on a misty mountain side in North Wales, the stone walls of 150 huts built in about 200 BC can still be seen today. Farming villages often had to be built on less protected lowlands, wherever the soil was good. In Ireland and Scotland, some villages were built on crannogs, artifical islands in lakes. The last of the Celtic invaders, the Belgae, built sizeable towns, such as St Albans and Colchester.

Inside the Celtic roundhouse, smoke drifted up to the rafters from the central hearth, and left through a hole in the roof. The timber posts may have been carved with ornate decorations. People slept on the ground in the cubicles, beneath warm animal skins.

THE CELTS AT HOME

ROUND HOUSES

Royal enclosures may have included large, rectangular halls, but most ordinary people in the western lands of the Celts lived in large round huts, which measured about 15 metres across. The roofs were cone-shaped with a heavy thatch. The walls were normally built of timber and wattle-and-daub (interlaced sticks covered in clay). Stone was used in areas where timber was scarce.

On the floor
Floors were of beaten earth or slabs. They could be strewn with sweet-smelling rushes or grasses.

The hearth
A wood fire in the centre of the hut was used for cooking and heating.

c100 BC	c100 BC	c90 BC	c75 BC	c75 BC	**27**
Lake village at Glastonbury, Somerset, England	Beautifully decorated hand mirrors become popular	First British coins, southern England	Thriving trade between Britain and Gaul	Large towns grow up in the lands occupied by Belgic Celts	

A LOVE OF FINERY

Celtic women wore long, loose dresses and tunics made of wool or linen, and wore shawls and cloaks fastened by brooches and pins. Men wore short tunics, cloaks and – a new fashion copied from the horse-riding warriors of Eastern Europe and Asia – trousers. Cloth was coloured with vegetable dyes and checked patterns were popular. Hair was often worn long and men favoured large, drooping moustaches. Both sexes loved to wear jewellery.

 A modern weaver recreates the Iron Age way of weaving. She passes a shuttle with yarn through the upright threads, which are stretched on an upright loom.

Livestock
Farm animals were kept in pens or even in the same huts as the villagers. They included sheep, goats, pigs, cattle and horses.

The loom
Looms (weaving frames) stood in most huts, for each household would produce its own cloth.

 The Iron Age diet was quite healthy. The Celts kept bees and honey was used to sweeten food and drink in the days before sugar was known in Europe.

Compartments
Each hut was really one single room, but the inside edge of the wall was divided into separate cubicles, used for storage of weapons and supplies or for sleeping.

WHAT'S FOR DINNER?

A big cauldron steamed over each hearth and the Celts were famous for enjoying their food. They might eat beef, mutton or pork, cheese or buttermilk. Bread and porridge were made from wheat, barley, rye or oats. Hunting and fishing provided boar, venison (deer meat) or salmon. Southern Europeans were amazed by the large amounts of alcohol drunk by Celtic men and women – imported wine, home-brewed ale and mead, a drink made from honey.

apples

wild boar

honey

nuts

c700 BC
Royal fort of Emain Macha, northern Ireland

c450 BC
First Iron Age phase of Maiden Castle, Dorset, England

c450 BC
South Barrule hillfort, Isle of Man

c300 BC
Celts in mainland Europe probably invent chain mail

c250 BC
War chariots introduced to the British Isles

WARRIOR HEROES

THE CELTS were famed as fighters through most of Europe. Far to the south of the British Isles, Celtic warrior bands were storming into Rome and Greece between 387 BC and 279 BC. Celtic tribes did take part in large pitched battles, but they preferred single combat, where champions from each army came out to fight each other. They belonged to an age which admired individual bravery more than organization or discipline. In the royal halls, warriors would boast of their exploits and drink to their dead companions.

Maiden Castle in Dorset, England, was already an important site during the New Stone Age. From about 450 BC, it was a major hillfort and the capital of a Celtic tribe called the Durotriges.

Timber defences
Heavy timbers were used to build fences and gates, the last line of defence against invaders.

High earthworks
The banks were staggered so that it was impossible to launch a direct attack on the gates. The fort was finally taken by the Romans.

The settlement
The settled area covered 18 hectares. Finds here have included Iron Age pots, sickles, combs made of bone and the skeletons of warriors who died in battle.

RATHS, DUNS AND BROCHS

Some forts were large defended settlements, but others were smaller and built more like castles. The remains of stone 'duns' may still be seen in Scotland and royal 'raths' in Ireland. The Picts, ancient inhabitants of northeastern Scotland who adopted the Celtic way of life, built 'brochs' – big stone towers which could be used as shelter in wartime.

A charioteer races his horses outside the dun, always ready for war.

CELTIC CHARIOTS

A new wave of Celtic warriors reached the British Isles in about 250 BC. With them came the light war chariot. Built of wood, it had iron-rimmed wheels and was pulled by two tough ponies, bred for their speed. It was driven by a non-fighting charioteer and was used to carry a fully armed warrior into battle. Some warriors who died were buried in their chariots.

CÚ CHULAINN, CHAMPION OF THE GAELS?

Some tales told by the ancient Celts were written down many centuries later, during the Middle Ages. The Irish tales tell of Sétanta, nick-named Cú Chulainn ('the Hound of Culain'), a legendary hero of Ulster in northern Ireland. As a boy he kills a fierce hound. As a youth he is trained in fighting by a female warrior called Scáthach. He has a magic spear and as a man takes on the invading army of Queen Medb of Connaught single-handed. Cú Chulainn represents everything the Celtic warrior wished to be. He is a cattle-raider, a warrior and a champion – swift, cunning, tireless and brave.

WEAPONS AND WARRIORS

Most Celts went into battle unprotected by helmets or armour. They often fought without any clothes at all, preferring to strip naked. Later, Celts on the European mainland did design very effective armour to use against the Romans. They may even have been the inventors of chain mail, armour made from linked rings of iron. Celtic warriors carried mostly long- or oval-shaped shields, spears, daggers and long slashing swords made of iron. Hillforts were defended with a hail of pebbles hurled from slings. Some Celtic warriors used lime to dress their hair into spikes and tattooed their skin with a blue dye, called woad – the name 'Picts' comes from the Latin for 'painted people'.

The Celtic warrior could use throwing spears and stabbing spears. His deadliest weapon was his long sword, which he whirled around his head and brought crashing down on the enemy.

30

@@ **200 BC**
Druidism already an ancient tradition amongst the Celts

@@ c**150 BC**
The Isle of Anglesey, North Wales, is the centre of druidism in Britain

@@ c**100 BC**
Cauldron from Gundestrup, Denmark, dedicated to Celtic god Cernunnos

@@ c**100 BC**
Sacred sanctuary built at Emain Macha, Northern Ireland

@@ **51BC**
Roman general Julius Caesar describes Celtic religious beliefs

DRUIDS AND MISTLETOE

THE LANDSCAPE was sacred to the ancient Celts, with holy mountains, mysterious woods and magical waters. Offerings were thrown into lakes and left by springs and wells. In parts of Ireland, Scotland and Cornwall today, it is still believed to be lucky to tie ribbons to trees near certain springs. Groves of sacred trees formed Celtic places of worship. There were also important religious enclosures called nemetons, although we do not know how they were used. Birds, snakes, fish and animals such as boars and stags were believed to have magic powers. Ancient Celtic tales are peopled with gods turning into animals, animals changing shape or becoming human.

The Celts made many sculptures of human heads in stone or wood. Some were double or triple heads. Celts believed that the human soul lived inside the head. Celtic warriors cut off the heads of their enemies and displayed them in halls and shrines. This custom may be the origin of the pumpkin and turnip heads people place in their windows at Halloween.

A MURDER MYSTERY

In 1984 a body was discovered in Lindow Moss, Cheshire, England. It had been preserved beneath the bog for over 1,900 years. The dead man wore an armband of fox fur. His stomach contained traces of burnt bread and mistletoe pollen. He had been hit over the head with an axe, strangled with a rope and cut across the throat. His hands were well cared for, so this was no warrior or labourer. Archaeologists have guessed that he was a druid who was sacrificed to the gods.

Lindow man

| ᴏᴏ cᴀᴅ 50 | ᴏᴏ cᴀᴅ 55 | ᴏᴏ ᴀᴅ 60 | ᴏᴏ cᴀᴅ 60 | ᴏᴏ cᴀᴅ 500s | 31 |
| First evidence of the Celtic calendar – a bronze plate from Gaul | Horned figure in bronze from Richborough, Kent, England | Roman invaders destroy sacred oak groves of the druids on Anglesey | Possible date for the sacrifice of Lindow Man, Cheshire, England | Druidism finally dies out in British Isles | |

WHO WERE THE DRUIDS?

The priests of the Britons and the Gaels were called druids. They came from noble families and some held more power than kings. They carried out sacrifices and other religious rituals, and may also have served as teachers, judges, peacemakers and secret messengers. They learned all kinds of secret lore about sacred plants such as the oak tree and the mistletoe.

oak leaf

mistletoe

GODS AND MYSTERIES

The oldest form of worship in the British Isles honoured the Earth Mother, bringer of fertility to the land. She was still honoured by the ancient Celts, under various names. They also believed in other gods and goddesses. Some belonged to a particular tribe or place. Irish gods included the Dagda, or supreme god, the goddess Dana, the shining Lug, Nuada of the Silver Hand, Morrigan, the terrifying raven goddess. Gods of the British Celts included a giant called Bran the Blessed, the powerful warrior Gwydion, Llew of the Strong Hand and the goddess Arianrhod. The Celts believed in other worlds, too, home of gods and the dead. Sometimes these were described as a happy island beneath the setting sun, sometimes as a mysterious fairy-world beneath the ground.

THE FIRES OF BELTAIN

The Celts held festivals throughout the year. On Beltain, 1 May, the dark hills were ablaze with bonfires. Lughnasa, for two weeks after 1 August, was a harvest festival in honour of Lugh. At Samhain, on the eve of 1 November, spirits from the other world were believed to walk the Earth. Imbolc, on 1 February, honoured the powerful goddess known as Brigit or Brigantia.

The Horned God, Cernunnos, was one of the most important Iron Age gods. He was worshipped throughout the Celtic world and is often shown surrounded by sacred animals. Later, Christians identified him with the devil.

32

⊚⊚ **55 BC**
The first Roman invasion of
Great Britain

⊚⊚ **54 BC**
The second Roman invasion
of Great Britain

⊚⊚ **AD 9**
Cunobelinus becomes
king of the Catuvellauni

⊚⊚ **AD 41**
Planned Roman invasion
fails to take place

⊚⊚ **AD 43**
The start of the
final Roman conquest

ROMAN INVASION

AFTER ABOUT 100 BC, the Celts in mainland Europe came under attack from German and Central European warriors. From Italy, too, Roman armies marched northwards to conquer the Gauls. In August 55 BC the Roman general Julius Caesar landed near Deal, in Kent, with 10,000 troops. He met with furious resistance, but returned the following year with at least 30,000 foot soldiers and 2000 cavalry. This time they crossed the River Thames and invaded the tribal lands of the Catuvellauni, Belgic Celts who had settled around St Albans. The Britons of southeast England were forced to pay tribute to Rome and Caesar withdrew.

JULIUS CAESAR

The conqueror of the Gauls and southern Britons was one of the most brilliant generals the world has known. Born in about 100 BC, his military campaigns made him the most powerful man in Rome. He made many enemies and was stabbed to death in 44 BC.

Gaius Julius Caesar

The Roman invasion of AD 43 brought Britain into a vast empire, which stretched from Spain into Western Asia, and southwards into North Africa. Its capital was Rome. Britain marked the northern limits of Roman rule. The Romans never conquered the far north of Scotland and Ireland too remained free.

THE ROMANS RETURN

After the second Roman invasion, the Catuvellauni grew more powerful. Their new king, Cunobelinus, conquered neighbouring tribes. When he died in AD 43, these tribes joined with an exiled son of the king to ask the Romans if they would curb the power of the Catuvellauni. They did more than that. The emperor Claudius ordered a full-scale invasion of Britain.

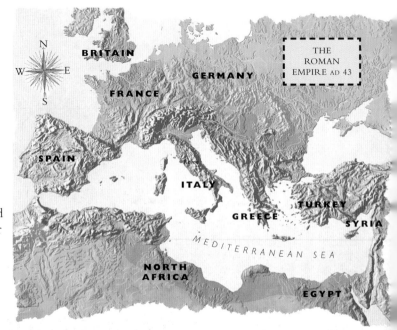

◎◎ **AD 48**
Caratacus leads resistance of the British Celts

◎◎ **AD 51**
Caratacus taken to Rome as a prisoner

◎◎ **AD 61**
Boudicca sacks Colchester, St Albans and London

◎◎ **AD 70**
The Romans attack the Brigantes tribe in Yorkshire

◎◎ **AD 84**
The Romans defeat the Caledonian tribes at Mons Graupius

33

THE CONQUEST OF BRITAIN

The new invaders numbered about 40,000 Roman troops and auxiliaries – units called in from other parts of the empire. They fought their way through Kent, crossed the Thames and captured Colchester. There were savage battles at hillforts such as Maiden Castle. It took four years for the Romans to take control of southern Britain, and over 30 more to conquer Wales and the West.

CARATACUS THE REBEL

Eleven British rulers immediately allied themselves with the Roman invaders. However Caratacus or Caradoc, a son of Cunobelinus, waged a fierce guerrilla campaign. Defeated, he sought refuge with Cartimandua, queen of the Brigantes, but she handed him over to the Romans. He was taken to Rome in chains, but in the end was pardoned. He died in AD 52.

A LONG STRUGGLE

In AD 60 a bloody rising began in what is now East Anglia. The queen of the Iceni, Boudicca, burned down Colchester, St Albans and the new town of London. She was defeated the following year and committed suicide. By the 70s, the Romans had advanced into northern England. In AD 84 they defeated the massed tribes of southern Scotland at Mons Graupius, near Inverurie. Calgacus, the defeated leader, said bitterly: 'They make a wilderness and call it peace.'

Boudicca was the wife of Prasutagus, king of the Iceni. He made a treaty with the Romans, but when he died they seized his lands and assaulted his family. This sparked off the great rebellion of AD 60-61.

In AD 122 building work started on Hadrian's Wall, a line of defences and forts 115 kilometres long. It ran from the Solway Firth to the River Tyne. The wall was more of a communications and trading network than a final frontier.

34

◎◎ AD 44
Romans capture Maiden
Castle

◎◎ AD 50
Camolodunum (Colchester)
is centre of military command

◎◎ AD 74
Roman fort built at Isca
Silurum (Caerleon)

◎◎ AD 75
Roman fort begun at
Segontium (Caernarfon)

◎◎ AD 79
Deva (Chester) a major
Roman army base

THE IRON LEGIONS

I T TOOK the Roman troops many years to gain
control of the lands now known as England and Wales
and they failed to hold Scotland. In AD 118, 34 years
after the battle of Mons Graupius, a whole Roman legion
– the Ninth – marched north and was never seen again.
Hadrian's Wall was built in AD 122 to keep out the Picts
and other northern tribes and this became the frontier of
the empire. In AD 142 more northerly defences were
raised along the River Clyde and beyond, but a second
'Antonine' Wall soon had to be abandoned. Ireland
remained unconquered.

Horses were used by
officers and by separate
cavalry units. These were armed
with long swords and spears.

THE ROMAN ARMY

Celts and Romans were very different
fighters. The Britons fought as heroic
individuals, the Romans as a ruthless
war machine. The Roman troops were
heavily armed and strictly disciplined.
They were organized into units called
legions, each with an eagle-headed
standard. At the time of the British
conquest each numbered about 5500
troops. Each legion was divided into
ten sections called cohorts and had
59 middle-ranking officers
called centurions.

When storming a hill fort,
Roman soldiers would
form a close unit, crouching with
shields covering their heads and
their sides. This formation was
called a testudo or tortoise.
Hillforts were also attacked with
huge catapults.

**BRITANNIA
(GREAT BRITAIN)**

Mare
Hiberniae
(Irish Sea)

ROMAN
BRITAIN

Mare
Orientale
(North Sea)

Luguvalium
Carlisle

Eboracum
York

Segontium
Caernarfon

Deva
Chester

Lindum
Lincoln

Ratae
Leicester

Camolodunum
Colchester

Glevum
Gloucester

Verulamium
St Albans

Isca Silurum
Caerleon

Londinium
London

Venta Belgarum
Winchester

Dubris
Dover

Isca Dumnoniorum
Exeter

Mare Austrum
(English Channel)

The new Roman province
was called Britannia. London
soon outgrew Colchester as the
most important town. Important
bases for the legions were built at
Chester and York in northern
England and Caerleon in South
Wales. After about AD 213
Britannia was divided into two
regions – Upper and Lower.

◎◎ AD 118
The Ninth Legion
disappears in Scotland

◎◎ AD 122
Work begins on
Hadrian's Wall

◎◎ AD 142
Building of the Antonine Wall
in Scotland

◎◎ AD 196
Northern frontiers are
overrun by British tribes

◎◎ AD 208
Romans try again to conquer
Scotland, under Emperor
Septimius Severus

35

Throwing spear
The legionary's spear was a weighted javelin, made of wood and iron.

Hand-fighting
The legionary carried a short sword in a scabbard and also a dagger.

Armour
Caesar's legions wore armour of mail, but by the time of Claudius, Roman foot soldiers wore armour made of metal plates.

Sandals
Sandals were made from leather and the soles were studded iron for the long marches.

LETTERS FROM THE WALL
Life on Hadrian's Wall was hard for the Roman legionaries and the foreign auxiliaries stationed there. Winters were cold, duties were dull or sometimes dangerous, always exhausting. Archaeologists have found orders for supplies, accounts, requests for leave, and even letters from home saying that the underpants and socks requested have been sent.

Marching baggage
The legionary marched with a heavy bundle slung over his shoulder. It included all sorts of digging tools, buckets and clattering tins as well as his basic food rations – biscuits, cheese and bacon.

Shield
Roman shields at this time were rectangular. They were made of wood, leather and linen, with a boss (central stud) of iron or bronze.

The Roman legionary was soldier, builder, engineer and labourer all in one.

A SOLDIER'S LIFE

The Roman legionary was a paid, professional soldier. Recruits were given very hard training. They learned parade-ground drill and battle formations. They were forced to march very long distances. They were taught how to fight with swords and throw javelins, how to pitch camp and dig defences. Punishments for disobedience were harsh. At the time of the conquest of Britain, legionaries were not allowed to marry whilst in service. After 25 years, however, they could retire. Many then settled around military camps and towns, often marrying a British woman and raising a family.

36

◎◎ **AD 43**
Roman legions build the first
proper roads in Britain

◎◎ **AD 45**
Pottery imported from Gaul
(Roman France)

◎◎ **AD 49**
Lead and silver being mined in
southwest England

◎◎ **AD 50**
The Roman town of
Londinium (London) is
founded on the River Thames

◎◎ **AD 62**
London is rebuilt after
Boudicca's revolt

ALL ROADS LEAD TO ROME

T HE ROMANS did not conquer Britain just for
the glory, or simply to protect their territories
in mainland Europe. They wanted to make a
profit. The island had precious metal ores, fertile lands
for farming and a large labour force. It could also
provide a new market for goods produced in Italy or
Gaul. Imports into Britain included pottery from Gaul
and wine from southern Europe and the Rhineland.
Exports included woollen cloaks, lead, silver, the black
stone called jet, oysters and hunting dogs.

SHIPS AND CARGOES

Creaking, square-sailed
wooden ships carried cargoes
and merchants across the
choppy waters of the North
Sea and the English Channel.
London, on the River
Thames, became Britain's
biggest port.

*Roman ships
followed
coastlines
whenever
possible*

ROMAN MONEY

Coins of gold, silver and brass
became common throughout
Britain. There was now a
single currency, or
money system,
across a vast area
of Europe,
Western Asia and
North Africa.

*a coin of the
emperor Constantine
(CAD 274-337)*

THE GROWING TOWNS

Celtic life had mostly been based in the country, but
Roman life was centred on towns with about 5,000
inhabitants. The Romans rebuilt many of the old
British settlements with straight streets and drainage.
They built large town halls, law courts,
markets, shops, bakeries, restaurants and
bars, even public toilets. Smaller
towns grew up around
military camps and forts,
or wherever there was
a need to trade.

*The materials
used to build
Roman roads varied
from one place to
another.*

Surveyors
The roads were
carefully surveyed
and measured
by army engineers

⊘⊘ **AD 70**
Romans start mining
gold in Wales

⊘⊘ **AD 100**
Open-cast coal mining near
Chester, England

⊘⊘ **c AD 175**
Pottery imported from
Cologne, in Roman Germany

⊘⊘ **c AD 200**
Large-scale pottery
manufacture in England

⊘⊘ **c AD 277**
Grape vines are grown in
southern regions of Britain

37

BUILDERS OF ROADS

The Romans built the first proper road system in Great Britain. In places such as Blackstone Edge, in Yorkshire, England, original Roman paving stones can still be seen today. The new Roman roads ran straight across the rolling countryside, providing fast, direct routes for marching soldiers, official messengers and merchants.

Paving
Closely fitted blocks of stone made the road surface. It was curved, or cambered, so that rain-water drained away

Verges
Forest was cleared back from the verges, to reduce the risk of an ambush

Milestones
Stones showing the distance to the next town were placed along the route

Foundations
Rocks were laid in a bed of sand and covered in gravel and cement

ON THE ROAD

The Romans built over 9000 km of roads in Britain. Some roads were built to be over 12 metres wide, others were minor routes. Transport included horses and mules, carts and heavy wagons pulled by oxen.

The first road workers and bridge builders were legionaries, but later city councils took over responsibility for building new roads and repairing old ones. Roman roads would not be bettered until the 1800s.

• **Ermine Street** linked London and York, joining Dere Street northwards to Scotland

• **Watling Street** ran through Kent to London, then northwest across the English Midlands to Chester

• From Exeter people could travel eastwards to London or join the **Fosse Way** which led northeast to Lincoln

BRITAIN'S ROMAN ROADS

York

Chester   Lincoln

London

Exeter   Dover

COUNTRY LIFE

Many Britons now worked on farms which were owned by the state or by wealthy landowners – British as well as Roman. The workers harvested grain, tended orchards and raised sheep. Slave labour was common on farms and in the mines. In the wilder lands of Cornwall, Wales and the Scottish borders, towns were few and far between and the old Celtic way of life was less influenced by Rome – even if crops were now carted off to feed soldiers at the local fort.

◎◎ **AD 75**
A splendid palace is built at Fishbourne, near Chichester, England

◎◎ **AD 78**
Aquae Sulis (Bath) already famous for its warm springs

◎◎ **AD 90**
A Roman theatre is built at Canterbury, Kent

◎◎ **c AD 90**
Large town houses being built in Britain for the first time

◎◎ **AD 100**
A Roman villa is built at Lullingstone, Kent, southern England

ROMAN PEACE

Gardens
Walkways with columns and statues passed through gardens of shrubs, herbs and fruit trees

B RITISH REBELS were sold into slavery, but local rulers and nobles who supported Rome prospered. Many of them adopted Roman ways and dress. They learned to speak Latin, the language of Rome. Roman rule was often harsh, but it did bring a period of peace to large areas of Europe.

BRITISH AND ROMAN

Romans who stayed in Britain for more than a few years were influenced in turn by the Celts. Although Romans worshipped their own gods and goddesses, they were also prepared to honour many of the Celtic gods. When the Romans built luxurious new public baths at Bath, in western England, these were dedicated both to the Celtic goddess Sulis and the Roman goddess Minerva.

The most impressive Roman villas were built in the AD 200s and 300s.

The hot springs at Bath, or Aquae Sulis, were believed to cure illnesses and injuries. The baths built there by the Romans attracted visitors from all over the empire.

ROMAN CRAFTS

British craft workers gradually learned to copy Roman skills such as making mosaics. These pictures, made from chips of coloured tile, decorated the floors of public buildings and the homes of the wealthy.

Mosaic from Fishbourne Palace, near Chichester, England

Roofs
Roofs were wooden framed and covered with tiles of baked clay

Roman dining
Guests ate lying down on couches around a low central table

In the kitchen
In the kitchen, cooks prepared dishes with food from the villa farm. Hunting in the forests provided wild game. Roman food was highly spiced.

Serving the master
The villa was kept running by a large team of slaves and servants

LIVING IN STYLE

Large country houses called villas were built for important Roman officials or for local British rulers who remained loyal to Rome. They were surrounded by large farm estates. Over the years, villas became more and more luxurious, with under-floor central heating, baths and dining rooms where visitors from Rome would be entertained with lavish banquets.

GODS FROM AFAR
New forms of worship arrived in Britain from distant lands. Mithras, the Persian god of light, was especially popular with the legions.

Mithras slays a bull

40

⊚⊚ **AD 280**
Start of Saxon raids on
southern and eastern Britain

⊚⊚ **AD 287**
Carausius rules Britain
independently

⊚⊚ **AD 297**
Rule from Rome is
restored in Britain

⊚⊚ **AD 306**
Constantine the Great is
declared Roman emperor
at York

⊚⊚ **AD 360**
The Mildenhall treasure is
buried in Suffolk

THE MIGHTY empire of Rome began to look less powerful after AD 200. There were bitter civil wars and struggles for power. In AD 286 the empire was divided into an eastern and western part. Britain was in the west, still ruled from Rome. However in AD 287 Carausius, commander of the Roman fleet in Britain, declared himself ruler of Britain. He was murdered by a fellow rebel, Allectus, in AD 293. Rome regained control in AD 297, but not for long. Frontier defences were now being breached all around the empire.

MAGNUS MAXIMUS

Magnus Maximus was a Spanish-born commander of the Roman troops in Britain. He made treaties with Celtic peoples such as the Votadini and Dumnonii to take on defending Britain against the Picts and Gaels. In AD 383 he marched with his troops to Rome and seized the throne. He was killed five years later. His memory survives in the folklore of Wales, where he is known as Macsen.

THE FALL · OF · ROME

INVADERS CHALLENGE ROME

Roman Britain now came under attack from all sides. In the far north the Picts overran Hadrian's Wall and advanced south. Western shores and shipping were under attack from the Gaels, the unconquered Celts of Ireland. The English Channel was plagued by pirates. Southern England and East Anglia were attacked by a people from Germany, the Saxons. From about AD 280 Romans built a chain of massive stone forts to defend southeastern coasts, which became known as the Saxon Shore.

A beacon blazes on top of a lighthouse as Roman ships patrol the English Channel. By AD 401 the legions were sailing away from Britain.

AD 367
Roman Britain invaded by
Picts and Gaels

AD 383
Magnus Maximus marches
on Rome

AD 401
The Roman legions start to
withdraw from Britain

AD 446
Last appeal by the British for
help from Rome

AD 476
The end of the Roman
empire in Western Europe

41

THE MILDENHALL TREASURE

In 1946 it was officially reported that four years earlier a Roman treasure hoard had been ploughed up at Mildenhall in Suffolk, England.

The pieces discovered were made of solid silver and dated from about AD 350. They may have originally been imported from Roman North Africa. They included spoons, splendid dishes, plates and wine goblets – 34 pieces in all.

In the days before banks and safes, people stored their wealth as precious metals. In times of war they would bury them at a secret spot, to prevent them falling into enemy hands. Hoards like this one suggest that by the 300s, Roman Britain was no longer a peaceful or secure place to live.

This splendid dish from the Mildenhall treasure hoard is now in the British Museum, in London.

The frieze
A picture strip around the cover of the dish features lions, boars and centaurs – strange creatures which are half-human, half-horse.

Decorated silver
Although the spoons in the treasure hoard had early Christian emblems on them, this fine dish is decorated with pictures of non-Christian gods.

END OF THE EMPIRE

Between AD 401 and 410, Roman troops were withdrawn from Britain as Germanic tribes crossed the River Rhine and poured into Gaul. Within the empire there were revolts and uprisings, and more attempts to seize local power. The economy collapsed. In AD 410 Rome itself was sacked by northern invaders called Goths. The emperor Honorius declared that from now on, the Britons would have to defend themselves. In AD 446 British leaders made one last appeal to Rome, but it was hopeless. It took just 30 more years for the Roman empire in Western Europe to come to an end.

The rim
The rim of the dish is finely patterned. None of the items were scratched or damaged by the plough.

3

RAIDERS AND SETTLERS

AD446–1066

THE WORLD AT A GLANCE

ELSEWHERE IN EUROPE

476
End of the Roman empire in western Europe

c500
Migrations of Slavs begin, to east, west and south of their homeland in eastern Europe

529
Justinian, emperor of East Rome or Byzantium (now Istanbul), draws up laws

711
Moslem Moors (Arabs and Berbers) invade Spain from North Africa

732
Charles Martel, ruler of the Franks, drives Arab invaders from France

800
Charlemagne, ruler of the Franks, is crowned emperor in Rome

912
The Viking warlord Rollo becomes Duke of Normandy in France

962
King Otto I of Germany becomes Holy Roman Emperor

ASIA

531
The Sassanid empire expands in Persia (Iran) under Chrosroes I

535
Collapse of the Gupta empire in India

552
The Buddhist faith reaches Japan from China

570
Muhammad the Prophet, founder of Islam, is born in Mecca, Arabia

610
A Grand Canal links China's two greatest rivers, the Huang He and the Chang Jiang

618
China is ruled by the Tang emperors, a golden age of arts and science

786
Harun al-Rashid is Caliph (ruler) of Baghdad and head of a vast empire

802
The Angkor kingdom is founded by Khmer rulers in Cambdodia

AFRICA

500
Bantu-speaking migrants arrive in southern Africa

531
A Christian Church is founded in Ethiopia, North Africa

600
Rise of the powerful gold-producing kingdom of Ghana, in West Africa

641
Arabs invade Egypt, beginning their conquest of North Africa

750
Trade across the Sahara desert between North and West Africa

900
Rise of Swahili culture on the coast of East Africa

969
Foundation of the city of Cairo, on the River Nile in Egypt

c1000
First settlement at Great Zimbabwe

"Monks take refuge as bands of warriors invade the islands."

Sutton Hoo helmet

NORTH AMERICA

500
Teotihuacán city in central Mexico has a population of about 200,000

700
Temple mounds built in the valley of the Mississippi river

700
Cahokia, the first town in the region now taken up by the United States

700
Hohokam, Anasazi and Mogollon peoples in the southwest

800
The 'Dorset' culture amongst Inuit hunters of Canada and Greenland

950
The Toltecs found the city of Tula in central Mexico

1000
Vikings try to found settlements in Labrador and Newfoundland

1050
The Anasazi build defensive settlements in the southwest

SOUTH AMERICA

500
Tiwanaku city, near Lake Titicaca, has a population of 40-100,000

600
The great Gateway of the Sun is raised at Tiwanaku

700
The Andean city state of Wari becomes very powerful

700
The decline of the Moche culture in northern Peru

750
The Nazca civilization of southern Peru comes to an end

800
The Chimú city of Chan Chan, northern Peru, covers an area of 15 sq km

900
The Chimú empire at the height of its power in northern Peru

1000
The city of Wari is abandoned

OCEANIA

c500
Polynesians settle in the southern Cook Islands

c700
Easter Islanders raise platforms of large stone blocks

c800
Earliest evidence for Polynesian hand clubs made of wood and whalebone

c850
The Maoris, a Polynesian people, settle New Zealand coasts

c850
Maoris begin to hunt large flightless birds such as the moa

c900
Aborigines mining rock for axes, Mount Isa, bartering routes across Australia

c1000
Last phase of Pacific settlement by Polynesian seafarers

c1000
Easter Islanders begin to raise huge heads of carved stone

✻ c AD 30
Crucifixion of Jesus Christ,
Jerusalem

✻ c AD 300
Execution of St Alban in
England

✻ c AD 313
Christians given full rights of
worship in Roman empire

✻ AD 390
St Ninian (Nynia) founds
church in southern Scotland

✻ AD 400
British monk Pelagius in Rome

SIGΠ ⊙ OF THE CR⊙SS

ONE of the new eastern religions that appeared in Britain towards the end of the Roman period was Christianity. Its founder, Jesus Christ, had been put to death by the Roman rulers of Jerusalem in about AD 30. Christians believed that there were not many gods, just one, and that Jesus was his son. They taught that people should love their enemies.

CHRISTIANS AND PAGANS

Many of the first Christians were killed by the Romans. In Britain, a Christian legionary called Albanus (St Alban) was executed in about AD 300. However the emperor Constantine made Christianity legal in AD 313 and himself became a Christian. The new faith spread among both Romans and Britons. As the ages passed, the old Celtic beliefs only survived as country customs. The word 'pagan', meaning non-believer, originally came from the Latin word for 'countryside'.

Jesus Christ was pictured in this floor mosaic found at a Roman villa in Hinton St Mary, Dorset, England. It dates from the early years of Christianity in Britain. The symbols in the background are the Greek letters Chi and Rho, the first two letters of the name 'Christ'.

Jesus Christ, like many condemned to death by the Romans, had been crucified – left to die on a wooden cross. The cross eventually became the most common symbol of Christianity. Early Celtic crosses are beautifully carved from stone.

IONA AND COLMCILLE

Colmcille, or Columba, was born in AD 521, into a noble Irish family. In the old days he would probably have been a druid, but instead he was an enthusiastic Christian. In AD 563 he set up a monastery and centre of learning on the island of Iona, in the Hebrides. He and his monks travelled through Scotland, founding churches and preaching Christianity to the northern Picts. It was another monk from Iona, Aidan, who set up a monastery at Lindisfarne, in Northumbria, in about AD 635.

❋ AD 433
St Patrick in northern Ireland

❋ AD 543
Death of St Petroc, who
preached in Cornwall

❋ AD 563
Colmcille or St Columba
founds church on Iona

❋ AD 574
Rome orders conversion of
Anglo-Saxons. Mission
postponed to AD 597

❋ AD 601
Death of St David (Dewi
Sant) South Wales

45

SPREADING THE WORD

After the Romans left Britain, raids by non-Christian Saxons increased in southern and eastern Britain. Christianity spread most rapidly in the west, in Wales and Cornwall. Many place names in these areas today begin with 'Llan-' or 'Lan-'. A *llan* was a religious enclosure, where monks would teach people about the life of Christ, farm the land and care for the sick.

THE CELTIC CHURCH

A type of Christianity grew up in Celtic lands which was rather different from that of Rome. It was influenced by the teachings of a British monk called Pelagius. He believed that people were basically good, that they were not born sinful. He also attacked wealth and privilege. It was AD 664 before the Celtic and Roman Churches finally came together.

THE AGE OF SAINTS

• St Patrick (cAD 385–460) was born in western Britain. Kidnapped by pirates, he escaped to Ireland and later studied in Gaul. In about AD 432 he went back to Ireland, probably to Armagh, to spread the Christian message.

St Patrick was made a bishop at the age of 45. He was probably sent back to Ireland by Pope Celestine I.

• St Ninian or Nynia (cAD 390) was a Briton born near the Solway Firth. He studied in Rome, became a bishop and founded a church in what is now Wigtownshire, Scotland. He converted the southern Picts to Christianity.

• St David or Dewi Sant (cAD 520–601) was born in southwest Wales. He founded religious centres in South Wales and the West of England and became Bishop at Menevia (St David's).

Monks of the early Celtic Church lived in beehive-shaped cells called clocháns. This style of building has been adapted to a rectangular stone chapel on the Dingle peninsula in Ireland. The Gallarus Oratory (chapel of prayer) may be 1,400 years old.

AD 430 Possible date for rule of Ambrosius (Emrys) over Britons

AD 448 Vortigern asks Hengist and Horsa to help him fight the Picts

AD 455 Hengist and Horsa attack Vortigern. Horsa is killed

AD 456 Hengist and his son Aesc defeat Britons in Kent

AD 477 A Saxon war leader called Aelle lands at Selsey and invades Sussex

THE AGE OF ARTHUR

THE thousand years between the fall of Rome and the start of modern European history are known as the Middle Ages. After Rome withdrew from Britain, the country was divided between local rulers. Many of them still tried to follow the Roman – and Christian – way of life. However trade was disrupted by war and grass grew through cracked pavements as Roman towns and villas fell into disrepair.

Dragons were used as emblems by the Britons after the Roman withdrawal. Dragons, originally an Asian design, were used on some Roman cavalry standards and may have appeared on the standard of Magnus Maximus. A red dragon remains the emblem of Wales today.

WHO WAS ARTHUR?

It cannot be proved that Arthur or Artorius, one of the most famous names in British history, existed at all. However many clues suggest that he was indeed a historical figure. If so, he was probably of noble birth, a British Celt and a Christian who followed the Roman way of life.

Arthur would have been a war leader or general rather than a king. He would have led a band of armoured, mounted warriors which could assist local defence groups, moving at speed to meet invading Saxons or Picts. He is linked with a great victory at somewhere called Mount Badon in about AD 516 and is said to have been killed at the battle of Camlan in AD 537.

During the later Middle Ages, tales about Arthur spread far and wide. Many of them mixed him up with ancient Celtic gods and heroes. He became a king in shining armour, famous for his bravery. Stories about Arthur and his companions were told in France, Germany and Italy.

Legend has it that Arthur was born at Tintagel, on the northern coast of Cornwall. This cliff-top site was inhabited in Roman times and by AD 500 had a Christian monastery. It also has the ruins of a castle from 500 years later.

NORTH SEA INVADERS

In eastern Britain there had been small settlements of retired auxiliaries from Germany since Roman times. Now roving Germanic warrior bands arrived across the North Sea. They were Angles, Saxons, Frisians and Jutes. They raided southern and eastern England and then seized the land. Their conflict with the Britons would last hundreds of years.

The British probably used small bands of cavalry to pursue the Saxon armies. They did slow down the Saxon advance, but they could not stop it.

ANCIENT TALES

The first mention of Arthur in literature comes in a series of fantastic tales, which were written down in Wales later in the Middle Ages. They had been passed down over the ages by word of mouth. Some are tales of ancient Celtic gods and the underworld, of severed heads and magical animals. Others refer to Magnus Maximus (Macsen), the age of Arthur and the Christian period. Today this group of tales is known as the *Mabinogion*.

BATTLING FOR BRITAIN

We know little of the kings and armies who defended Britain against the new invaders. Emrys or Ambrosius seems to have been a very powerful ruler in about AD 430, possibly later. In AD 449 another king called Vortigern invited two Jutes called Hengist and Horsa to help him fight the Picts, in return for land.

By AD 455 they had turned against Vortigern and were waging war on the Britons.

48

⊛ **AD 559**
Glappa becomes king of
Bernicia (Northumbria)

⊛ **AD 560**
King Ceawlin drives the
Britons from Wessex

⊛ **AD 560**
Ethelbert becomes king
of Kent

⊛ **AD 604**
Earliest record of a Saxon
land charter

⊛ **AD 644**
Northumbria is made up of
Deira and Bernicia

SAXON·SWORDS

T HE invasion of southern and eastern Britain by Angles, Saxons, Frisians and Jutes was just one part of a great movement of Germanic peoples across Europe. German lands in Central Europe were being invaded by fierce warriors from the east, such as the Huns and the Slavs. The Germanic peoples who lived there looked westwards at the crumbling defences of the old Roman empire. There they saw rich farmland for the taking and a chance to carve out new kingdoms for themselves. Germanic tribes poured into France, Italy, Spain and North Africa.

CELTS AND SAXONS
The Britons believed that the Angles and Saxons were savages. These peoples had never experienced the civilisation of Rome, nor were they Christians. In reality, however, the Germanic invaders were not so different from the British Celts. They shared similar European origins and lived in small kingdoms. They depended on farming and fishing. They shared the same technology and were fine craft workers.

THE DAY OF WODEN
The newcomers brought with them worship of the ancient Germanic gods. These survive in English names for days of the week. Tuesday is named after Tiw, god of war. Wednesday is the day of Woden, the chief god. Thursday is the day of Thor, god of thunder. Friday is from Frigg, goddess of love.

Woden, also known as Wotan or Odin

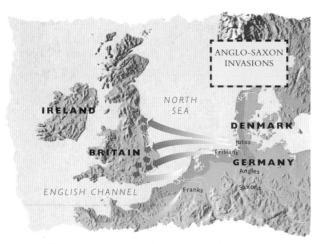

ANGLO-SAXON
INVASIONS

IRELAND

NORTH
SEA

DENMARK

BRITAIN

Jutes

Frisians

GERMANY

Angles

ENGLISH CHANNEL

Franks

Saxons

The invaders came from the lands now occupied by Germany, Denmark and the Netherlands. They crossed the North Sea and English Channel in wooden boats and fought their way westwards.

THATCH AND TIMBER
The various Germanic invaders can be grouped together under the general name 'Anglo-Saxons'. It was their language which eventually became English. They built small farming villages, many of whose names survive as English place names today. Their houses were rectangular, with walls of timber planks and pitched roofs covered in a heavy thatch. These were surrounded by a fenced yard. In some regions, huts seem to have been raised over sunken pits, which may have been boarded over.

✵ **AD 625**
Probable date of the Sutton Hoo burial in East Anglia

✵ **AD 625**
First Anglo-Saxon coins to be minted in England

✵ **AD 642**
Penda of Mercia kills Oswald of Northumbria at Maserfeld

✵ **AD 655**
Penda of Mercia killed by Oswiu of Northumbria at Battle of the Winwaed

✵ **AD 668**
Ine becomes king of Wessex, first records of Anglo-Saxon laws

49

ANGLO-SAXON LANDS

Modern names for counties and regions of England recall the first advances of the Anglo-Saxons. Essex comes from East Seaxe, land of the East Saxons. Sussex come from Suth Seaxe, land of the South Saxons. East Anglia was East Engle, the eastern territory of the Angles. By AD 550 the Anglo-Saxons controlled large areas of eastern and southern Britain. The Britons still ruled in the west and much of the north.

◀ Anglo-Saxon warriors of the AD 400s and 500s might be armed with a battle axe, a long sword, a spear, or a long knife called a sax. They wore woollen tunics over trousers and carried round shields. Chieftains wore helmets and shirts of mail.

A ROYAL SHIP BURIAL

In 1939 a grave was discovered at Sutton Hoo, near Woodbridge in Suffolk, England. It was a royal burial, probably that of Raedwald, a ruler of East Anglia who died in about AD 625. He was buried in a ship beneath a mound of earth. His ship was 27 metres long and was rowed by 40 oars. Inside a wooden chamber in the boat was a rich treasure hoard. There were buckles and fasteners of shining gold, a jewel-covered purse containing 37 gold coins. There was a musical instrument called a lyre. There was a sword, a shield and the remains of a splendid helmet made of iron and bronze.

◀ The ornate Sutton Hoo helmet shows the influence of Roman styles on European design 200 years after the collapse of the Roman empire.

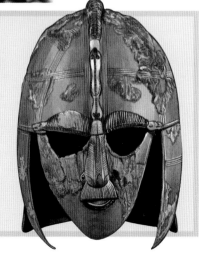

50

❀ c AD 500
The founding of the kingdom
of Dál Riada by Fergus Mór

❀ AD 574
Colmcille crowns Aedán
MacGabráin High King
of Dál Riada

❀ AD 604
Strathclyde and Dál
Riada defeated by Angles
at Degsástan

❀ AD 642
Owain of Strathclyde defeats
Dál Riada at Strathcarron

❀ c AD 650
Dál Riada loses its territories
in northern Ireland

THE MAKING
OF SCOTLAND

SCOTLAND takes its name from a people whom the Romans called Scoti. These 'Scots' were Gaels who sailed from northern Ireland to raid Britain's western coasts and islands as the Roman empire collapsed. By AD 500 they had founded a kingdom called Dál Riada on the Scottish mainland. For many years the Scots battled with the Picts, who still controlled the lands of the northeast, around Aberdeen. The monk Colmcille (Columba) was an Irish-born Scot, and he hoped that once these northern Picts had become Christian, the two peoples could live in peace.

Picts were one of four groups of people living in Scotland at this time.

BATTLE FOR THE LOWLANDS

The Angles who had founded Bernicia (later part of Northumbria) soon pushed further northwards, into the Scottish Lowlands. The Britons living in the Lowlands were under pressure from all sides. They made an alliance with the Scots to fight the Angles, but were defeated at the battle of Degsástan (perhaps near Jedburgh) in AD 603. The Angles now controlled the Lothian region – eastern Scotland below the Firth of Forth. This left the Britons of the Lowlands isolated in their kingdom of Strathclyde. Their lands to the south were also being overrun by Angles and they were soon cut off from their fellow Britons in Wales.

For hundreds of years after the Picts first built brochs, they used these round towers for shelter when attacked by enemies. This is Don Carloway Broch on the Isle of Lewis.

✽ AD 685
Picts stop northern advance
of Angles at Nechtansmere

✽ AD 736
Victories of Picts under King
Óengus I against Scots
of Dál Riada

✽ AD 768
King Áed Find of Dál Raida
invades Pictish kingdom of
Fortriu

✽ AD 841
Kenneth I MacAlpin becomes
King of Dál Riada

✽ AD 843
Scots and Picts unite in
Kingdom of Alba

51

This beautiful wooden box, the Monymusk Reliquary, is decorated with gilt and silver. It was made in the 600s or 700s and is said to have contained the remains of Colmcille (Columba).

THE KINGDOM OF ALBA

In AD 685 the Picts halted the northward advance of the Angles with a desperate battle at Nechtansmere, Dunnichen. But it was not until AD 843 that northern Scotland finally became united. That was when a ruler of the Scots called Kenneth MacAlpin ('mac' meaning 'son of') joined his kingdom with that of the Picts.

The centre of the Christian Church in Scotland now moved eastwards from Iona to Dunkeld, in Perthshire. The new kingdom was called Alba and it linked up most of the region lying to the north of the Firth of Forth and the River Clyde.

It was one of the most important kingdoms in the Celtic world and formed the chief building block of the future kingdom of Scotland. Alba rarely knew peace, for it was under constant attack by Anglo-Saxons from the south and by Scandinavians around its coasts.

DÁL RIADA

The new kingdom of Dál Riada included part of northern Ireland, islands such as Iona, and the Argyll region of the Scottish mainland. By about AD 650 the Scots had lost their lands back in Ireland. Cut off from their homeland, the dialect of Irish that they spoke gradually developed into the Gaelic language still spoken today in the islands and highlands of Scotland.

Kenneth I succeeded his father Alpin as King of the Scots in AD 841. Two years later he united the lands of the Scots and the Picts. He died in AD 858.

THE STONE OF DESTINY

A ceremonial slab of sandstone was brought by the Scots from Ireland to Iona. From there it was taken to Dunstaffnage and later to Scone, near Perth. This 'Stone of Destiny' was used at the coronation of the kings of Alba and of united Scotland. In 1297 the English King Edward I stole the stone and took it south to London. There it stayed until 1950, when it was reclaimed by four Scottish students. The stone was recovered in Arbroath and returned to England. However in 1996 it was officially installed in Edinburgh Castle.

52

❋ c AD **540**
The voyages of Brendan
around North Atlantic coasts

❋ c AD **550**
Start of the age of the
monasteries in Ireland

❋ AD **561**
Brendan founds Clonfert
monastery, Galway

❋ c AD **600**
Ogham script now replaced
by the Roman alphabet

❋ c AD **600**
The royal house of Uí Néill
becomes the most powerful in
Ireland

A LİGHT İN İRELAND

HISTORIANS used to call the period after the fall of Rome the 'Dark Ages', because European civilization was torn apart by war. However the darkness did not cover all of Europe. Ireland, in the far northwest, was a shining example. It had escaped Roman rule and trade now prospered with Cornwall, Brittany and southwestern Europe. Between about AD 700 and 800, Celtic arts and crafts reached the high point in their history.

◗ The Tara brooch is made of gilded bronze and silver and is decorated with glass and amber. It probably dates from about AD 700.

ART OF THE MONKS

Christian monasteries in Ireland became great centres of learning. They also held great political influence. Important monasteries grew up at Clonmacnois in County Offaly and Clonard in County Meath. Derry, Durrow and Kells were linked with the church at Iona. Armagh was another great Christian centre. The Irish monasteries inspired beautiful works of art and craft. In the Book of Kells, produced before AD 800, religious texts are decorated with elaborate patterns, animal designs and pictures.

◗ The Book of Kells may have been produced on the island of Iona, but finished in Ireland.

❀ c AD 650	❀ c AD 650	❀ AD 697	❀ c AD 700	❀ c AD 800	53
The *Book of Durrow*, start of the golden age of Celtic Christian art	Irish laws begin to be written down (to AD 750)	Synod of Birr discusses Christian treatment of women and children	Fine metal working, such as the Tara brooch and Ardagh chalice	The *Book of Kells*, the masterpiece of Celtic Christian art	

KINGS, LORDS AND PEASANTS

Irish society was divided into three classes. At the bottom were the commoners. These included some slaves, serfs (labourers who were not allowed to leave the land) and freemen who owned their farms. Life for poor people was very hard. They lived largely on a diet of porridge and oatcakes. Hunger and disease were common. They toiled on the land. Commoners had to declare their loyalty to the lords and the lords to the kings. There were many minor kings, but real power lay with the regional kings of Ulster, Meath, Munster, Leinster and Connaught. A High King was based at the ancient royal site of Tara, but rarely ruled all Ireland because of the endless wars between Ireland's royal families.

OGHAM SCRIPT

A kind of alphabet made up of criss-cross lines was carved on Irish stones from about AD 300. It is called ogham. Ogham fell out of use as Christian monks in the 600s and 700s introduced the letters of the Roman alphabet.

THE VOYAGES OF BRENDAN

Brendan or Brandan was born in Tralee, in County Kerry, in AD 484. A Christian saint, he is said to have founded Clonfert monastery in Galway in AD 561. Tales about him were written down later in the Middle Ages, describing his sea voyages. Brendan seems to have been a navigator who sailed the North Atlantic Ocean and knew its eastern coasts. A description of the 'mouth of hell' suggests that he may have seen volcanic eruptions off the coast of Iceland.

This chalice, a cup used during Christian worship, was dug up at Ardagh, in County Limerick, in 1868. It is one of the finest pieces of metal working produced in Europe during the early Middle Ages. It is made of silver and gilt bronze, with a central stud of rock crystal. It dates from about AD 700.

❋ AD 577
West Britons defeated by
Wessex at the Battle of
Dyrham

❋ AD 600
Earliest known Welsh poetry,
the *Gododdin*

❋ AD 607
The battle of Chester.
Aefelfrith of Northumbria
defeats the Britons

❋ AD 632
Cadwallon I of Gwynedd
allies with Penda of Mercia to
defeat Northumbria

❋ AD 635
The West Britons start to
call themselves *Cymry*
– the Welsh

THE MAKING · OF WALES

MANY Britons now found themselves ruled by
Anglo-Saxons. Others fled westwards. So many
sailed off to northwestern France that it later
became known as 'Little Britain' or Brittany. Britain
itself only became known as 'Great' by way of
comparison. After the Battle of Dyrham in AD
577 the Britons of Devon and Cornwall
were cut off from those to the north.
The last strongholds of the
Britons were the Cornish
peninsula and the
mountainous west,
the land that came to
be known as Wales.

At the courts of the Welsh
kings, harpists praised
rulers for their wisdom and
bravery, or lamented their defeat
by the Anglo-Saxons.

WELSH RULERS

Houses of Gwynedd,
Powys and Dyfed
✤ Rhodri Mawr ('the Great')
  AD 844–78
✤ Anarawd AD 878–916
✤ Hywel Dda ('the Good')
  AD 915–950
✤ Iago ab Idwal AD 950–979
✤ Hywel ab Ieuaf AD 979–85
✤ Cadwallon II AD 985–986
✤ Maredudd ap Owain
  AD 986–999
✤ Cynan ap Hywel
  AD 999–1008
✤ Llywelyn ap Seisyll
  1018–1023
✤ Iago ap Idwal ap Meurig
  1023–39

A great dyke, or
earthwork, was raised
along the Welsh borders by King
Offa of Mercia in about AD 784.
It can still be seen today.

❀ **AD 654**
Last ties broken between the Britons in Wales and the Old North

❀ **AD 784**
Offa's dyke marks the eastern border of Wales

❀ **AD 844**
Rhodri Mawr becomes king of Gwynedd and extends its power

❀ **AD 855**
The royal house of Powys comes to an end

❀ **c AD 945**
The Laws of Hywel Dda are written down

55

THE OLD NORTH

In Welsh history, the lands of the northern Britons are known as the Old North. This region was divided into several kingdoms. They included Elmet (around the hills of the Pennines), Rheged (Cumbria), Manaw Gododdin (around Edinburgh) and the kingdom of Strathclyde. All but the last were invaded by the Angles. An Anglo-Saxon victory at Chester, in AD 615, drove a wedge between Wales and the Old North. Links between the two were finally broken after AD 654.

"MEN WENT TO CATRAETH..."

Welsh poetry has a very long history. Some of the earliest and finest verse was written down later in the Middle Ages. The story of the *Gododdin* comes from the Old North and is dated to about AD 600. It describes a British war band which sets out, perhaps from Edinburgh, to attack the Angles at Catraeth (today's Catterick, in Yorkshire). The war band suffers a terrible defeat.

THE LAWS OF HYWEL

Hywel ap ('son of") Cadell was a grandson of Rhodri Mawr. He came to rule most of Wales and made peace with the Anglo-Saxons. In AD 928 he went on a pilgrimage to Rome. Hywel is famed as a law-maker, for it was in his reign that the ancient laws of Wales were written down. The laws deal with property, murder, theft and the rights of women. They describe compensation for crimes, oath-taking and the part played by witnesses. Welsh law was carried out by trained judges and remained in use for over 500 years. Hywel died in AD 950 and is remembered as Hywel Dda ('the Good').

◀ *Surviving copies of Hywel's laws are in Welsh and Latin, and are illustrated with pictures. They give us a fascinating glimpse of life in the Middle Ages. We learn about farming, fishing, hunting, bee-keeping, about the life of families and communities*

WELSH KINGDOMS

Even when Wales was cut off by the Anglo-Saxons, its merchants and monks could still sail to Ireland, Cornwall, Brittany and beyond. Wales was made up of rival kingdoms. Gwynedd was in North Wales. This kingdom became the most powerful under the rule of Rhodri Mawr ('the Great'), who died in AD 877. In southwest Wales, an area settled by Irish invaders, was the kingdom of Dyfed. It later joined with Ceredigion to make a kingdom called Deheubarth. The royal house of Powys in mid-Wales was said to have been founded by Vortigern. Gwent and other small kingdoms of southeast Wales joined together to form Morgannwg (Glamorgan).

◀ *This tombstone records the death of King Cadfan of Gwynedd in AD 625. The words are written in Latin and his name is made Roman (Catamanus). The words mean 'King Cadfan, wisest and most renowned of all kings'.*

❊ AD 597
Augustine becomes first
Archbishop of Canterbury

❊ AD 634
Oswald becomes king of
Northumbria, introduces
Celtic Christianity

❊ AD 664
Synod of Whitby unites
Roman and Celtic Churches
in England

❊ AD 680
Christian poetry in
English written by
Caedmon at Whitby

❊ AD 698
The Lindisfarne Gospels
produced by monks in
Northumbria

THE MAKING OF ENGLAND

ANGLO-SAXON KINGDOMS

Celts

Northumbria   NORTH SEA

Anglo-Saxons

East Anglia

Celts   Mercia

Essex

Kent

Wessex   Sussex

Celts

ENGLISH CHANNEL

ANGLO-SAXON kings such as Offa of Mercia held great power. They constantly attacked neighbouring kingdoms in their search for wealth and more land. Kings demanded personal loyalty and support from their lords, who were called thanes. Many of the peasants were conquered Britons. They included free men called ceorls, as well as serfs and thralls (slaves). Anglo-Saxon merchants traded across the English Channel, the North Sea and the Baltic.

Kent, Sussex and Essex ruled the southeast. Wessex, in the southwest, grew more and more powerful. Mercia, occupying the English Midlands, was the biggest kingdom. The kingdoms of Deira and Bernicia united as Northumbria, taking in all northern England and Lothian.

ANGLO-SAXON LIFE

At first the Anglo-Saxons were not great builders of towns, but Canterbury, Southampton, Winchester and York all thrived and the port of London (then in the kingdom of Essex) continued to grow. Some of the land was still covered in thick forest. The sound of axes rang through the trees, as farmers cleared the land for building and ploughing with oxen. They grew peas, beans and barley, wheat or rye. They baked bread and brewed beer. Pigs snuffled under the oak trees, searching for acorns.

An Anglo-Saxon farmstead was surrounded by a few large fields cleared from the forest. Within these, farmers worked their own strips for cultivation and harvest.

✿ **AD 700**
The Old English poem of
Beowulf is written down

✿ **AD 731**
Bede writes his history of the
English Church

✿ **AD 735**
York becomes an
archbishopric

✿ **AD 757**
Offa makes Mercia the most
powerful Anglo-Saxon kingdom

✿ **AD 798**
Cenwulf of Mercia lays
Kent to waste and tortures
Kentish king

57

BEOWULF AND THE MONSTER

In about AD 700 an exciting tale was told and retold in the halls of the Anglo-Saxon kings. It was written down in the Old English language of the Anglo-Saxons. It took the form of a long poem about a monster called Grendel, which terrorises the Danes until they are saved by a hero called Beowulf. The verse is alliterative, which means that it plays on repeated sounds.

CHRISTIAN ENGLAND

In AD 597 St Augustine and 40 of his monks arrived from Rome with a mission – to convert the Anglo-Saxons to Christianity. King Ethelbert of Kent, who had a Christian wife, became a Christian too. England's first cathedral was built at Canterbury. In Northumbria, however, the Roman teachings clashed with the Celtic version of Christianity, as preached by the monks of Lindisfarne. In AD 664 a meeting or synod was held at Whitby. Here the Celtic Church agreed to recognize the Roman Church.

BEDE'S HISTORY

Bede or Baeda was born in about AD 673 at Monk-wearmouth, in County Durham. He became a monk at Jarrow in AD 703 and studied Latin, Greek, Hebrew, medicine and astronomy. In AD 731 he wrote *The Ecclesiastical History of the English People* in Latin. It was translated into Anglo-Saxon and still serves as a very useful guide to early English history. Bede was buried at Jarrow in AD 735 and his remains were later moved to Durham.

As Christians, the Anglo-Saxons built many fine churches of timber and of stone. St Lawrence's is at Bradford-on-Avon in Wiltshire, England. It was first raised by St Adhelm in the 700s, and then re-built later in the Anglo-Saxon period.

❀ AD 789
First Viking raids on
southern coast of England

❀ AD 793
Vikings attack the monastery
of Lindisfarne

❀ AD 795
First Viking raids on Ireland

❀ AD 795
First Viking attack on the
monks of Iona

❀ AD 806
Vikings kill 68 monks in Iona

SEA WOLVES

IN AD 793 the monastery of Lindisfarne was
ransacked and burnt down. A few years later
the island of Iona came under attack and its
monks were slaughtered. The raiders were
known as Northmen or Danes. They are
often called Vikings, from an Old Norse
word meaning 'sea raiders'. Vikings came
from the lands of Scandinavia – Denmark,
Norway and Sweden. No sight in Europe was
feared more than the sails of their ships coming
over the horizon.

Shields
Shields were round and
made of wood, ringed
with iron or leather. They
were used as a weapon
as well as for defence.

BERSERK!
Viking warriors believed that a heroic death in battle
would bring them glory and a place in Valholl, the
heavenly hall of the Germanic gods whom they still
worshipped. They despised the Christian monks. Vikings were
masters of the surprise attack and raiding from beach or river.
When cornered in a pitched battle, they would form a wall of
shields and fight to the bitter end. Leading warriors would
work themselves up into a frenzied rage before battle. They
were called *berserkir*, or 'bearskin shirts', after their dress.

*Many Vikings spent most of
the year farming and fishing
before joining a war band for the
sea voyage. Some hired themselves
out as mercenaries – soldiers who
fight for a wage.*

Helmets
Helmets were conical and
made of hardened leather
or iron. Some had a bar to
protect the nose.

Weapons
Swords were double-edged in
steel. Many were given pet
names by their owner. The
battle-axe was another favourite
weapon and every ship carried
bundles of spears and arrows.

Battle dress
Most Viking warriors wore simple
tunics, trousers and cloaks. The
wealthier ones wore mail shirts.

Wind power
The mast was made of pine. It carried a rectangular sail made of linen or wool.

The prow
The high front of the ship was often finely carved.

The crew
The longship was rowed by 30 or more warriors. They sat on benches or on sea chests containing their weapons, food and cloaks.

Wooden wall
Shields could be slung along the side of the ship as extra protection against enemy arrows.

The keel
The central beam of the ship was made of oak and might be over 18 metres long.

THE VIKING RAIDS

Whalers and seal hunters from Norway had already settled many of the bleak islands to the north and west of Scotland. Norse Vikings came seeking more southerly lands too. Their homeland had barren mountains, forests and cold, dark winters. The milder climate and more fertile lands of the British Isles offered rich prizes. Danish Vikings attacked eastern and southern Britain in search of wealth and adventure. They kidnapped slaves from coastal villages and stole jewellery, silver and gold. They looted the precious chalices, plates and even the bells from churches and monasteries.

The Vikings were expert seafarers. They sailed to war in streamlined wooden vessels called longships.

LANDS IN PERIL

Soon no region of the British Isles was safe from the Vikings. They raided along all English Channel and North Sea coasts. They attacked villages and towns in Wales, Scotland, Ireland and the Isle of Man. They sailed along the costs of Germany, the Netherlands, France and Spain. Vikings travelled east into Russia and down to the Middle East. They sailed west, settling Iceland and Greenland. They even reached North America.

A ship in full sail is shown on this carved stone from Gotland in Sweden. Above it the god Odin rides his eight-legged horse to Valholl.

60

⚜ **AD 800**
Vikings occupy Orkney and Shetland Isles

⚜ **AD 830s**
Increased Viking raids on Ireland

⚜ **AD 841**
Start of Viking settlement at Dublin

⚜ **AD 850**
Viking settlements on Isle of Man

⚜ **AD 850**
Viking raiders over- winter in England for the first time

JORVIK TO DUBLIN

DURING the 800s, many areas of the British Isles were permanently settled by Vikings. They included the isles of the Shetlands, Orkneys, and Hebrides and the northern and western coasts of the Scottish mainland. They invaded the Isle of Man and occupied the northern Irish coast. After the 830s the Vikings founded settlements at Dublin and other places in southern Ireland, too. Dublin Vikings later married into the royal family of Gwynedd, in North Wales. In England, Vikings captured York, which they called Jorvik, in AD 867. Three years later they invaded East Anglia and killed King Edmund. Their next prize was the Midland kingdom of Mercia.

VIKINGS ON THE MAP

Many place names in the British Isles date from the age of the Vikings. Scandinavian settlements often end in *-by* or *-thorp*. Examples include Duncansby in Scotland or Grimsby and Mablethorpe in England. The ending *-ey* means 'island'. It can be seen in the Channel Islands of Alderney or Guernsey, or in Caldey and Anglesey in Wales. Personal names are also to be found. Knutsford is named after Knut or Cnut.

IN A VIKING TOWN

A typical Viking settlement in the British Isles was built around quays on a coast or river bank. Moored at the jetties there might be a *knarr*, a broad-beamed merchant ship. A small four-oared *færing* might be seen rowing in from a day's fishing, followed by squawking gulls. Buildings were rectangular and normally made of wattle and daub or oak planks. In the northern islands, stone and turf were common building materials.

◀ *Inside the home there was a central hearth, hung with cooking pots. There was a loom for weaving and a clutter of barrels and chests used for storage.*

🌸 **AD 851**
Norwegian and Danish Vikings
battle for control of Dublin

🌸 **AD 867**
The Vikings take York (Jorvik)
which becomes their chief
settlement

🌸 **AD 914**
New wave of Viking attacks
on Ireland

🌸 **AD 950**
Death of Erik Bloodaxe, last
Viking king of Jorvik (York)

🌸 **AD 980**
Christianity begins to spread
through Viking homelands

61

 Fragments of Viking clothing
have been discovered by
archaeologists at York, including
boots, shoes and socks.

Hair
Viking men
wore their hair
long or tied
back.

The Vikings
made fine
jewellery, including
bracelets, brooches,
rings and necklaces.

Plaits and scarves
Women's hair was worn
long. It was tidied with a
comb made of horn or
bone before being plaited
or covered by a scarf.

BLACKSMITHS AND WOODCARVERS

Viking settlements included smithies,
where sparks flew as the blacksmith
forged swords and spears on the anvil
and repaired iron tools for the farm.
Metalworkers and jewellers produced
finer craft, working with gold, silver,
pewter (an alloy of lead and tin),
with black jet and yellow amber.
The Vikings carved wood, stone
and whale bone, often using
intricate designs of animals. Vikings
often formed a business fellowship
called a *felag*, which was rather like
a company. The members, who
might be craft workers, merchants
or mercenaries, put up money and
shared the risks and the profits of the
enterprise.

Dress
Viking women
wore a shift of
linen or wool
covered by a long
woollen tunic with
shoulder straps
fastened by
brooches.

Tunic
Men wore a knee-
length long-sleeved
tunic over trousers.
Cloaks would be
worn against the
cold.

THE TYNWALD

Vikings passed laws and settled disputes at a
public assembly called a *Thing*. The Isle of
Man assembly met at a grassy mound called
the Tynwald. This is still the name of the
Manx parliament today. It claims to be the
world's oldest legislative (law-making)
assembly with an uninterrupted history.
Viking assemblies were attended by all free
men, but not by women or slaves.

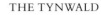 A Viking chieftain rides to the assembly.
Here there would be discussion about new
laws and judgements to be passed.

62

✴ **AD 829**
Egbert of Wessex overlord of
the Anglo-Saxon kingdoms

✴ **AD 866**
The Grand Army of 'Danes'
arrives in England

✴ **AD 871**
Alfred becomes the king of
Wessex

✴ **AD 879**
Treaty of Wedmore. Alfred
recognizes the Danelaw

✴ **AD 901**
Edward the Elder starts
Anglo-Saxon conquest of
England

DANELAW

THE Scandinavian conquest of East Anglia,
Mercia and Northumbria was not carried out
by small bands of raiders but by a Grand Army
of Danes – an alliance of warriors recruited from many
different Viking settlements. Their chief enemy was
Wessex, in southern England, for in AD 829 King
Egbert of Wessex had become overlord of all the other
Anglo-Saxon kingdoms. Now, in AD 871, Egbert's
grandson, Alfred, came to the throne. If the Danes
conquered Wessex, all England would be in their grasp.

The Vikings' permanent
settlements in England were
known as the Danelaw. The relentless
advance of the 'Danes' was first
reversed by Alfred of Wessex.

ALFRED FIGHTS BACK

A great army of Danes
descended on Wessex again in
the winter of AD 876. Alfred
took refuge at Athelney, in the
marshes of Somerset. He then
fought back and defeated the Danes in
AD 878. They gave up the lands of southern
Mercia and their leader Guthrum agreed to
become a Christian – but Alfred had to
recognize the rule of Danelaw to the north.

THE ANGLO-SAXON
CHRONICLE

During the reign of Alfred,
a history of England since the
Roman conquest was written
down by Christian monks. The
Anglo-Saxon Chronicle is not just
a record of English history but
the record of a language.
The writing continued into the
1100s and so it shows how the
Old English language
developed and changed.

King Alfred is named on
this jewelled ornament
found at Athelney.

DANEGELD

Shortly after Alfred became king
of Wessex, his army was defeated
by the Danes. Alfred could think
of only one solution – bribery.
He paid the Danes money to
leave Wessex alone. They did –
but only for four years. A later
king adopted the same policy.
Ethelred II, who came to the
throne in AD 978, brought in a
tax called Danegeld ('Dane
money') to keep the Danes out
of the south. Needless to say, they
kept coming back for more.
The name Ethelred means 'wise
counsel' or 'good advice'. He
of course became known as
'Redeless' – meaning 'ill-advised'.

In the 700 and 800s, the Anglo-
Saxons began to produce large
numbers of silver pennies and other coins.
Many of these found their way
back to Scandinavia.
Viking settlements
minted their own
coinage as well.

					63
✹ **AD 926**	✹ **AD 991**	✹ **1009**	✹ **1016**	✹ **1042**	
Athelstan brings the Britons of Cornwall under Anglo-Saxon rule	Danes win Battle of Maldon. Payment of Danegeld by Ethelred	Vikings under Olaf the Stout pull down London Bridge	Battle of Ashingdon. England under Danish rule	Witan appoints Edward the Confessor as English king	

RULERS OF WESSEX AND ENGLAND
Houses of Cerdic and Denmark

✤ Egbert	AD 802–839	✤ Eadwig	AD 955–959
✤ Ethelwulf	AD 839–855	✤ Edgar	AD 959–975
✤ Ethelbald	AD 855–860	✤ Edward 'the Martyr'	AD 975–978
✤ Ethelbert	AD 860–866	✤ Ethelred II 'the Redeless'	AD 978–1016
✤ Ethelred I	AD 866–871	✤ Edmund 'Ironside'	AD 1016
✤ Alfred	AD 871–899	✤ Cnut I	1016–1035
✤ Edward 'the Elder'	AD 900–924	✤ Harold I 'Harefoot'	1037–1040
✤ Athelstan	AD 924–939	✤ Cnut II 'Harthacnut'	1040–1042
✤ Edmund I	AD 939–946	✤ Edward 'the Confessor'	1042–1066
✤ Eadred	AD 946–955	✤ Harold II	1066

Alfred learned many lessons from the Vikings. One was the importance of ships in warfare. He was the first English ruler to build a fleet. He also reorganized the fyrd, the Anglo-Saxon peasant army.

ALFRED'S LEGACY

Alfred proved to be a wise ruler. He encouraged learning and wrote down the laws of England. In the 890s he planned a new type of stronghold called a *burh* and built many of these to hold back the Danes. His lands grew wealthy from trade. Alfred's daughter Ethelflæd of Mercia fought the Danes in battle and Alfred's good work was continued by his sucessors Edward the Elder, Athelstan and Edgar. However peace broke down after AD979 and Ethelred II provoked a major Danish invasion by the Danish king Svein 'Forkbeard'.

ENGLAND UNITES

After many battles and treaties, in 1016 England came under the rule of Svein's son, Cnut I (Knut or Canute). He married Ethelred II's widow, Emma, and went on to reign over Denmark and parts of Sweden and Norway as well. The appointment of Anglo-Saxon kings had to be approved by a council of nobles, called the Witan. In 1042 the Witan chose Edward, the son of Cnut I and Emma. The ruler of a united England, he was a devout Christian and is remembered in history as 'the Confessor'. He founded Westminster Abbey near the growing city of London.

64

🌸 **AD 866**
High King Áed Finlliath drives
Vikings from northern coast

🌸 **AD 919**
Vikings defeat the Irish at the
Battle of Dublin

🌸 **AD 951**
Death of Cenéttig, father of
Brian Boru

🌸 **AD 971**
Brian Boru rules both
Munster and Leinster

🌸 **AD 999**
Leinster-Viking alliance defeated
at battle of Glenn Máma

VIKING TOWNS IN IRELAND

The Vikings' chief town was Dublin, but there were also settlements at Strangford, Carlingford, Limerick, Waterford, Wexford, Cork and Youghal. The Irish Vikings were known as Ostmen ('men from the east').

The Viking hold on Ireland was less complete than that of the Engish 'Danelaw', being made up of scattered settlements and coastal and river ports.

BLOODSHED AT CLONTARF

THE Viking attacks on Ireland came in several waves. At first, in the 800s, the Scandinavians – mostly from Norway – came to plunder. Later they built permanent camps and then settlements and towns. The Vikings met fierce resistance from the Irish kings and often from the monks, too. After AD 914 there was another great wave of Viking invasions, and in AD 919 King Niall Glúundúb, along with many lords of Ireland's most powerful family, the Uí Néill, were killed at the Battle of Dublin.

OSTMEN AND IRISH

In these times of trouble, tall, round towers were built at many Irish monasteries, such as Glendalough in the Wicklow mountains. They served as lookouts and shelters against Viking raiders. Sometimes however the invaders joined forces with one Irish king to fight another. The Vikings had great effect on Irish life. They influenced Irish arts and crafts and encouraged long-distance trade. They also taught the Irish their boat-building and sailing skills.

Brian Boru, born in AD 926, was a ruthless fighter who spent as much time battling with other Irish kings as with the Ostmen.

BRIAN BORU, HIGH KING

During the 900s, the royal family of Munster, the Eóganacht, lost pride of place to a dynasty from North Munster, called the Dál Cais. Their king, Cennétig, died in AD 951. One of his sons was called Brian Bóruma, or Boru ('Brian of the Tribute'). By AD 976 Brian had gained control of Munster. By AD 984 he was king of Leinster and by 1002 he ruled all Ireland as High King, going on to conquer the settlements of the Vikings.

🌼 **1002**
Brian Boru rules all Ireland as
High King

🌼 **1014**
Brian Boru defeats Viking-
Leinster alliance at Clontarf

🌼 **1014**
Death of Brian Boru.
Máel Sechnaill II regains
High Kingship

🌼 **1014**
End of Viking power in Ireland

🌼 **1022**
Power of the Irish High Kings
fragments

65

THE BATTLE OF CLONTARF

The people of Leinster had never been happy with the
rule of Brian Boru, and he soon faced revolt on many
sides. Brian's son was sent to subdue Leinster in 1013.
Leinster allied with the Dublin Vikings and in the
spring of 1014 there was a fierce battle at Clontarf, to
the northeast of Dublin. The ageing High King's forces
won the day, but he was murdered after the battle.
Clontarf marked the end of Viking power in Ireland.
The *Ostmen* who remained gradually took on Irish
ways and language.

This beautiful
crozier or staff
belonged to the abbot of
Clonmacnois in the
1100s. In the century
after Clontarf, the
powerful Irish Church
was reformed by Rome.

IRELAND FRAGMENTS

With the death of Brian Boru, the office
of High King passed back to Máel
Sechnaill II of the Uí Néill, who had
been High King before Brian rose to
power. He died in 1022. After that, real
power passed back to the kings of the
provinces. It was they who laid
down the law and taxed the
people heavily in order to fight
the endless wars they waged
upon their rivals.

HIGH KINGS OF IRELAND

House of Niall of the Nine
Hostages (Tara)

✦ Máel Sechnaill I	AD 842–862
✦ Áed Findliath	AD 862–879
✦ Flann Sinna	AD 879–916
✦ Niall Glúundub	AD 916–919
✦ Donnchad Donn	AD 919–944
✦ Congalach Cnogba	AD 944–956
✦ Domnall ua Néill	AD 956–980
✦ Máel Sechnaill II	AD 980–1002
✦ Brian Boru	1002–1014
✦ Máel Sechnaill II	1014–1022

The battle of
Clontarf was brutal
and bloody, even by the
standards of the day.

✵ 1018
Battle of Carham. Malcolm II
defeats Northumbrians

✵ 1034
Duncan I becomes king
of all Scotland

✵ 1034
British kingdom of Strathclyde
joins Scotland

✵ 1039
Duncan I launches attack on
the English city of Durham

✵ 1040
Macbeth kills Duncan I and
seizes throne

MACBETH'S SCOTLAND

I N 1018 Macolm II, King of Alba, marched southwards across the River Tweed and defeated the Northumbrians at the battle of Carham. Lothian was now in Scottish hands. In 1034 another piece of the jigsaw puzzle fell into place when King Duncan of Strathclyde, (the kingdom of the Britons in the southwest) inherited the throne of Alba. The kingdom of Scotland had now been created and within it were Scots, Britons and Angles. However Norwegian Vikings still held on to the northern and western fringes of the kingdom, and the southern border would be fought over for hundreds of years.

Duncan's son Malcolm avenged his father's murder, killing Macbeth at Lumphanan in 1057.

NORSE AND GAELIC

In the Hebrides, the old Gaelic way of life was now mixed with the Norse. A group of independent chieftains arose, part Scots and part Norwegian. They sailed in longships and answered to no king. It was not until the 1100s, when Somerled, ancestor of the Macdonald clan, gained control of the islands, that the Viking way of life finally began to disappear. But even then, the islanders were a law to themselves.

The island of Skye is part of Gaelic Scotland, but the strong Norse presence there is confirmed by many place names and by hoards of coins.

STRUGGLES FOR POWER

The lands of Scotland may have been united under the rule of Duncan I, but all around the throne there were old scores to settle and quarrels betwen rival groups or factions. One faction was led by Macbeth, the Mórmaer (chief) of Moray who married Gruoch, granddaughter of Kenneth III. He defeated and killed Duncan in 1040 and banished Duncan's sons, Malcolm and Donald Bán, from the kingdom.

❁ 1045
Duncan's father, Crínán, fails
in revolt against Macbeth

❁ 1057
Malcolm Canmore
kills Macbeth

❁ 1070
Margaret marries Malcolm
Canmore at Dunfermline

❁ 1093
Malcolm Canmore
killed at Alnwick.

❁ 1093
Death of Queen
Margaret of Scotland

67

DEATH AND REVENGE

The famous play *Macbeth* was written in England by
William Shakespeare hundreds of years after the real
Macbeth ruled Scotland. In the play, Macbeth is a
murderous villain, driven by personal ambition. In
reality, Macbeth may have been no more villainous than
many other kings of his day. His motives for killing
Duncan were probably part of a family feud. Macbeth
went on a Christian pilgrimage to Rome and Scotland
prospered under his rule. However Duncan's son,
Malcolm, supported by his uncle Earl Siward of
Northumbria, returned to kill Macbeth in 1057.

MALCOLM CANMORE

Malcolm III came to the Scottish throne in the
following year. He was nicknamed Canmore, from the
Gaelic *Ceann Mor*, which could mean either 'big head'
or 'great chief'! He built a new palace at Dunfermline,
which was now the Scottish capital. Malcolm's long
reign was marked by endless wars south of the border,
with Cnut I and the kings of England that followed
him. He was killed at Alnwick in 1093.

RULERS OF ALBA AND SCOTLAND	
House of MacAlpin	
✤ Kenneth I MacAlpin	AD 843–858
✤ Donald I	AD 858–862
✤ Constantine I	AD 862–877
✤ Aed	AD 877–878
✤ Eochaid and Giric	AD 878–889
✤ Donald II	AD 889–900
✤ Constantine II	AD 900–943
✤ Malcom I	AD 943–954
✤ Indulf	AD 954–962
✤ Dubh	AD 963–966
✤ Culen	AD 966–971
✤ Kenneth II	AD 971–995
✤ Constantine III	AD 995–997
✤ Kenneth III	AD 997–1005
✤ Malcolm II	AD 1005–1034
✤ Duncan I	1034–1040
✤ Macbeth	1040–1057
✤ Lulach	1057–1058
✤ Malcolm III 'Canmore'	1058–1093

MACBETH'S
SCOTLAND

NORSE
LANDS

ALBA
(SCOTLAND)

NORTH
SEA

Dál Riada

Pictland

Strathclyde

Lothian

IRISH
SEA

ENGLAND

*Scotland was fashioned out of four
smaller kingdoms Dál Riada, Pictland,
Strathclyde and Lothian. Its southern borders
were constantly shifting.*

MARGARET, QUEEN AND SAINT
Malcolm Canmore's first wife was
Ingiborg, the widow of a powerful Norse
leader called Thorfinn, Earl of Orkney. She
died and in about 1070 there was another
royal wedding, at Dunfermline.
The bride was 24 year-old
Margaret, daughter of an exiled
claimant to the English throne,
called Edward the Ætheling. Born
in Hungary, Margaret brought the
customs of mainland Europe to the
Scottish court. Her palace shone with
gold and silver, but she was a careful
manager of finances. She founded
many monasteries and was later
made a saint.

*Under Margaret's
influence, Roman forms
of Christian worship replaced
traditions of the Celtic Church
which had survived in Scotland.*

4

CASTLES AND KNIGHTS

AD1066–1509

THE WORLD AT A GLANCE

ELSEWHERE IN EUROPE

1220
King Frederick II of Sicily and Germany becomes Holy Roman Emperor

1226
Louis IX (St Louis) comes to the throne in France

1237
Mongol armies invade East and Central Europe (to 1241)

1378
A split in the Roman Church, with one Pope in Rome and another in Avignon, France

1453
Turks capture Constantinople (Istanbul). End of the Byzantine empire

1462
Lorenzo de Medici rules over splendid court at Florence, Italy

1480
Ivan the Great, first Tsar of Russia, expels the Mongols and unites his country

1492
Christians finally reconquer all of Moslem Spain, rule of Ferdinand and Isabella

ASIA

1096
European Crusaders attack Moslems in the Near East and found Christian kingdoms

1170
The Hindu Srivijaya kingdom rules Java, Southeast Asia

1190
Temujin (Genghis Khan) starts to create the Mongol empire

1192
Yoritomo Minamoto becomes first Shogun (military dictator) in Japan

1206
The Islamic Sultanate rules in Delhi, India

1271
Mongol ruler Kublai Khan becomes the emperor of China

1368
Ming emperors rule China, capital at Nanjing

1405
Death of Timur the Lame (or Tamberlaine), Tatar ruler of a vast Asian empire

AFRICA

1200
The rise of the state of Mali in West Africa

1200
Rise of Hausa city-states in northern Nigeria and Kanem-Bornu in Lake Chad region

1250
Rise of the Benin empire in southern Nigerian forests

1250
High stone enclosures built at Great Zimbabwe, in southeast Africa

1300
Founding of the Kongo kingdom in southern Central Africa

1400
Chinese, Arab and Indian traders along East Africa's Swahili Coast

1400
Fine heads made from bronze in the Benin empire

1450
Height of Songhai power in southern Sahara, university at Timbuktu

"The peasant toils, the king rules – and God is in His heaven..."

Llywelyn Fawr

NORTH AMERICA

1100
Thule culture of the American Arctic, based on whaling

1150
The Anasazi people settle Mesa Verde in the southwest

1170
Collapse of Toltec rule in Mexico, period of wars and strife

1300
The Maya people return to power in Mexico, with capital at Mayapán

1345
Aztecs build the great city of Teotihuacan on the modern site of Mexico City

1428
The Aztec empire expands and becomes very powerful

1492
Christopher Columbus, in the service of Spain, lands in the Caribbean

1493
The Spanish settle on the Caribbean island of Hispaniola

SOUTH AMERICA

1100
The city of Cuzco, Peru, is founded by the first Inca emperor

1370
The Chimú empire expands in northern Peru

1450
The founding of the Inca town of Machu Picchu, high in the Andes

1470
The Incas conquer the Chimú empire

1492
The Incas conquer northern Chile

1493
The Treaty of Tordesillas. Spain and Portugal divide up the Americas.

1498
The Inca empire is at its greatest extent under ruler Wayna Qapaq

1500
The Portuguese claim Brazil

OCEANIA

1100
Increased farming and irrigation begins on the Hawaiian islands

1200
Powerful chiefdoms grow up in Polynesia

1200
The Tu'i Tonga dynasty rules the Tongan Islands and part of Samoa

1200
Large numbers of stone platforms and houses built in the Society Islands

1250
Funeral of the Melanesian ruler Roy Mata on the island of Retoka

1300
Giant moa is hunted to extinction in New Zealand, increase in agriculture

1350
Classic Maori period begins on New Zealand, large fortresses

1400s
Malay fishermen camp on shores of northern Australia

70

♣ 1064
Harold swears to support
William of Normandy

♣ 1066
Harold II chosen as King of
England

♣ 1066
King Harald III of Norway
defeated at Stamford Bridge

♣ 1066
Norman invasion. Harold II
defeated at Battle of Hastings

♣ 1067
William I starts to build the
Tower of London

HASTINGS 1066

WHO WERE THE NORMANS?

The Anglo-Saxon kings were not the only ones who attempted buy off the Vikings. In AD 911 Charles 'the Simple', King of France, offered a Viking warlord called Rollo part of northern France in a desperate bid to win peace. It became called Normandy ('land of the Northmen'). Rollo became a duke and married Giselle, a French princess. Like their Viking ancestors, Norman warlords stormed their way around Europe. They invaded the Italian island of Sicily in 1060.

IN the summer of 1066 a large fleet assembled along the French coast. Its commander was William, Duke of Normandy. Ships wallowed at anchor in choppy seas, waiting for the northerly wind to turn. Norman lords galloped to and fro on horseback. Carts trundled along the beach loaded with spears, swords, arrows and axes, iron helmets, shields and coats of mail. This would be the last major invasion of England in the Middle Ages.

Archers
The bow used by the Normans was about 1.5 metres long and was drawn to the chest. It was said that a Norman arrow pierced King Harold's eye and killed him.

Wooden weapons
Bows were made of elm, but arrows of ash. The flights were made from goose feathers.

 The Battle of Hastings remains the most famous event in English history. Its shockwaves were felt right across the British Isles.

CLAIMS FOR THE THRONE

Harold of Wessex was the son of a powerful Anglo-Saxon earl called Godwin. In January 1066 the Witan named Harold as King of England, but their decision was challenged at once. Edward the Ætheling, nephew of Edward the Confessor, claimed the throne. So did Harold's own brother, Tostig. A third claimant was King Harald III of Norway, known as 'Hardraade', 'the Ruthless'. The fourth was William of Normandy. William swore that in 1064 Harold had made a solemn vow to support the Norman claim.

RULERS OF ENGLAND	
House of Normandy	
♣ William I 'the Conqueror'	1066–1087
♣ William II 'Rufus'	1087–1100
♣ Henry I 'Beauclerk'	1100–1135
♣ Stephen	1135–1154

✤ 1068
Norman conquest of
northern and western England

✤ 1069
Anglo-Saxon uprising, led by
Edward the Ætheling

✤ 1070
Rebellion in East Anglia by
Hereward 'the Wake'

✤ 1085
William I orders compilation
of the Domesday Book

✤ 1087
War with France, William I
dies after he falls from horse

71

ONE BATTLE TOO MANY

Harold II's troops were waiting for the Normans when word
came that Harald III of Norway had joined forces with Tostig.
Harold marched northwards at speed. He defeated and killed
them both at Stamford Bridge, near York. Just three days later,
Norman troops landed in Sussex. Harold had to march his
exhausted army south again. On 14 October 1066, the two
great armies clashed at Senlac Hill, near Hastings. All day, wave
after wave of Normans broke against the Anglo-Saxon shields.
Harold's men stood firm but, scenting victory, they broke rank
too soon. The victory belonged to William – 'the Conqueror'.

THE DOMESDAY BOOK

Exactly 19 years after his
coronation, William I
announced that all the lands in
England south of the rivers
Ribble and Tees (and
excluding the cities of London
and Winchester) were to be
registered in a great book.
From 1086 onwards, royal
officials travelled from one
estate to another. They wrote
down the details of buildings,
land and resources, so that
they could be taxed.

Shield
The long kite-shaped
shield was developed
by the Norman cavalry

Helmet
The iron, cone-shaped
helmet was worn over a
hood of mail, called a coif.

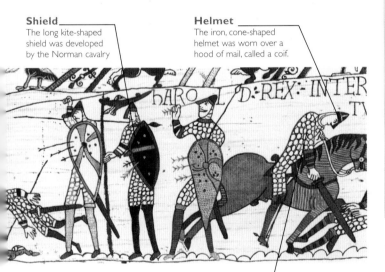

This tapestry of wool on a linen
backing has a 70-metre long 'strip'
format, which tells the story of the Norman
invasion of England. It can still be seen
today in Bayeux, Normandy.

Coats of mail
Norman warriors protected
themselves with a mail shirt
worn over a tunic.

The Tower of London
was added to over the
ages. It played a central role
in English history, with many
famous prisoners being
locked up in its dungeons.

THE CONQUEST

On Christmas Day 1066, William I was crowned
king in Westminster Abbey. Within months of his
coronation, William ordered the building of a new
fortification by the River Thames, in London. Its
great keep, or stronghold, was the White Tower.
This became the centre of the Tower of London.

Within two years most of England was under his
control. Revolts led by Edward the Ætheling and
an Anglo-Saxon lord called Hereward the Wake
('the Watchful') were crushed.

72

✛ **1066**
The Norman Channel Islands come under the English crown

✛ **1072**
William I of England leads army into Scotland

✛ **1092**
Normans build castle at Pembroke in South Wales

✛ **1094**
'Marcher' Lordships established in the Welsh borders

✛ **1094**
Norman invasion of North Wales

THE MAILED FIST

THE Norman kings of England and their successors wanted to be recognized as overlords of all the British Isles. Their fleets sailed north and their armies were soon battling with the Scots. Norman warlords were given territories on the Welsh borders (the 'Marches'), and stormed into North and South Wales. Within a hundred years, their great castles of stone could be seen in Ireland, too.

Braided hair
Norman ladies often wore their hair in plaits. Heads were sometimes covered with a short veil, secured by a circlet of silver or gold.

A cloak
A long woollen cloak was worn for warmth, fastened across the front by a cord.

The girdle
A cord or jewelled belt was worn around the waist.

A flowing dress
A long-sleeved shift was covered by a long tunic called a bliaut, which was laced at the side.

◗ *A Norman lady*

◗ *Dermot, the Irish ruler of Leinster, needed the support of Strongbow (right). In return he offered him the hand of his daughter, Aoife, and succession to the throne of Leinster*

THE NORMANS IN SCOTLAND

After repeated Scottish invasions of his new kingdom, William I marched into Lothian at the head of a large army in 1071, but he made peace with Malcolm Canmore at Abernethy. In 1092 the Normans took Cumbria from the Scots, but a full-scale invasion of Scotland never occurred. Norman settlers did arrive, bringing their ways to the Lowlands and to the Scottish court. Later Scottish kings, including Robert Bruce and the Stewarts, were of Norman descent.

Supplies
Weapons and equipment had to be carried with the troops. Food and grain could be seized by force along the way.

✤ 1097
Normans defeat
Donald III of
Scotland

✤ 1100
William II of England is killed,
possibly murdered, in the
New Forest

✤ 1106
Henry I of England defeats
and imprisons his brother
Robert in Normandy

✤ 1166
Dermot MacMurrough of
Leinster invites Normans into
Ireland

✤ 1170
Normans invade from
Baginbun, Wexford

73

WALES AND THE MARCHES

The Norman kings did not intend to rule Wales directly, but they wished to control it. As early as 1067 William I gave land on the borders to William Fitzosbern, Roger Montgomery and Hugh d'Avranches. These 'Marcher Lords' were a law to themselves. They launched savage raids into North Wales in the 1080s. By the 1090s Norman warlords were gaining control of large areas of South and West Wales. They met fierce resistance, but this was a period when the Welsh kingdoms were at war with each other. The Normans were defeated in 1096 at Gelli Carnant, Gwent, but they kept their foothold in Wales.

GWENLLIAN GOES TO WAR

Gwenllian was the daughter of Gruffudd ap Cynan, ruler of Gwynedd in North Wales. She married another Grufudd, son of Rhys ap Tewdwr, ruler of Deheubarth. In 1136 her husband went to meet her father, to plan a rising against the Normans in South Wales. While he was away, Gwenllian led a warrior band to storm Kidwelly castle. They were beaten back and defeated by Maurice de Londres. Gwenllian was killed in the attack.

Horse power
The Normans used highly mobile forces to control their conquests.

Metal in motion
The mounted knight was the key to Norman success.

STRONGBOW'S IRELAND

In Ireland, warring between provincial kings gave a chance for descendants of the Normans to invade. In 1166 Dermot MacMurrough, King of Leinster, appealed to Henry II of England for help. He had lost his lands in the wars between Ireland's provincial kings. Henry authorised Norman lords to carry on this fight independently.

In 1169 Richard fitz Gilbert de Clare, Earl of Pembroke, agreed to help Dermot in return for land. De Clare, half Norman and half Welsh, was known as 'Strongbow'. His invasion of Ireland was successful – too much so for Henry II, who was jealous of Strongbow's new-found power. The English king and his army arrived in Ireland in 1171.

 The Norman invasion did not stop at the borders of England.

✤ 1086
Population of 2 million in area surveyed by the Domesday Book

✤ 1086
Domesday Book records over 2 million hectares of land as cultivated

✤ 1191
First record of windmills being used for grinding wheat

✤ 1200s
Rapid growth of towns and cities

✤ 1300s
Feudal system begins to be replaced by a money-based economy

THE FEUDAL SYSTEM

THE division of society into classes of serfs, free men, nobles and rulers had started earlier in the Middle Ages. The Normans were the first to enforce this 'feudal' system rigidly. The king was at the top, ruling by the will of God. He parcelled out land to his lords in return for their support. The land was worked by free men and serfs (or 'villeins'), who provided the nobles with food and served in their armies. In return, the poor were, in theory at least, protected by their lord.

Kings of the Middle Ages held extreme power over their subjects. Every royal document was marked with a personal badge called a seal, pressed into soft wax. This one belonged to Henry III of England.

OATHS OF LOYALTY

The feudal system was a series of two-way contracts, reinforced by oaths of loyalty. The loyalty was not to a nation, but to a noble or royal family. A lord could even insist that 'his' people take up arms against their own countrymen. The feudal system crossed national borders. Europe's ruling classes were allied with each other, rather than with the peasants who worked for them. If a king from one royal family married the princess of another, the lands they ruled might be joined together, regardless of public opinion or geography.

Field use
One field might be for oats and another for wheat. The third might lie 'fallow' (uncultivated) and be grazed by cattle. Field use changed from year to year so that the goodness in the soil was not all used up.

The feudal economy was based on land and services rather than money. It only worked if people stayed on the land. Villeins were not allowed to leave their village and were forced to work on their lord's estates.

✤ **1300s**
Rise of a middle class made up of merchants and craft producers

✤ **1300s**
Cloth production moves out of towns, water power needed for fulling

✤ **1300s**
Spinning wheels introduced into the British Isles

✤ **c1330**
The *Luttrell Psalter* includes illustrations of everyday English life

✤ **1349**
Ordinance of Labourers tries to limit English wages

75

WOMEN IN THE MIDDLE AGES

In the medieval (Middle Ages) period, most women in Europe had few rights. Strict vows bound together man and wife, just as society was bound by oaths of feudal loyalty. It was the men who held real power and wealth. Despite this, many women were strong characters and became widely respected in their own right. There were powerful queens and noblewomen, abbesses and nuns, scholars and poets, and able working women in every village. In the later Middle Ages, poets began to sing the praises of women, but in a very idealized way.

Women may have been honoured in medieval poetry but in reality had hard lives. Many died in childbirth.

RICH AND POOR

The Norman lords who had supported William I during the invasion of England profited hugely. They were rather like the lottery winners of today, only their new-found wealth was based on land rather than money. This created problems for kings that followed, for there were now many very powerful lords who could challenge their rule. At the other end of the scale were the villeins. They had to labour on the lord's land for, say, three days a week. They also had to pay taxes and supply farm produce to the lord. The Church too demanded one-tenth (a 'tithe') of their harvested crops.

Windmill _____
Windmills, originally an Asian invention, were first built in Britain during the 1190s. They were mounted on an upright post, and could be turned so that the sails caught the wind. They were used for grinding grain into flour.

Harrow
A harrow was a spiked frame used for preparing the soil ready for the seeds to be scattered by the sower.

76

✛ 1100
Death of William II of England, called 'Rufus'

✛ 1106
Battle of Tinchebrai. Henry I regains Normandy

✛ 1120
Prince William, heir to the English throne, is drowned

✛ 1135
Stephen is crowned English king. Start of civil war

✛ 1148
Matilda leaves England, Stephen rules

IS MIGHT RIGHT?

I N the days of William the Conqueror, life was short and violent. The road to kingship was not through election or consent. It was often through murder and battle. Even the laws reflected the belief that 'might is right'. A legal dispute might be settled by an official fight – 'trial by combat' – or by making the accused grasp a red hot bar of iron – 'trial by ordeal'. God, it was believed, would punish the guilty and protect the innocent.

A KING'S NIGHTMARES

In 1100, William II of England was killed in a hunting accident in the New Forest. Or was it murder? Nobody knew for sure. Six years later his successor, Henry I, imprisoned his own brother for 28 years. A series of pictures drawn in the 1140s shows Henry I haunted by royal nightmares. Haughty bishops, armed knights and angry peasants all protest by his bedside.

Armed might invades the peace of Canterbury Cathedral in 1170. Four knights have burst in to murder English archbishop Thomas Becket while he prays.

THE FIGHTING EMPRESS
When Henry I's son was drowned at sea in 1120, he named his daughter Matilda as his heir. She lived in Germany at that time, for she had been betrothed (engaged to be married) at the age of just seven to the Emperor Henry V. She had married him in 1114, aged twelve. Widowed in 1125, Matilda soon remarried another very powerful but younger man, Geoffrey of Anjou. She fought desperately for the English throne until 1148.

Matilda flees from Oxford. She was unpopular with the English people. At one time she captured Stephen, but was never crowned queen.

A TIME OF TERROR
Henry I did manage to keep order in the land, but after his death in 1135, there was chaos. Before his chosen heir, Matilda, arrived back in England, the throne was seized by Stephen, a grandson of William I. There followed 13 years of war between the two. It was a terrible period for the common people, as lord fought lord and armies looted the land.

✤ **1154**
Henry II comes to throne, legal reform

✤ **1170**
Murder of Thomas Becket, Archbishop of Canterbury

✤ **1215**
Barons force King John to sign *Magna Carta*

✤ **1258**
Henry III hands over power to a council of barons

✤ **1265**
De Montfort calls the first English parliament

77

TRIAL BY JURY

A fairer legal system was brought in by Henry II of England during the 1100s. Punishments for crimes were still often brutal, but now courts were held around the country in the king's name. Juries were called to decide guilt or innocence. In those days, juries were not independent members of the public but people who may have known the accused or witnessed the crime.

BISHOPS AND BARONS

The Roman Church was very powerful. Popes believed that as God's representatives they had the right to control European politics. Quarrels between kings and the Church became common. In 1170 supporters of Henry II of England murdered Thomas Becket, the Archbishop of Canterbury. Another challenge to royal power came from barons (powerful nobles). In 1215 English barons forced King John to agree to recognize their legal rights. The agreement was known as *Magna Carta* ('the great charter'). The barons did not need protection, but at least the law was now recognized as more important than the word of kings and queens.

King John was a weak ruler. In 1215, at Runnymede, near the River Thames, he caved in to the demands of his rebel barons and signed the Magna Carta.

A SUMMONS TO PARLIAMENT

Magna Carta may have been one of the first moves towards social justice, but its immediate effect was to make the warring barons even more powerful. When Henry III of England came to the throne in 1216, he was only a child. In 1258 he was forced to hand over power to the barons.

Their leader was Simon de Montfort, Earl of Leicester and brother-in-law of the king. He imprisoned Henry III at Lewes, Sussex, in 1264. The next year de Montfort called a great council, or 'parliament'. Each county sent a knight and each town sent a burgess (leading citizen).

De Montfort was killed in 1265, but parliaments were again summoned by later kings. By 1352 parliment had two sections or 'chambers'. The House of Lords was for the nobles and the bishops, while the House of Commons was for knights and burgesses.

78

♣ 1128
Matilda marries Geoffrey
of Anjou

♣ 1152
Henry of Anjou marries
Eleanor of Aquitaine

♣ 1154
Henry II is crowned first
Plantagenet king of England

♣ c1167
Students start to
study at Oxford

♣ 1198
Richard I 'Cœur de Lion' dies
from a crossbow wound

THE ANGEVIN EMPIRE

ALTHOUGH Matilda failed to win the throne of England, her son was crowned King Henry II in 1154. His royal line is sometimes called Plantagenet, named after the sprig of broom (in Old French, *plante genêt*) that his father Geoffrey wore in his cap. Henry II ruled over a huge area of western Europe called the Angevin (Anjou) empire.

WHICH LANGUAGE?

The English spoken today began to take shape in medieval England. It grew out of several languages. The court used French, while scholars and the Church used Latin. Most ordinary people spoke dialects of English. Other languages spoken in the British Isles at this time included Cornish, Welsh, Scots Gaelic, Irish and Norse.

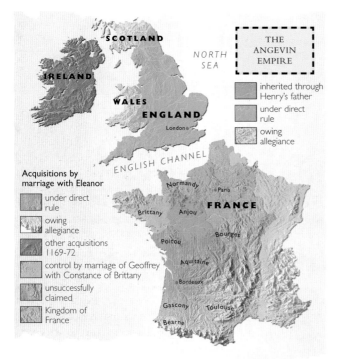

THE ANGEVIN EMPIRE

inherited through Henry's father

under direct rule

owing allegiance

Acquisitions by marriage with Eleanor

under direct rule

owing allegiance

other acquisitions 1169-72

control by marriage of Geoffrey with Constance of Brittany

unsuccessfully claimed

Kingdom of France

SCOTLAND
IRELAND
WALES
ENGLAND
London
NORTH SEA
ENGLISH CHANNEL
Normandy
Paris
Brittany
Anjou
FRANCE
Poitou
Bourges
Aquitaine
Bordeaux
Gascony
Toulouse
Béarne

ROYAL LANDS

Henry II's lands stretched from the sunny vineyards of Bordeaux in southwest France, to the rainy Scottish borders. He had inherited Anjou from his father and gained Poitou, Aquitaine and Gascony on marrying Eleanor of Aquitaine. Henry also claimed to be overlord of Brittany, Wales, Scotland and Ireland.

RULERS OF ENGLAND
House of Anjou (Plantagenet)

♣ Henry II 'Curtmantle'	1154–1189
♣ Richard I 'Cœur de Lion'	1189–1199
♣ John 'Lackland'	1199–1216
♣ Henry III	1216–1272
♣ Edward I 'Longshanks'	1272–1307
♣ Edward II	1307–1327
♣ Edward III 'of Windsor'	1327–1377
♣ Richard II	1377–1399

THE EMPIRE UNRAVELS

Henry II of England was energetic and fiery-tempered. He was a very able ruler, but he quarrelled bitterly with his wife and with his sons. They rebelled against him and the great empire began to break up. Royal power lessened under Stephen and John, but the struggle to control France would continue for hundreds of years.

✤ 1205
England loses Normandy to France

✤ 1215
Cambridge University is founded

✤ 1267
Opus Majus ('great work') by Roger Bacon

✤ 1283
First record of a mechanical clock in England

✤ 1326
First record of spectacles being used in England

79

ELEANOR OF AQUITAINE

Eleanor of Aquitaine was one of the most remarkable women in medieval Europe. She was born in about 1122. She became Duchess of Aquitaine in 1135, when she married the heir to the French throne. He was crowned Louis VII two years later. Eleanor was unconventional and beautiful. She and a troop of women, dressed as classical warriors, joined the Second Crusade (one of the wars between Christians and Moslems in the Near East). After her marriage was annulled (cancelled) in 1152, Eleanor married young Henry of Anjou, who became King Henry II of England. Their love soon turned sour and when Henry was unfaithful she supported his sons in rebellion against him. She was imprisoned from 1174 until the death of Henry in 1189. She died in 1204.

◀ The lute was widely played in western Europe in the Middle Ages. Musicians performed at court and poets and singers travelled from one castle to another.

◀ Eleanor's court in Poitou attracted poets, musicians and scholars from all over Europe.

SCHOLARS AND INVENTORS

Under Plantagenet rule in England, few people could read or write. Some children were taught in church schools or were tutored by monks or nuns. University students may have been studying at Oxford as early as 1167, and Cambridge University was founded in 1215. One scholar who studied at Oxford and Paris was Roger Bacon (c1214–1292). He was a scientist who predicted the use of flying machines and telescopes. At this time all sorts of exciting new inventions were arriving in Britain from abroad, including gunpowder, clocks and spectacles.

FOOD FOR A ROYAL BANQUET

England's medieval language divide has survived in the kitchen today. English-speakers raised 'sheep', but the French-speaking nobles who ate them called them 'moutons'. 'Mutton' later became used for the cooked meat.

Medieval feasts or banquets included huge pies and tarts, jellies, fish such as eels and lampreys, roast goose or swan and venison. Dishes were served with great ceremony.

◀ boar's head

✤ AD 632
Death of Muhammad, founder
of Islam, in Arabia

✤ 1075
Moslem Turks capture the holy
city of Jerusalem

✤ 1095
Pope Urban II calls for a holy
war or 'Crusade'

✤ 1096
The First Crusade leaves
Europe for the Holy Land

✤ 1099
Crusaders capture Jerusalem,
massacre 40,000 Jews and
Moslems

THE CRUSADES

IN 1075 the city of Jerusalem was captured from its Christian rulers by Turkish Moslems. Twenty years later, Pope Urban II appealed to all Christian knights to launch a holy war, or Crusade. Its aim was to recapture Jerusalem and the 'Holy Land'. The First Crusade began in 1096 and Jerusalem was taken after three long years.

Moslem lands stretched from Spain through North Africa to Southwest Asia. The Christian lands of Europe were known as Christendom. The Christian lands of the Near East were called Outremer ('overseas').

JEWS, CHRISTIANS, MOSLEMS

By now, most of Europe was Christian. The Moors (Moslem Berbers and Arabs) had conquered much of Spain, but were under constant attack by Christian armies from the north. There were communities of Jews in many parts of Europe, too. Their ancestors had been expelled from Jerusalem by the Romans in AD 70. In Moorish Spain, Moslems, Christians and Jews lived peaceably together. However in most of Christendom, religious hatred against Moslems and Jews ran rife. Jews were persecuted terribly in England and in 1290 they were expelled by Edward I.

RICHARD THE LION HEART

One of the most famous English kings, Richard I spent only 10 months of his reign in England and probably spoke only French. In 1189 he became King of England. In the following year he joined the Third Crusade, at first with King Philippe Auguste of France. In 1191 he captured the city of Acre. Richard's exploits brought him fame and the nickname *Cœur de Lion* ('Lion Heart'). Journeying home, Richard was shipwrecked and forced to cross the lands of his enemy, Duke Leopold of Austria. He was captured and handed over to Emperor Henry VI. A huge sum ('a ransom') had to be paid for his release and it was the English people who had to find the money. Richard was killed fighting against France in 1199.

Richard I, son of Henry I and Eleanor of Aquitaine, spent most of his reign at war.

✤ 1099
Christian kingdom founded at Jerusalem

✤ 1148
The Second Crusade fails to capture Damascus in Syria

✤ 1189
The Third Crusade is launched, Richard I pledges support

✤ 1202
Crusaders attack the Christian city of Constantinople

✤ 1291
The fall of Acre, end of crusading against the Saracens

81

The Crusader
Crusaders were armed with swords, lances, axes and maces. Their armour varied over the years. Chain mail gave way to solid plate armour.

RELIGIOUS WARS

There were several further Crusades between 1096 and 1270. These shameful wars poisoned relations between Christianity and Islam into modern times. Religious motives soon gave way to looting and land-grabbing. Moslems were not the only enemy. In 1204, Crusaders turned aside to sack the Christian city of Constantinople. In 1208 a Crusade was launched against Christians in southern France, who differed from Rome in their beliefs. German Crusaders invaded Poland and the Baltic lands in the 1200s.

Saracen weapons
The Saracens had swords of the finest steel, spears and round shields. Archers fired arrows from small bows while riding.

Saracen armour
Moslem troops either wore tunics which were padded or sewn with metal plates, or coats of mail.

Fighting in the dry heat and dust of the Near East, when weighed down with armour and weapons, was often an ordeal. Although the Crusades were meant to be 'holy' wars, the citizens of besieged towns were often slaughtered without mercy. The Crusades left a bitterness between Christianity and Islam that still affects the politics of Southwest Asia today.

CRUSADERS AND SARACENS

Crusaders came from all over Europe, including the British Isles. Some joined international 'orders', such as the Knights of St John (founded in 1099), or the Knights Templar (1119). The Moslem soldiers of the 'Holy Land' were called Saracens and included Arabs, Turks and Kurds. Their most famous leader was Salah-ed-din Yussuf ('Saladin',1137-1193). He earned the respect of many Crusaders. Contact with Arab civilization opened the eyes of many Europeans to the wider world.

82

✤ **1066**
Norman knights wear long
tunic of mail ('hauberk')

✤ **1099**
The Order of the Knights of
St John is founded

✤ **1119**
The Order of Knights Templar
is founded

✤ **1200s**
Horses protected with
padded or mail coats called
trappers

✤ **1292**
Statute of Arms lays down
rules for English tournaments

KniGHTS in ARMOUR

I N the 700s, a simple invention had reached Europe from Asia – stirrups. They supported the legs of a horseback rider and made it possible for mounted soldiers to charge the enemy really hard, without falling. By Norman times, horse soldiers called knights had become the most important part of most armies. Even lords and kings had to learn how to be good knights. In the 1100s and 1200s, almost every battlefield shook to the thundering hooves of great war-horses leading a cavalry charge.

Knights might be away at the wars for years on end. Castles and households were often managed by their ladies.

HERALDRY

In a tournament or a battle, it was hard to tell one armoured knight from another. Knights began to use personal badges or emblems, which were displayed on surcoats (tunics worn over armour), on shields and standards. These emblems were passed down from one generation of a family to another. They became known as coats-of-arms and can still be seen carved on castle stones or coloured in the stained glass of old churches. The rules for drawing up coats-of-arms are known as heraldry.

Heraldic design and colouring followed strict rules. It used various geometric patterns as well as emblems such as the fleur-de-lys ('lily flower', above right).

A fine display
Fancy crests, plumes and scarves were worn at tournaments to impress the spectators.

Jousting helmet
The 'great helm' worn for tournaments was padded with straw.

Coats-of-arm
In tournaments and battles even the horses displayed coats-of-arms.

THE AGE OF CHIVALRY

In the high Middle Ages, knights developed a code of behaviour, called 'chivalry'. It was based on Christian virtues. A knight vowed to protect the weak, honour women, keep his word and respect his enemies. These ideas were admired by many later generations, but they were only ever an ideal. Battles may have had strict rules, but they were still brutal affairs. Respect was certainly not extended to peasants or to enemy foot soldiers, who were slaughtered without mercy.

✣ 1300s	✣ 1330s	✣ 1334	✣ 1400s	✣ c1490	83
'Coat of plates' – armoured plates stitched to tunics	Solid breastplate encases the upper part of the body	Edward III of England founds knightly Order of the Garter	Full plate armour covers whole body	James IIII of Scotland founds knightly Order of the Thistle	

Helmets
Now protected the whole face as well as the skull.

Pauldrons
Shielded the shoulders from heavy blows.

Gorgets
Were plates which prevented the throat being stabbed.

Cowters
Covered the elbows.

Breastplates
Covered the ribs.

Gauntlets
Were jointed, armoured gloves.

Skirts
Plate strips protected the waist.

Cuisses
Protected the thighs.

Poleyns
Protected the kneecaps.

Greaves
Protected the shins and lower leg.

Sabatons
Were pointed, armoured shoes.

● By the 1400s, plate armour encased the knight's whole body.

● Weapons used in hand-to-hand fighting included clubs (called 'maces') and all kinds of swords and daggers.

BECOMING A KNIGHT

Young boys started to learn how to be a knight at about the age of seven, when they were sent to serve as a page in a castle. They were taught to fight, ride and use weapons. At about 14 they became an esquire, or assistant to a knight, and could go into battle. At about 21, or earlier if they showed great courage, esquires would be made full knights.

Sword
A double-edged blade like this was used in the 1300s.

Mace
Knights used clubs like this one after about 1250.

SPLENDID TOURNAMENTS

More than 800 years ago, knights turned their military training into a sport. They fought mock battles called *mêlées* and later fought one-to-one, galloping at each other with lances raised. This was called jousting. It was a very violent sport and deaths were common. Grand competitons called tournaments were held, at which young knights sought fame and fortune. Before they took part, they dedicated their fight to a lady of the court.

● Two knights clash in a joust. After the 1400s, their horses would be separated by a low wooden fence called a tilt.

✦ cAD 950
Motte-and-bailey castles
built in France

✦ 1066
Normans bring castle
building to the British Isles

✦ 1100s
Castle defences centred on
massive stone towers called
keeps

✦ 1180s
Castles built with square wall
towers

✦ 1220s
Castles built with
round wall towers

THE AGE OF CASTLES

FORTRESSES had been built in Britain in Roman times. After the Normans invaded England in 1066, powerful kings and lords began to build new kinds of fortresses, called castles. Castles served as homes, as well as military bases and centres of government. They were used to control conquered lands and show off the power of their owner. Kings and lords sometimes owned several castles and moved from one to the other during the year.

The first castles were wooden towers called baileys, on top of earthen mounds called mottes. By the 1100s, castles were being built with thick stone walls.

Arrow loops
Archers could shoot arrows through loops, narrow slits in the castle walls.

Outer walls
Thick stone walls were fireproof and hard to knock down.

LIFE IN A CASTLE

The centre of activity in the castle was the Great Hall. This was where banquets and important meetings were held. In the kitchens, meat sizzled on spits in front of the fire. The bedrooms and the main living room (called a 'solar') were often cold and draughty. Fresh reeds were strewn on the stone floors, as there were no carpets. There were rooms for the servants, guard rooms and stables.

During a siege, armed knights could ride out from 'sally ports' – small gates at the side of the castle – to launch a counter-attack.

Peasants worked the fields around the castle, supplying it with food. Grain was stored inside the castle walls, in case a siege cut off supplies.

HISTORIC CASTLES

Massive stone castles were built all over England, Wales, Scotland and Ireland. Many of them can still be seen today. Some of them are ruined, but you can still see the holes where joists once supported floors and timbers, or the arrow loops in the walls. Some castles are still in use as museums or private homes.

Edinburgh, Scotland, was fortified in ancient times. Parts of its castle date back to the 1000s.

✤ **1290s**
Concentric castles, built with rings of walls and towers.

✤ **1320s**
The age of gunpowder begins, new threat to castles

✤ **1350s**
Bricks begin to be used in building some castles

✤ **1450s**
Castles start to be replaced by fortified homes and palaces

✤ **1600s**
Last military use of castles in British Isles

85

Battlements

The walls were topped by battlements. These walk-ways were defended by stone blocks called merlons and firing gaps called crenels.

Machicolations

Chutes overhung the outer walls, for dropping missiles on the enemy.

Gatehouse

A strong gate called a portcullis could be dropped to seal off the entrance to the castle.

KING OF THE CASTLES

Beaumaris castle is on the Isle of Anglesey, in Wales. Work on it began in April 1295 and cost a fortune. It employed no fewer than 2,000 labourers, 200 stonemasons and 400 quarrymen. Beaumaris was the last in a powerful chain of castles built by King Edward I of England to secure his conquest of North Wales. He was the greatest castle builder of his day.

Stonemasons and carpenters were recruited from all over the Kingdom of England.

Castles were built with rings of defences and were hard to attack. They were garrisoned by footsoldiers, archers and men-at-arms.

SIEGE WARFARE

An army trying to attack a castle tried to surround it and cut off its supplies, so that the defenders starved. This was called a siege. Blazing arrows were shot into roof timbers. The walls were pounded with boulders from giant catapults, or undermined with tunnels dug beneath the foundations. More sieges ended by treaty or agreement than by the fall of the castle.

The first cannon were very unreliable, but by the mid-1400s they were used to deadly effect.

Bodiam, Sussex, England, 1386. This castle had holes for firing handguns as well as arrow loops.

86

♣ 1080
Building of York Minster,
England

♣ 1136
Melrose Abbey, Scotland, is
built

♣ 1154
The only English pope,
Hadrian IV (to 1159)

♣ 1171
Pilgrimage to Canterbury
Cathedral begins

♣ 1172
Christchurch Cathedral,
Dublin

TO THE GLORY OF GOD

I N later medieval Europe, the
Christian faith was part of everday
life. It was expressed in the great
stone cathedrals and abbeys which were
raised all over the British Isles in the
Middle Ages. Building styles changed
over the years. Some cathedrals had
massive, awe-inspiring towers. Others
were graceful, with tall spires pointing
to heaven. Inside, gold glittered in
candle light and coloured ('stained')
glass windows glowed like precious gems.

Durham Cathedral, towering
above the River Wear in the
northeast of England, was started by
the Normans in 1093. It contains the
tombs of St Cuthbert and Bede. During
the Middle Ages the bishops of Durham
were as warlike as any barons and had
great political power.

In the Middle Ages, the language of
the Roman Church was Latin, which
few ordinary people could understand.
Most were unable to read either. Stained
glass windows were an ideal way of telling
worshippers stories from the Bible or the
lives of the saints.

✣ **1180**
St David's Cathedral, Wales, is rebuilt

✣ **1215**
Roman Church and Pope at height of power

✣ **1221**
Friars enter England for first time

✣ **1250**
Westminster Abbey is rebuilt near London

✣ **1380s**
Bible first translated into the English language

87

Monks and nuns lived in monasteries and convents. Some cared for the sick or taught young people. Some travelled from one town to another, living on charity. Religious orders such as the Franciscans ('Grey Friars') or the Dominicans ('Black Friars') were founded in the 1200s.

MONKS AND NUNS

By about 1215 the Roman Church was at the height of its power and wealth. It was at that time that an Italian monk called Francis of Assisi called for Christians to give up riches and help the poor and the sick. By the 1220s his ideas were being spread through the British Isles by wandering monks, or friars. However many church officials remained greedy and corrupt. They were condemned by an English priest called John Wycliffe, who gained many followers in the 1300s.

LETTERS OF GOLD

Before the days of printing, books had to be copied out by hand. The work was often done in monasteries. The pages were made of vellum (animal skin) and decorated with elaborate letter designs and small pictures, called 'illuminations'. Books were such rare and precious objects that they were often chained to the shelf.

Illuminated letters were decorated with coloured paint and gold leaf. They were works of art in themselves.

MYSTERIES AND MIRACLES

CANTERBURY PILGRIMS

Many people went on pilgrimage to holy sites, such as the tomb of Thomas Becket in Canterbury. They prayed for healing or forgiveness of sins. Between 1387 and 1400 a poet called Geoffrey Chaucer wrote about these pilgrims and of the stories they told to pass the time. The *Canterbury Tales* was one of the first and greatest works of English literature.

Many people believed in miracles or in the healing power of relics such as saints' bones (which were often fakes). Some Christians became hermits, living alone to meditate. A woman called Julian of Norwich wrote about the meaning of religious visions she had in 1373. At that time a poem called *Piers Plowman* was also written, which celebrated the simple faith of ordinary people. The Bible was not translated into English until the 1380s. One way people could learn about the scriptures was through acting. Religious ('mystery') plays, featuring angels and devils, were performed outside many cathedrals.

Amongst Chaucer's pilgrims were a knight, a nun, monks, a miller, a lawyer, a merchant and a doctor – a cross-section of medieval society.

88

♣ 1063	♣ c1115	♣ 1164	♣ 1165	♣ 1176
Death of Gruffudd ap Llywelyn, having briefly united Wales	Welsh princes start to build their own castles	Founding of Strata Florida abbey (Ystrad Fflur)	Owain Gwynedd resists Henry II of England	Eisteddfod held at Cardigan Castle

THE WELSH PRINCES

WALES in the 1100s and 1200s was a rural land, with few large towns. People farmed and hunted, travelling by narrow tracks through the mountain passes. The princes were guarded by castles built by the Welsh rulers. They also endowed (funded) great monasteries such as Strata Florida (Ystrad Fflur) in the Teifi valley and Llanfaes, on Anglesey. There was a rich tradition of music, and a great gathering of poets (an *eisteddfod*) was held at Cardigan in 1176.

Rhys ap Grufudd ('the Lord Rhys' of Deheubarth) weakened Norman power in South Wales during the chaotic reign of King Stephen in England.

WHO HOLDS POWER?

Under rulers such as Rhys ap Gruffudd in the south and Owain Gwynedd in the north, Norman power in Wales declined. The Marcher Lords still held the borders, however, and the English kings regarded themselves as overlords of the Welsh. The division of Wales into separate kingdoms played into the hands of the English. In 1157 Madog ap Maredudd of Powys helped King Henry II of England invade Wales, in order to weaken his rivals in Gwynedd.

St David's Cathedral came under the control of Norman bishops in 1115. It was rebuilt in 1182.

GERALD OF WALES

Gerald de Barri was born in about 1146. His ancestry was part Norman, part Welsh. Gerald became a talented writer in Latin and a great churchman. In 1188 he travelled through Wales with Archbishop Baldwin, and his *Journey Through Wales* and *Description of Wales* give us lively and good-humoured pictures of Wales in the high Middle Ages. He died in 1223 and has gone down in history as Giraldus Cambriensis, or Gerald of Wales.

✤ 1188
Gerald de Barri travels
through Wales

✤ 1216
Llywelyn Fawr summons
parliament at Aberdyfi

✤ 1250
Coal being mined at
Margam, in South Wales

✤ 1267
English recognize Llywelyn ap
Gruffudd as Prince of Wales

✤ 1283
Llywelyn ap Gruffudd killed in
skirmish with English, Cilmeri

89

RULERS IN WALES

- ✤ Gruffudd ap Llywelyn   1039-1063
- ✤ Bleddyn ap Cynfyn   1063-75
- ✤ Trahaearn ap Caradog   1075-1081
- ✤ Gruffudd ap Cynan   1081-1137
- ✤ Owain Gwynedd   1137-1170
- ✤ Dafydd ap Owain Gwynedd 1170-1194
- ✤ Llywelyn 'Fawr' ('the Great') 1194-1240
- ✤ Dafydd ap Llywelyn   1240-1246
- ✤ Llywelyn ap Gruffudd   1246-1282

Llywelyn II's death near Cilmeri in 1282 marked the end of Welsh independence. He is remembered in Wales as 'The Last Prince'.

THE GREAT LLYWELYN

In 1170 three sons of Owain Gwynedd fought each other at Pentraeth, on Anglesey, for the throne of Gwynedd. Hywel was defeated by Rhodri and Dafydd and the kingdom was divided. By 1194 all Gwynedd had come under the rule of Llywelyn ap Iorwerth, 'the Great'. Llywelyn married Joan or Siwan, daughter of King John of England, but the two rulers later became enemies. Llywelyn was the most powerful ruler in medieval Wales, a strong supporter of the Church and the law.

This stone head is believed to represent Llywelyn Fawr, 'the Great'. He held court at Aberffraw, on Anglesey.

THE LAST PRINCE

Llywelyn was succeeded by his younger son, Dafydd, but he died in the sixth year of his reign. He was to be followed by his nephews Llywelyn and Owain, but the former seized the throne for himself and gained control of all Wales. Llywelyn II ap Gruffudd was recognized as Prince of Wales by the English in 1267. However he would be the last Welsh prince. He quarelled with King Edward I and after long wars, was killed in a skirmish with English troops near Cilmeri. His severed head was displayed in London.

THE CONQUEST

King Edward I of England was now the undisputed ruler of Wales. His castles ringed the land. English criminal laws replaced Welsh ones and the *Statute of Rhuddlan* (1284) divided Wales into counties, along English lines. In 1301 Edward I's son (the later Edward II) was declared Prince of Wales, and ever since then the title has been held by the eldest son of the English monarch.

Conwy castle

✤ 1130s
Norman families gain estates
in the Lowlands

✤ 1174
William I of Scotland forced
to recognize English king as
overlord

✤ 1264
Norwegian invasion defeated
at Largs

✤ 1266
Scotland gains Norwegian
territories on mainland and
Western Isles

✤ 1296
Edward I of England defeats
John Balliol at Dunbar

SCOTTISH FREEDOM

IN the 1100s, Scotland saw great changes. Norman families gained Scottish lands. Three sons of the great Queen Margaret ruled the country in turn – Edgar, Alexander I and the great David I. Many fine churches and abbeys were built during their reigns, and around them developed prosperous 'burghs' (large towns). Peasants lived in small farming villages called 'touns'.

RULERS OF SCOTLAND

✤ Donald III Bán	1093-1097
✤ Duncan II	1094
✤ Edgar	1097-1107
✤ Alexander I 'the Fierce'	1107-1124
✤ David I 'the Saint'	1124-1153
✤ Malcolm IV 'the Maiden'	1153-1165
✤ William I 'the Lion'	1165-1214
✤ Alexander II	1214-1229
✤ Alexander III	1249-1286
✤ Margaret 'Maid of Norway'	1286-1290
✤ Throne disputed	1290-1292
✤ John (Balliol)	1292-1296
✤ Edward I of England	1296-1306

House of Bruce

✤ Robert I Bruce	1306-1329
✤ David II	1329-1371
✤ Edward Balliol	1306 & 1333-1336

SCOTLAND STANDS FIRM

In 1174, William I of Scotland was captured by English troops and forced to recognize Henry II as his overlord. It was an act never forgotten by the English – or the Scots. Alexander III, who came to the throne as a boy, had another old enemy to deal with – Norway. The Norwegians invaded in 1263, but were forced to withdraw and finally lost their mainland and island territories.

David I was succeeded by his young son Malcolm IV, who died before he was married.

SCOTLAND FALLS

Tragedy now struck the Scots. In 1286 Alexander III fell from his horse and was killed. Four years later his successor, the young girl Margaret of Norway, also died. Who should reign next, was unclear. The Scots turned to Edward I of England for advice. His candidate was John Balliol, a distant descendant of David I. Edward I thought he could control his chosen man, but instead Balliol turned and made an historic alliance with France. Edward I stormed into Scotland in 1296 and defeated Balliol at Dunbar.

William Wallace blocked the northern advance of English forces at Stirling Bridge in 1297 and became Edward I's most hated foe.

LORDS OF THE ISLES

In the Highlands and Western Isles, the old Gaelic way of life continued. Here, first loyalty was to the chief of the clan (a group sharing descent from a common ancestor). The lands of Clans Dugall, Donald and Ruairi became known as the Lordship of the Isles. The first Lord of the Isles was John of Islay of Clan Donald, who died in 1387. The Lordship was in constant conflict with the Scottish kingdom and was brought to an end in 1493.

Legend has it that Robert Bruce was inspired to keep fighting the English by watching a spider try time after time to rebuild its web. At last it succeeded. Bannockburn was the turning point, although the war continued for another 14 years.

WAR OF INDEPENDENCE

Resistance to English rule was fierce. Its champion was William Wallace, who defeated an English army at Stirling Bridge, but was himself defeated at Falkirk in 1298. Captured in 1305, Wallace was horribly executed in London. Parts of his body were sent to Newcastle, Berwick, Stirling and Perth. The fight was taken up by Robert Bruce (who had stabbed his chief rival, John Comyn, to death). Robert was crowned king by the Scots in 1306. Edward I died in the following year and at Bannockburn, on 24 June 1314, Bruce turned the tide and defeated 20,000 troops of Edward II.

92

✤ 1175
Treaty of Windsor. Rory
O'Connor recognizes Henry
II as overlord.

✤ 1210
Irish kings submit to King
John of England

✤ 1235
Normans complete conquest
of western Ireland

✤ 1257
Irish attack Normans in Sligo
and Thomond

✤ 1315
Edward Bruce invades
Ireland from Scotland

THE PALE AND BEYOND

THE word 'pale' means fence or enclosure. In medieval Ireland it came to mean the area of the country which was directly controlled by the kings of England. It lay in the east of the country, around Dublin. Within the Pale, English language, laws, fashions, architecture and customs became normal. The Pale was settled not just by English royal officials, but by merchants and labourers too, from across the Irish Sea.

THE ENGLISH
PALE IN
IRELAND

The Breac Maedhóc is a bronze shrine from Drumlane, County Kavan. Its figures show the Gaels of Ireland in the 1100s. The men have long hair and beards and wear long cloaks. The women wear their hair in ringlets.

The area of the Pale varied greatly during the later Middle Ages. By 1464 it included the counties of Dublin, Kildare, Louth and Meath.

THREE WORLDS, ONE LAND

Beyond the Pale, lay the lands of two other groups – the Irish-speaking Gaels and the powerful, independent Norman families who had seized Irish land. Over the years, many of the latter adopted Irish ways. The English kings, however, firmly believed that civilization ended 'beyond the Pale'. This phrase is still sometimes used today to describe unacceptable or uncouth behaviour. From time to time the English attempted to expand their rule by founding colonies beyond the Pale. These were English settlements protected by soldiers.

THE STATUTES OF KILKENNY

From the early days of English rule in Ireland, the official policy was one of separation and apartness. In 1366 the English, under Prince Lionel of Clarence, called a parliament at Kilkenny and passed a wide range of statutes (laws).

According to these, English colonists were not allowed to marry into Irish families, or to adopt Irish dress or customs. They were not to speak Irish or use the ancient Irish legal system, known as Brehon Law.

✤ **1318**
Edward Bruce killed at Battle of Faughart

✤ **1320**
University founded in Dublin, first in Ireland

✤ **1333**
English crown loses control of Connaught and Ulster

✤ **1366**
Statutes of Kilkenny are proclaimed

✤ **1394**
Richard II of England regains control of Ireland

93

BARLEY FOR THE TAKING

When Henry II of England landed in Ireland in 1171, his chief aim had been to make sure that 'Strongbow' and his adventurers did not set up a Norman kingdom in Ireland to rival his own. As the years went by, the English found another reason for staying in Ireland. The lush, green pastures and fields of ripe barley were a valuable economic resource. Grain from Irish estates could be exported to England or mainland Europe for rich rewards.

KERN AND GALLOGLASS

Ireland saw wave after wave of English invasion. John came in 1185 as prince and again in 1210 as king. Richard II arrived in 1394–1395 and again in 1399. There were long battles between the old Norman families and amongst the Irish kings. By recognizing the English kings, some Irish royal families managed to survive and even thrive in this changing world. The poor peasants experienced endless warfare. All sides used roving bands of troops who would fight for anyone who paid and fed them. These mercenaries included Norman men-at-arms, Irish footsoldiers called kerns and Scottish adventurers called galloglass, meaning 'foreign warriors'.

The Rock of Cashel is crowned by splendid buildings from the Middle Ages. Cormac's Chapel dates from 1127-34, while the great cathedral was built about 100 years later.

These stone carved tombs represent two of Ireland's most powerful families at the close of the Middle Ages. They may be seen in St Canice's Cathedral, Kilkenny. They belong to Piers Butler, Earl of Ossory and Ormond, and his wife Lady Margaret Fitzgerald.

94

✤ c1170
Major period of
town building begins

✤ 1176
London Bridge is
rebuilt in stone

✤ 1233
Piped water supply to
Westminster, near London

✤ 1250s
Zoo animals including lions in
Tower of London

✤ c1300
Town building starts to decline

A MEDIEVAL TOWN

Towns were now beginning to grow quickly. They were noisy, rowdy places and often foul-smelling, too, for there was no proper drainage. Water had to be carried to each house from wells. Carts brought vegetables to market and cattle were herded though the muddy streets. Women tied wooden platforms called pattens to their shoes, to walk through the puddles. Travellers slept huddled together on straw mattreses, in flea-infested inns.

Rich merchants began to build with stone. The Jew's House in Lincoln is over 800 years old and has a hall on the first floor.

WALLS AND CHIMNEYS

Medieval cities were surrounded by walls and at night the gates were locked and barred. Tall wooden-framed houses were crowded together. House fires were common and straw thatch was often banned in favour of slates and tiles, which could not blaze. All cooking fires had to be covered each night – the time of 'curfew' (from the Old French *cuevre-feu*). At first smoke came out through holes in the wall. It was not until the 1400s that chimney pots topped the roofs.

By the 1250s, most of the English population lived within 25 kilometres of a market town. Modern cities that were founded during the Middle Ages include Liverpool, Hull, Leeds, Newcastle upon Tyne, Portsmouth.

Timber houses
In the Middle Ages, most houses were still built with timber frames and walls of wattle-and-daub. Some of these may still be seen in Britain today.

Open sewers
Waste was thrown into the street and streams were used as open sewers. Birds and dogs scavenged rubbish tips.

✤ c1350
Average town has a
population of about 3,000

✤ c1350
Rapid growth in the woollen
cloth trade

✤ 1411
Guildhall rebuilt in the City
of London

✤ 1463
First record of eating with
forks in Britain

✤ 1463
Playing cards in use
in Britain

95

OLD LONDON BRIDGE

The first versions of London Bridge were made of wood, and they really did keep falling down, just as it says in the old nursery rhyme. However a 19-arch stone bridge, built between 1176 and 1209, lasted until 1831. On this bridge there were rows of houses and even a chapel. Sometimes the bridge was used for jousting. Traitors' heads were often displayed on the bridge after they had been chopped off.

The wealth of merchants began to compete with that of the nobles and the Church.

MONEY AND MERCHANTS

Merchants became wealthy. In London there were great warehouses owned by the Hanseatic League, a powerful organization which traded right across Germany to the Baltic Sea. Bankers lent money in return for payment of interest. Even kings borrowed from them to pay for their wars. When bankers became richer than kings, it was clear that the old feudal system was breaking down. Craft workers formed trading guilds which controlled the marketing of their wares. Young lads came to stay in the house of the master of their trade and learned how to be a weaver, a tailor or a goldsmith. They were called apprentices.

Shop signs
When most people people couldn't read, shop signs had to be visual. A boot might hang above a cobbler's shop, or a horse-shoe above a smithy. A green bush was the sign of an inn.

Animals to market
Even large cities echoed to the sound of cattle, sheep and geese being driven through the streets to market.

FOOTBALL HOOLIGANS

Apprentices were an unruly lot and often tried to avoid work. They formed gangs on the streets. One of their favourite sports was football. A blown-up pig's bladder served as a ball. There were no rules and the game was played on the street. It was very rough. In 1314 the sport was banned by King Edward II of England.

96

✦ 1314
Weather destroys harvests,
major famine

✦ 1315
Harvests fail yet again,
starvation

✦ 1348
Black Death appears in
England and Wales

✦ 1349
Black Death reaches Scotland,
kills one in five

✦ 1351
England attempts to freeze
workers' wages

THE HARD LIFE

O N 14 April 1360 the weather was so foul and bitter that many horseback riders were reported to have died of cold, frozen to death in their saddles. There were few comforts in the Middle Ages. Castles were draughty and stank of sewage from the cesspit or the moat. People rarely bathed and disease was common. Many women never survived childbirth and children often died when small.

MEDIEVAL MEDICINE

Medical knowledge had grown little since the days of the Romans. Surgeons could mend bones and monks grew herbs to make medicines. Some of these cures worked, but many didn't. One common treatment was bleeding – taking blood from the patient.

A leper's clapper

"OUR DAILY BREAD"

While the nobles ate fine wheaten bread, the poor ate crusts of coarse rye. Rye crops were sometimes spoiled by a fungus disease called ergot. People who ate flour made from mouldy rye became sick and saw strange visions. Country people preserved their own food, salting fish and smoking bacon. They ate eggs and caught hares and waterfowl. If the harvests failed and prices rose, then people starved.

Food supply was seasonal and depended on good harvests. Famine was common.

Leprosy was an infectious disease. Lepers had to carry a wooden clapper, to warn people that they were coming along the road.

SINNERS AND LEPERS

Natural disasters and illnesses were often believed to be punishments sent by God, because of human sinfulness. One of the most feared diseases was leprosy, which causes lumps, discoloured patches and ulcers to form on the body. Fingers and toes would sometimes become numb and fall off. Sufferers (lepers) were banned from public places and were only allowed to watch church services through a slit in the wall.

Rats and fleas were all too common in medieval towns and cities. The plague was first brought to England by the black rats which used to infest almost every ship.

♣ **1361**
A second outbreak of the plague in Britain

♣ **1369**
A third outbreak of the plague in Britain

♣ **1377**
Poll tax introduced in England

♣ **1381**
Peasants' Revolt in England led by Wat Tyler

♣ **1390**
The plague returns for the fourth time

97

THE BLACK DEATH

In August 1348 a new disease appeared at the port of Weymouth, in the southwest of England. It was known as the Pestilence, later as the Black Death. This terrible plague, spread by rats and their fleas, had already devastated Central Asia and Europe. Soon it was raging across England, Wales, Scotland and Ireland. The Black Death took various forms. One poisoned the bloodstream and caused horrid swellings and boils on the body. Another affected the lungs and could be passed on by coughing and sneezing.

In medieval Europe, knowledge of diseases and medicine had not advanced since Roman times. The sick were sometimes cared for by nuns. The Black Death killed many of the carers as well as the patients. Soon, plague victims were being buried in mass graves and there were no priests left to pray for their souls.

A LABOUR SHORTAGE

In the years 1347 to 1351, the plague may have killed 75 million people in Asia and Europe. Many villages in the British Isles lost half to two-thirds of their population. In some there were no survivors at all. There was a great shortage of labour, so workers now found that they could demand high wages. The English government passed harsh laws in a desperate bid to keep wages at the same level, in 1349 and 1351.

THE PEASANTS' REVOLT

In England after 1377, people had to pay more and more poll taxes (standard payments demanded from all citizens). In 1381 angry peasants from Kent and Essex, led by Wat Tyler and a priest called John Ball, stormed London. Fourteen year old King Richard II rode out to meet the rebels and offered to take up their cause. But Wat Tyler was cut down by the Mayor of London and the rising was savagely suppressed.

Twenty thousand peasants marched on London in 1381. They burnt the palace of John of Gaunt, Duke of Lancaster. They killed the archbishop, captured the Tower of London and set prisoners free.

98

✣ 1337
Edward III of England declares himself King of France

✣ 1340
Naval battle off Sluys won by England

✣ 1346
English defeat the French at Crécy

✣ 1347
English troops capture the French port of Calais

✣ 1356
The Black Prince defeats the French at Poitiers

THE HUNDRED YEARS' WAR

THE period we know as the Hundred Years' War was a long drawn out, bloody struggle between England and France. It took place across the muddy battlefields of northern France and Flanders (in what is now Belgium). It was never really one war, but a series of raids, battles, campaigns and treaties. Nor did it last 100 years, but from 1337 until 1453.

WHO RULES FRANCE?

King Edward III of England was related to the French royal family and in 1337 he claimed the throne of France as his own. England had fought for its lands in France ever since the days of the Normans and the Angevin empire. What was more, France was now a close ally of Scotland, England's enemy. The result was a war which cost Edward III's subjects dearly. They had to pay for it with taxes, loss of trade – and their lives.

🔽 In October 1415, Henry V found his route blocked by a huge French army (foreground) at the village of Agincourt. His 6,000 troops were sick with dysentery and greatly outnumbered, but he won a great victory. The French knights became bogged down in mud, while flight after flight of arrows whistled through the air.

🔽 Edward 'the Black Prince', was the eldest son of Edward III. His nickname came from the colour of his armour. Edward was a brilliant soldier who made a name for himself when he was only 16, at the Battle of Crécy. In 1356 he won a great victory at Poitiers. He died in 1376.

🔽 The crossbow was a much more accurate weapon than the ordinary bow.

WEAPONS AND TACTICS

For campaign after campaign, the English raided and plundered northern France. Long columns of battle-weary knights, waggons, footsoldiers and archers trailed across the countryside. Some carried new-fangled handguns, others hauled early cannon. When it came to pitched battles, England's great strength lay in its use of archers, armed with deadly longbows. They could fire up to 12 arrows a minute.

✢ 1360
The Peace of Brétigny
between England and France

✢ 1415
Henry V of England wins the
battle of Agincourt

✢ 1420
The *Treaty of Troyes*. Henry
V becomes heir to the
French throne

✢ 1431
The English burn Joan of Arc
as a witch at Rouen

✢ 1453
English defeat at Castillon, end
of the 100 Years' War

99

THE GAME OF CHESS

The English were not alone in their attacks on the French kings. At times they were allied with the Bretons of the northwest, at times with powerful barons from Burgundy, in the east. At first the English achieved some great victories. At Poitiers in 1356 the French king, Jean II ('the Good'), was captured. Three years later, the *Treaty of Brétigny* offered Edward III one-third of France if he gave up his claims to the throne.

THE TABLES ARE TURNED

Peace did not last. When Henry V came to the throne of England, he led his army back across the Channel and was victorious. In 1420 the *Treaty of Troyes* made him heir to the French throne – but within two years he was dead. French fortunes now began to turn. Their knights were inspired by a peasant girl called Joan of Arc. She claimed that voices of the saints had called her to free her homeland. The English accused her of witchcraft and burned her alive in 1431. However by 1453 France had regained most of the English-occupied lands.

"DEAR KATE"

In Shakespeare's play *Henry V*, she is called 'dear Kate'. 'Kate' was Catherine de Valois, daughter of Charles VI of France. In 1420 she married Henry V of England, at the height of his success, but her husband became sick while away at the wars and died in 1422. Nine years later, Catherine secretly married a handsome young Welsh courtier. His name was Owain Tudur or Tudor, and it was their grandson, Henry VII, who founded the most famous dynasty in English history.

Catherine de Valois married Henry V at Troyes. She was crowned Queen of England and gave birth to a son, the future Henry VI, in 1421. Her eldest son by Owain Tudor was Edmund, Earl of Richmond, and he was father to Henry VII, the first Tudor monarch.

100

✦ 1296
The Welsh Revolt under
Madog ap Llywelyn

✦ 1316
Llywelyn Bren revolts in South
Wales

✦ 1369
Owain Lawgoch gains support
in France

✦ 1400
Owain Glyndŵr rises against
English rule

✦ 1403
Welsh and English rebels
defeated at Shrewsbury

THE WELSH RISE UP

W ALES was changing under English rule. Towns had already been developing in the days of the Welsh princes. Now, new shire or county towns controlled all local trade, and they prospered. In the Welsh heartlands, the new towns took the form of colonies, settled by incomers from England, France or Flanders. Welsh citizens were often forcibly removed to other settlements.

TROUBLED TIMES

Many Welsh people protested against the taxes and laws brought in by the English. An uprising began in 1294, led by Madog ap Llywelyn, but it was put down in 1295. In 1317 there was a revolt in South Wales, led by Llywelyn Bren. Perhaps the greatest danger to English rule came from Owain Lawgoch, grandson of Llywelyn Fawr. He fought as a mercenary for the French, who called him Yvain de Galles. He planned to reconquer Wales with French help, but was murdered by a secret agent in 1378.

Harlech Castle, completed by King Edward I of England in 1289, was besieged and captured by Owain Glyndŵr's rebels in the spring of 1404. It remained in Welsh hands until 1409.

Love and life in fourteenth century Wales is described in the poems of Dafydd ap Gwilym.

POET OF LOVE AND NATURE

Dafydd ap Gwilym is believed by many to be the greatest ever writer in the Welsh language. He was born in the parish of Llanbadarn Fawr, near Aberystwyth, and wrote his masterpieces between 1320 and 1370. He broke with traditional Welsh verse forms and was influenced by French literature. Dafydd wrote light-hearted and joyful poems, many of them about his sweethearts, Morfudd and Dyddgu. He wrote about nature, too, describing the grace of a seagull's flight in a way that still seems very modern today.

✚ 1404
Owain Glyndŵr summons
first of three parliaments

✚ 1404
Welsh treaty with Charles VI
of France

✚ 1408
English start to regain
control of Wales

✚ 1413
The end of the Welsh
uprising, English rule restored

✚ 1415
Owain Glyndŵr goes into
hiding and disappears

101

A SPARK CATCHES FIRE

In 1400 Lord Grey of Ruthin, a personal friend of the English king, Henry IV, siezed some land from his neighbour in the Marches of northeast Wales. Owain Glyndŵr was a middle-aged Welsh nobleman of royal descent. He appealed to the English parliament for justice, but they reacted with contempt, declaring the Welsh to be 'barefoot rascals'. A simple land dispute rapidly became a full-scale national uprising. Owain was supported by all ranks of Welsh society, including monks and bishops. Welsh labourers and students hurried back from England to join him.

The longbow was a deadly weapon in the hands of Welsh archers.

Owain Glyndŵr had studied law in London and fought with the English army, but he now became leader of a Welsh uprising. He summoned Welsh parliaments at Machynlleth and Dolgellau.

THIRTEEN YEARS OF WAR

Owain was declared Prince of Wales and by 1401 most of his country had joined the uprising. Castles were captured and towns were sacked. Owain joined forces with rebel English barons Henry Percy ('Hotspur') and Edmund Mortimer, but they were defeated at Shrewsbury in 1403. Owain was also supported by the Scots and the French, who sent troops to support him. By 1408, the English were regaining control, but resistance continued until 1413.

MASTERS OF THE LONGBOW

Welsh archers are said to have been the first to develop the longbow. Unlike the shorter Norman bow, it was the full height of a man. It was normally made of yew and had a pull of about 40 kilograms. Arrows were about 78 cm long, made of ash with long metal tips. Goose-feather flights made them spin as they flew through the air. They could even pierce armour. The English used companies of Welsh archers to devastating effect during the Hundred Years' War with France.

102

✣ **1399**
Henry IV, son of John of Gaunt, is first Lancastrian king

✣ **1453**
Henry VI suffers from mental illness

✣ **1454**
Richard, Duke of York appointed Protector

✣ **1455**
Battle of St Albans. Wars of the Roses begin

✣ **1461**
Edward of York is proclaimed King of England

WARS ·OF· THE ROSES

Lancaster

As battle-hardened soldiers returned from the French wars, many entered the service of powerful English lords. Their job was to bully peasants for payment of taxes, or to fight in private armies. There was no shortage of work for them. For thirty years, from 1455 until 1485, there were civil wars as rival branches of the royal family fought for the throne of England.

 *A red rose stood for the House of Lancaster. A white rose was the badge of the House of York. When Henry VII came to the throne, he combined both designs in a red-and-white 'Tudor rose'.*

York

ENGLISH KINGS

House of Lancaster
✣ Henry IV   1399-1413
✣ Henry V   1413-1422
✣ Henry VI   1422-1461 & 1470-1471

House of York
✣ Edward IV   1461-1470 & 1471-1483
✣ Edward V   1483
✣ Richard III   1483-1485

House of Tudor
✣ Henry VII   1485-150

LANCASTER AND YORK

The Houses of Lancaster and York were both descended from Edward III. Their rivalry came to a head when a Lancastrian king, Henry VI, became too mentally ill to rule. In 1454 Richard, Duke of York, was appointed Protector. When Henry VI got better, Richard would not give up his new-found power, and went to war. Henry VI was defeated at St Albans in 1455, but then Richard was killed at Wakefield in 1460.

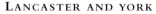

Richard III was killed at the battle of Bosworth in 1485. This brought about the end of the Wars of the Roses.

✤ 1470
Henry VI restored as King of England

✤ 1471
Lancastrians led by Queen Margaret defeated at Tewkesbury

✤ 1483
Young Edward V and his brother disappear

✤ 1483
Parliament asks Richard of Gloucester to become king

✤ 1485
Henry Tudor defeats Richard III at Bosworth

103

WARWICK 'THE KINGMAKER'

The most powerful man in England at this time was not the weak king, but Richard Neville, Earl of Warwick. It was he who had Richard's son proclaimed Edward IV in 1461, the first Yorkist king. Henry VI was imprisoned and exiled. Later, Warwick fell out with Edward and brought Henry VI back to the throne. No wonder he was remembered in history as the 'kingmaker'. Edward returned to seek revenge. Warwick was killed in battle and Henry was murdered in the Tower of London in 1471.

WHO MURDERED THE PRINCES?

Did Richard III murder the princes in the Tower? He had every reason to. Skeletons were found in the Tower in 1674 and buried in Westminster Abbey. However some historians believe that Richard III was not such a villain as he is often made out to be. Might Henry VII have been the true murderer?

THE AGE OF PRINTING

In 1471 an Englishman called William Caxton travelled to the German city of Cologne. There he learned about a new technology, which had been invented in China and developed in Germany and the Netherlands. It was called printing, and it would change the world. Caxton set up his own printing press at Westminster in 1476 and produced about 100 titles.

THE MARCH TO BOSWORTH

Edward IV died in 1483. His heir, Edward V, was too young to rule for himself, so he and his young brother were left in the care of their uncle, Richard of Gloucester. They went to live in the Tower of London, but mysteriously, were never seen again. Gloucester was crowned Richard III in the same year, at the request of parliament. He did not rule for long. In 1485 the Earl of Richmond, a Lancastrian, landed in Wales. His name was Henry Tudor and he defeated and killed Richard III at the battle of Bosworth, near Leicester. Henry VII married Elizabeth of York, and brought peace and prosperity to England.

5

PALACES AND PLAYERS

1509–1714

THE WORLD AT A GLANCE

ELSEWHERE IN EUROPE

1512
Michelangelo completes painting of the Sistine Chapel, in Rome

1517
German monk Martin Luther starts the Protestant Reformation

1571
Naval Battle of Lepanto, Christian fleet led by Venice defeats the Turks

1618
Religious strife in the Holy Roman Empire leads to the Thirty Years War

1643
Louis XIV the 'Sun King' becomes ruler of France

1648
Spain recognizes independence of the Netherlands, art and trade flourish

1701
Frederick I becomes first King of Prussia, in east Germany

1703
Peter the Great, Tsar of Russia, builds new capital at St Petersburg

ASIA

1526
Babar defeats Delhi and founds the Moghul empire in northern India

1566
The Ottoman (Turkish) empire is at its greatest extent

1581
The Russians begin their conquest of Siberia (northeast Asia)

1587
Abbas I 'the Great' rules Persia, a golden age of arts and crafts

1603
Tokugawa Ieyasu becomes Shogun, brings all Japan under his rule

1619
The Dutch found colonial empire in the East Indies, based at Djakarta

1644
Manchurian emperors now rule China: the Qing dynasty

1707
The death of Emperor Aurangzeb, decline of Moghusl power in India

AFRICA

1546
Songhai destroys the empire of Mali in West Africa

1517
Egypt is conquered by the Turks and becomes part of the Ottoman empire

1575
Portuguese found Luanda and settle the coast of Angola

1578
Moroccans defeat Portuguese in North Africa

1600
The Oyo state is at the height of its power in Nigeria

1632
Emperor Fasilidas closes Ethiopia to foreigners

1662
Portuguese defeat the kingdom of Kongo, southern Central Africa

1700
Rise of Ashanti power in Ghana, West Africa

"New faiths, new nations and faraway lands..."

Robert Hooke's microscope

NORTH AMERICA

1510
First African slaves begin to arrive in North America

1519
Spanish begin conquest of Aztec empire in Mexico

1570
Northeast Native Americans form an alliance, the Iroquois Confederacy

1607
English found a permanent settlement at Jamestown, Virginia

1608
French colonists found a settlement at Québec, in Canada

1625
Dutch settle New Amsterdam (later New York City)

1684
French explore the Mississippi region and claim Louisiana

1692
Port Royal, Jamaica, a notorious pirate haven, is destroyed by earthquake

SOUTH AMERICA

1519
Portuguese Ferdinand Magellan explores the Strait named after him

1532
The Spanish invade and defeat the Inca empire of Peru

1536
The first Spanish settlement at Buenos Aires, Argentina

1541
The Spanish found a settlement at Santiago, in Chile

1545
Spanish develop silver mining in the Andes mountains

1560
The Portuguese lay out sugarcane plantations in Brazil

1620
Dutch West India Company settles Guyana, northern South America

1667
Dutch colonists take Suriname, in northern South America

OCEANIA

1519
Portuguese explorer Ferdinand Magellan enters the Pacific Ocean

1526
Portuguese explorer Jorge de Menezes visits New Guinea

1600
Decline of Easter Island culture due to over-population and warfare

1600
Tu'i Kanokupolu dynasty comes to power in Hawaiian islands

1606
Dutch explorer Willem Jansz sights Cape York Peninsula, Australia

1616
Dutch crew under Dirck Hartog lands in Western Australia

1642
Dutch explorer Abel Tasman reaches Tasmania and New Zealand

1643
Tasman sails to the Pacific islands of Tonga and Fiji

106

⚙ **1509**
Henry VIII marries Catherine of Aragon (Spain)

⚙ **1512**
Henry VIII claims French throne. War with France.

⚙ **1520**
English-French meeting at Field of the Cloth of Gold

⚙ **1530**
Wolsey falls from power over divorce crisis

⚙ **1533**
Henry VIII marries Anne Boleyn

KING HARRY'S DAYS

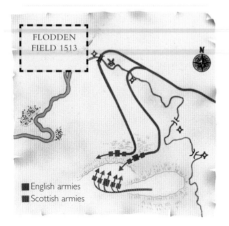

FLODDEN FIELD 1513

■ English armies
■ Scottish armies

YOUNG Henry VIII, crowned King of England in 1509, loved to fight tournaments in gleaming armour. In 1520 he met François I of France at the Field of the Cloth of Gold, near Calais. Both sides wore the most splendid clothes imaginable. Standards fluttered in front of luxurious tents. However although royal courts still dreamed of chivalry, the period we call the Middle Ages had already slipped away.

In 1513, while Henry VIII was away fighting in France, the Scots invaded England. They were defeated at Flodden. Ten thousand were killed, including James IV, who was married to Henry's sister Margaret.

Henry VIII's personal life led to an historic break with the Church of Rome.

THE EARLY TUDORS

Henry VII had been a skillful ruler, who survived false claims to the throne and rebellions over his harsh taxation. His sickly eldest son, Arthur, died young. However his second son, who became Henry VIII, was strong and energetic. In the new Europe, nations were competing for power and trade. Henry was a cunning statesman, as was his Lord Chancellor, a bullying, arrogant churchman called Thomas Wolsey.

THE KING WITH SIX WIVES

The young Henry VIII cut a fine figure, but by the time of his death in 1547 he had become bloated, overweight and diseased. He married no fewer than six times. His marriages were marked by passion, political intrigue, jealousy, rage and selfishness. Henry's love for a beautiful courtier called Anne Boleyn led him to demand a divorce from Catherine of Aragon. The Pope refused and this led to a crisis which changed the direction of English history.

MONEY, LAND AND SHEEP

While Henry VIII spent lavishly on court life and on wars, ordinary people suffered extreme hardship. The Spanish were now mining gold and silver in the Americas, and this upset the economy of other European countries.

Prices began to rise and rents with them. For many years common land, that had always been used by the public for farming and grazing, was seized by greedy landlords. Many poor people were forced off the land, to become beggars and outlaws.

In July 1549 Robert Kett, from Wymondham in Norfolk, led a rebellion against the enclosure of common land for sheep pasture. Kett attracted 16,000 supporters to his cause and they killed 20,000 sheep as a protest. They occupied the city of Norwich, but Kett was captured and hanged.

The Guildhall at Lavenham in Norfolk, East Anglia, was built in 1529. Lavenham was a centre of the wool trade and wool was the mainstay of the English economy.

DIVORCE AND REBELLION

When Henry VIII demanded something, he usually got it. Thomas Wolsey was unable to persuade Pope Clement VII to agree to Henry's divorce with Catherine of Aragon, so he was thrown out of office. In 1534 a law was passed making Henry VIII head of the Church in England, so that he could decide his own fate. The arrogance of the king and his officials led to many uprisings. In 1536-37 there was a major rebellion in Yorkshire and Lincolnshire, called the Pilgrimage of Grace.

RULERS OF ENGLAND

House of Tudor (continued)
+ Henry VIII   1509-1547
+ Edward VI   1547-1553
+ Mary I   1553-1558
+ Elizabeth I   1558-1603

Catherine of Aragon was the widow of Prince Arthur. Henry demanded a divorce.

Henry married Anne Boleyn in 1533, but they quarrelled and she was executed in 1536.

Henry married Jane Seymour the day after Anne was executed. She died in childbirth.

The fourth marriage was for political reasons and Henry found Anne of Cleves too unattractive.

After another divorce, Henry married Catherine Howard, but executed her too, for being unfaithful.

Henry's sixth wife, Catherine Parr, was a wise queen, who survived Henry's death.

1517
Martin Luther starts
Protestant movement in
Germany

1521
Henry VIII is made Defender
of the Faith by the Pope

1531
English priests recognise
Henry VIII as head of the
Church in England

1534
Henry VIII breaks ties with
the Church of Rome

1535
Thomas Cromwell starts
to seize Church wealth for
the state

CLASHES ⊙ OF FAÏTH

I N 1521, Pope Leo X had honoured Henry
VIII of England with the title 'Defender of
the Faith', because of his support for the
Roman Church. Within 13 years, however,
Henry had broken with Rome and made
himself head of the Church in England – all
because of his divorce with Catherine of
Aragon. This marked the start of centuries of
religious conflict in the British Isles.

The English nursery rhyme 'Little Jack Horner' has its origins in history.
Horner was steward to the Abbot of Glastonbury. When Henry VIII was
busy seizing the wealth of the monasteries, Horner stole the deeds
(ownership papers) to a manor house called Mells, in Somerset, and gave
them to Henry VIII. The 'good boy' was rewarded with the land – a real 'plum'.
The last abbot of Glastonbury, Robert Whiting, was executed in 1539.

THOMAS MORE'S *UTOPIA*

Thomas More's perfect land of
Utopia was far removed from
the realities of Henry VIII's England

Sir Thomas More was appointed Lord
Chancellor of England in 1529. He did
not want the job, but he carried it out
dutifully. Although More wished to see
many changes in the Roman Church,
he refused to accept Henry VIII as
head of the English Church. More was
beheaded for treason in 1535. In 1516
More wrote a book in Latin, which
compared the social problems of
his day with an imagined island
where there was an ideal
society. The name of the book
was *Utopia* – from the Greek
words for 'nowhere'.

THE PROTESTANTS

New ideas were entering the British Isles from mainland Europe during the reign of Henry VIII. They came from people who were known as Protestants, because they were protesting against the Roman 'Catholic' (meaning 'universal') Church, its teachings and its customs. Leading Protestant campaigners included a German called Martin Luther and a Frenchman called John Calvin. Their demands for reform led to this period of European history being called the Reformation.

The year 1539 saw the 'dissolution' (closing down) of Roman Catholic monasteries in England and Wales. The property was mostly sold off to nobles, raising huge amounts of money for Henry VIII. The operation was organized by Thomas Cromwell, another powerful politican who ended up having his head chopped off.

The early Tudor period produced some beautiful church architecture. The roof of King's College Chapel, Cambridge, fans out into a delicate tracery of stone. It was completed in 1515.

AN ENGLISH CHURCH

Henry VIII broke with Rome for political reasons, rather than because of his religious beliefs. He had little sympathy for the English supporters of Martin Luther and intended the English Church to follow basic Catholic teachings. During the reign of Henry's successor, Edward VI, the Church in England did adopt Protestant policies.

Knox had a very strong character and was an influential campaigner. In an age of powerful queens, he claimed that it was against the will of God for women to be rulers.

THE SCOTTISH REFORMER

John Knox was born at Haddington, Lothian, in about 1513. He became a Catholic priest in 1540, but soon fell under the influence of the Lutheran George Wishart. Wishart was burnt for his beliefs in 1547, and Knox became a Protestant minister. He spent some time in England in the service of Edward VI and then went to Switzerland, where he studied the teachings of John Calvin. Knox returned to Scotland in 1559. Despite the efforts of the Scottish Catholics, a Protestant Church of Scotland was recognized in 1560.

⊛ 1498
Henry VII rebuilds palace at Richmond, Surrey

⊛ 1515
Thomas Wolsey builds Hampton Court palace

⊛ 1526
German artist Hans Holbein makes portraits of the Tudor court

⊛ 1533
Anne Boleyn gives birth to Elizabeth at Greenwich palace

⊛ 1536
St James's Palace is built in London

A TUDOR PALACE

I N Tudor times, the River Thames was the lifeline of the growing city of London. Rowing boats called wherries carried passengers across to the south bank and sometimes a splendid royal barge could be seen, its oars dipping in the water. It would leave the royal landing stage by Whitehall Palace and beat upstream to the royal palaces at Richmond or Hampton Court, or downstream to the grand palace of Greenwich.

The court of Henry VIII followed French fashions, with rich velvets, satins and brocades for both men and women.

LIVING IN LUXURY

Nobles no longer lived in draughty castles. They built fine country houses, often of brick, surrounded by beautiful gardens. These were laid out in complicated patterns, their gravel paths and sunny flower beds being hedged with lavender or box shrubs. The most impressive buildings of all were the royal palaces, built near the capital. They were decorated by the finest craftsmen in Europe. Hampton Court, in Surrey, was built by Thomas Wolsey. He offered it to Henry VIII as a present, when it looked as though he might be falling from favour.

OAK AND PLASTER

In Tudor country houses and palaces, there were wooden panels and great carved staircases. Furniture include cupboards and heavy chests of oak. Ceilings were often decorated with raised plaster patterns, which were sometimes picked out in bold colours. Rich tapestries on the walls might show scenes of hunting or woodland views. Fireplaces were enormous, leading to high, ornate chimney pots.

Feather beds were enclosed by a carved four-poster frame, hung with heavy curtains.

1538
Building begins of Nonsuch
royal palace in Surrey

1540
The astronomical clock installed
at Hampton Court palace

1553
Longleat House is built in
Witlshire, southern England

1572
A royal firework display is
staged at Warwick Castle

111

COURT AND CULTURE

In the 1500s there was a great renewal of interest in learning, in the civilizations of ancient Greece and Rome, in painting and sculpture and in invention. This period, called the Renaissance or 'rebirth', began in Italy, but its influence was also felt in northern Europe. The Tudor rulers were well educated and intelligent. Artists such as the great German painter Hans Holbein the Younger came to the English court.

Henry VIII and his courtiers loved music, dancing and playing royal or 'real' tennis, a version of the game which was played in an indoor court. They also loved to hunt deer in the royal parks and forests.

Henry VIII studied music as a boy. He later composed religious music and popular songs.

TIME, SUN AND EARTH

The ingenious clock at Hampton Court was made for Henry VIII by Nicholas Oursian, in 1540. It not only tells the time, but shows the month, the number of days since the year began, high tides, phases of the Moon and signs of the zodiac. It also shows the Sun moving around the Earth. A book by the Polish astronomer Nicolaus Copernicus, explaining that actually it is the Earth which moves around the Sun, was not published until 1543.

The Tudor rulers moved from one palace to another during the year. Hampton Court was their favourite.

112

☒ **1485**
Henry Tudor flies red dragon
standard at battle of Bosworth

☒ **1523**
Poets gather at Caerwys for
an *eisteddfod*.

☒ **1536**
The first Act of Union. Wales
is annexed by England

☒ **1542**
The second Act of Union
becomes law

☒ **1547**
The first book to be printed
in the Welsh language

WALES UNDER THE TUDORS

WALES during the reign of the Tudors was still mostly a land of farms and villages, of windmills and water wheels. Women spun and wove their own cloth. Few towns had more than 2,000 inhabitants. There was little industry, although coal was being mined in South Wales during the reign of Elizabeth I. Ships traded with Ireland, with other parts of Great Britain, France and Spain.

WELSH CONNECTIONS

Henry VII was of Welsh descent and fought under a red dragon standard at the battle of Bosworth. The green and white background on the modern Welsh flag represents the family colours of the Tudors. During the reign of Henry VII, many fortune-seekers arrived in London from Wales. The Seisyllt family, who came from the Welsh borders, became one of the most powerful families in Tudor England, changing their name to Cecil.

A stained glass window in the church at Penmynydd in North Wales recalls that this was the ancestral home of the Tudor family. The window is decorated with the Tudor rose emblem and symbols of royal power.

This fine map of Wales was published in 1573, during the reign of Elizabeth I. It was made by the cartographer Humphrey Llwyd who was born in Denbigh, North Wales, in about 1527. He was educated at Oxford University and died in 1568. The place names are shown in three languages – Latin, English and Welsh.

SCHOLARS AND BISHOPS

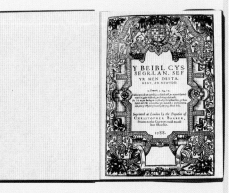

William Morgan, born in 1545, was the first to translate the whole of the Bible into Welsh. He was a scholar who understood Latin, Greek and Hebrew. He died at St Asaph, North Wales, in 1604.

In 1571 Hugh Price, an expert in Church law from Brecon, founded Jesus College, in Oxford, England, for Welsh students. Over the ages it kept its special links with Wales.

After 1588, students would have been able to read the Bible for the first time in the Welsh language. The brilliant translation was by William Morgan, who in 1595 became Bishop of Llandaff. Morgan's masterpiece helped to shape the Welsh language and keep it alive into modern times.

THE ACTS OF UNION

The Tudors may have been proud of their Welsh ancestors, but as rulers of England they demanded total control of their lands. By the Acts of Union, passed in 1536 and 1542, Wales and the Marcher lordships were annexed, or taken over, by England. In doing this, Henry VIII took the first step towards creating a United Kingdom. Welsh law and Welsh customs were to be abolished. No Welsh person could hold public office unless they could speak English, a ruling which excluded 95 percent of the population. Otherwise, Welsh citizens did now have equal rights with English citizens before the law, and were represented in the English parliament.

Roofs and gables
The roof was supported by massive wooden beams and tiled with slate. The stepped design of the gable ends was copied from Flanders.

Servants' bedrooms
Servants slept in male and female dormitories in the attic.

The cellars
Barrels of ale and wine were stored in the basement.

One of the finest Tudor town houses in Britain survives at Plas Mawr, in Conwy, North Wales. It was built in 1577 for a wealthy local gentleman named Robert Wynn.

The great chamber
The chief reception room had decorated plasterwork, showing Tudor roses and coats of arms.

Preparing food
On the ground floor was the kitchen, the pantry and the brewhouse.

114

1547	1549	1549	1550	1553
Somerset becomes Protector as Edward VI is still a boy	First Book of Common Prayer is printed in English	Rebellions in Cornwall and East Anglia	Somerset is overthrown, replaced by Warwick	Edward VI dies. Lady Jane Grey declared queen

PROTESTANT OR CATHOLIC?

Edward VI was a sickly boy, who died young.

H ENRY VIII died in 1547. Would England become Protestant or Roman Catholic? Living through the years that followed was like riding a see-saw, as rulers swung from the one faith to the other. There were fierce struggles between powerful nobles. Many people suffered economic hardship.

THE BOY KING

Edward VI was just 10 when he came to the throne. The son of Henry VIII and Jane Seymour, he was raised as a strict Protestant. He was very clever and learned Greek, Latin and French. His uncle Edward Seymour, Duke of Somerset, governed as Lord Protector in his place. However Somerset was overthrown and executed in 1552, to be replaced by John Dudley, Duke of Northumberland. Edward VI died from tuberculosis in 1553.

THE GRAMMAR SCHOOLS

Now that there were no more monks to carry out teaching work, schools became more and more important. Many new schools were named after the Tudors, others after the rich merchants who funded them. It was mostly boys who received formal schooling. The school day lasted from six in the morning until four or five in the afternoon. Pupils learned to write using slates. They learned to read and did sums and were beaten if they made mistakes. A lot of the time was spent learning Latin grammar, so these were known as 'grammar schools'.

The grammar school in Stratford-upon-Avon was named after Edward VI. Its most famous pupil in Tudor times was a young lad called William Shakespeare.

⊠ **1553**
Jane Grey is imprisoned. Mary I becomes queen.

⊠ **1554**
Sir Thomas Wyatt's rebellion fails. Jane Grey is executed

⊠ **1554**
Mary I of England marries King Philip II of Spain

⊠ **1555**
Persecution of Protestants begins. 300 executed

⊠ **1558**
England loses Calais, its last French possession

115

QUEEN FOR NINE DAYS

The Duke of Northumberland had persuaded the young king to make his daughter-in-law, Lady Jane Grey, heir to the throne of England. She was crowned queen in 1553, but within just nine days had been forced from the throne by the supporters of the rightful heir, Mary Tudor. Jane was imprisoned. After Sir Thomas Wyatt the Younger started a rebellion in her name, she was beheaded in the Tower of London in 1554, at the age of 16.

Jane was a quiet, intelligent girl, a Protestant and a great grand-daughter of Henry VII. Against her will, she became a pawn in a deadly game of power politics.

BLOODY MARY

Mary Tudor was the daughter of Henry VIII and Catherine of Aragon. Her father had forced her to sign a document stating that his marriage to her mother had been illegal. Mary remained a very unhappy woman for most of her life. She was a Roman Catholic and in 1554 married King Philip II of Spain. He spent little more than a year in England and the marriage was very unpopular. Mary began to bring back the Catholic faith. During the last three years of her reign, 300 leading Protestants were burned alive. This earned her the nickname of 'Bloody Mary'.

PRINCESS ELIZABETH

Mary I had a young half-sister, the daughter of Henry VIII and Anne Boleyn. Princess Elizabeth loved learning as well as playing music, dancing and riding. She was raised as a Protestant and this aroused the suspicion of Mary, who imprisoned her for a time. Elizabeth had to tread very, very carefully. However when Mary died without a child, in 1558, it was Elizabeth who became Queen of England.

Protestant churchmen who went to their death in the years 1555-1556 included Hugh Latimer, Nicholas Ridley and Archbishop Thomas Cranmer.

116

⊠ **1558**
Elizabeth I becomes Queen of England

⊠ **1558**
William Cecil is appointed Secretary of State

⊠ **1559**
The Church of England is established

⊠ **1569**
Roman Catholic rebellion led by northern earls

⊠ **1570**
Pope expels Elizabeth I from the Roman Catholic Church

THE RED QUEEN

ELIZABETH, pale-skinned with flaming red hair, was crowned Queen of England in January 1559, dressed in heavy robes of gold and ermine fur. She was 25 years old. The new queen was warmly welcomed by the people, who longed for an end to religious strife and struggles for power.

STATESMEN AND SPIES

During the reign of Mary I, Elizabeth had learned how to survive in a world of plots and intrigue. As a queen, she possessed all the diplomatic and political skills that Mary had lacked. She surrounded herself with cunning statesmen such as William Cecil (who became Lord Burleigh) and set up a secret service under Sir Francis Walsingham. Elizabeth, like her father, enjoyed power and would let nobody stand in her way.

Although Elizabeth I never married, she had her favourite courtiers, such as Robert Dudley, Earl of Leicester (left), Christopher Hatton and, until they quarrelled, Robert Devereux, Earl of Essex.

Elizabeth I was much loved, and knew how to win public approval. However when she was crossed, she showed a fierce temper.

THE VIRGIN QUEEN

Who would the new queen marry? The throne of England was a rich prize. Elizabeth kept everyone guessing, playing off one suitor against another in order to gain political advantage. In the end, she married no one. She said that she was already married – to the English people.

Elizabeth I left no heir to the throne and so became known as the Virgin Queen. The newly formed North American colony of Virginia was named in her honour.

1588
31 Roman Catholic priests are executed in England.

1596
Robert Cecil is appointed Secretary of State

1601
Last parliament summoned by Elizabeth I

1601
Poor Laws, to support the poorest in society

1603
Elizabeth I dies of pneumonia at Richmond Palace

GLORIANA

Elizabeth I ruled over a glittering court. It was like a continuous dramatic performance, in which all eyes were drawn to her. She is said to have owned over 1,000 dresses. Courtiers competed for her approval and greatly feared falling from favour.

Elizabeth I inspired a great poetical work by Edmund Spenser, called *The Faerie Queene*. Characters in the book, which was written between 1590 and 1596, were meant to represent virtues and vices. Elizabeth is called Gloriana, the ideal queen.

At the court of Elizabeth I both men and women wore starched collars called ruffs. Later in her reign, women wore wide skirts stretched over hoops called farthingales.

Elizabeth's signature was scrawled across the page in ink, with a quill pen. The R stands for regina, which is Latin for 'queen'. The loops are intended to prevent any one else adding an extra message to the bottom of the document.

AT HOME AND ABROAD

The court moved around the country, making royal 'progresses'. Elizabeth's hosts had to spend a fortune on her entertainment and food. These journeys helped Elizabeth find out what was going on in her kingdom and made her aware of any local problems or needs. It also showed off her power and authority. Elizabeth I could speak Latin, French and Italian fluently, and she also knew ancient Greek and some Spanish. She spoke to foreign ambassadors directly – and often very forcibly – in protection of English trading interests.

Large areas of land were set aside as royal parks and forests. The queen and her courtiers would attend stag hunts, breaking off to enjoy open-air picnics and entertainments.

118

■ 1559
Robert Dudley is patron of a players' company

■ 1560s
Plays are acted in the yards of London inns

■ 1572
A law is passed classing actors as rogues and beggars

■ 1576
The Theatre in Shoreditch, the first commercial stage

■ 1583
Elizabeth I becomes patron of a players' company

PLAYS AND PLAYERS

ELIZABETH I loved the theatre, and she and her courtiers set up their own companies of players (actors). The first players had performed in the yards of inns and been generally regarded as rogues. Some private theatres were set up, but soon the first commercial theatres were also being built in London. These were rowdy, exciting places.

Play in progress
A flag was flown to show if a play was about to begin. The stage extended into the yard, so the audience and the actors were very close. There was no curtain.

Tiring house
This was where the actors changed their costumes and prepared for the show.

KIT MARLOWE
Christopher ('Kit') Marlowe was born in 1564, the son of a shoemaker. He went to King's School, Canterbury, and studied at Cambridge. He was very intelligent but also loved drinking and brawling. He was rumoured to be an atheist, someone who does not believe in God. Marlowe wrote poetry and several great plays, including *Tamburlaine, The Tragical History of Dr Faustus, The Jew of Malta* and *Edward II*. He may have worked as a secret agent and was killed in a fight in a tavern ('pub') in 1593.

Christopher Marlowe led life to the full, but died in a drunken brawl.

WELCOME TO THE GLOBE
An actor groans as he brandishes his sword, while cannonballs (rolled across wooden boards) make the sound of thunder. The actress is really a boy wearing a wig, for an actor's life is said to be too disreputable for a woman. In front of the stage, the audience is packed into an open-air yard, entrance fee one penny. They laugh, roar and shout out during the play. The better-off members of the audience watch from the covered galleries which ring the yard.

⊠ c1587
William Shakespeare arrives in London

⊠ 1593
Christopher Marlowe stabbed to death in a tavern brawl

⊠ 1599
The Globe Theatre is built by the Burbage brothers

⊠ 1612
John Webster writes *The White Devil*

⊠ 1616
William Shakespeare dies in Stratford-upon Avon

119

▶ William Shakespeare lived until 1616. His great plays still speak directly to us today, wherever we live in the world.

◀ The Globe Theatre was built in Southwark, on the south bank of the River Thames, in 1599.

Galleries
Covered galleries ringed the yard. Plays were performed in daylight, normally during the afternoon.

WILLIAM SHAKESPEARE

Out of the taverns, theatres and royal courts of the Elizabethan age came some of the finest plays ever written. The master playwright and most brilliant poet was William Shakespeare. Born at Stratford-upon-Avon, Warwickshire, in 1564, he came to London in about 1587. In 1594 he bought a shareholding in a new company of players called the Lord Chamberlain's Men, whose leading actor was Richard Burbage. Shakespeare wrote witty comedies and heartbreaking tragedies, many of them based on British history.

POETRY, ART AND MUSIC

The late 1500s and early 1600s were a rich period for the arts in England. Several of Elizabeth I's courtiers, such as Sir Philip Sidney and Sir Walter Raleigh, were poets. The playwright Ben Jonson worked with Shakespeare in the 1590s and John Webster wrote the first of his tragedies, *The White Devil*, in 1612. The artist Nicholas Hilliard was making exquisite miniature paintings at the royal court, while Thomas Tallis and William Byrd were composing music for church and palace.

▶ This house in Shottery, Stratford-upon-Avon, was the family home of Anne Hathaway, who married William Shakespeare in 1582.

120

⊠ **1494**
The body of English law now applies in all Ireland

⊠ **1504**
The Earls of Kildare (Fitzgeralds) control Ireland

⊠ **1534**
Rebellion in Ireland led by Lord Offaly

⊠ **1557**
Mary I starts 'plantation' in Laois and Offaly

⊠ **1573**
Elizabeth starts 'plantation' of Ulster

İRELAND REBELS

DURING the early Tudor period, the most powerful people in Ireland belonged to an old Norman family, the Fitzgeralds. As Earls of Kildare, Gerald Mór (1478-1513) and Gerald Óg (1513-1534) came to control most of the country. England was happy for the Fitzgeralds to look after the royal interests in Ireland – but only so long as they did not challenge English rule.

This well-to-do lady comes from the Pale, the English-speaking area around Dublin.

RELIGIOUS DIVISIONS

The political divisions of Ireland were further complicated when Henry VIII broke with the Roman Church. The Irish-speaking Gaels remained faithful to Rome. Of the rest, some remained loyal to the king, but could not accept him as head of the Church. Others accepted the new order, and did well for themselves, as they profited from wealth seized from the Church.

In 1534 the Fitzgeralds declared themselves for the Pope. One of them – Thomas, Lord Offaly – rose up against Henry VIII but was defeated by an English army.

In the Gaelic west, long-haired mercenary soldiers, the 'kern', were armed with long swords and daggers. Their home villages were made up of simple thatched houses, often grouped around a fortified tower.

⊞ **1579**
Rebellions in Munster and
(1580) Leinster

⊞ **1593**
Hugh O'Neill leads rebellion
in Ulster

⊞ **1601**
English defeat O'Neill's
rebellion

⊞ **1603**
Treaty of Mellifont confiscates
lands of Irish nobles

⊞ **1607**
Flight of the Earls. Irish nobles
flee to mainland Europe

121

THE PIRATE QUEEN

During the 1560s, shipping off the west coast of Ireland came under attack from a fleet of pirate ships. These were based in Clew Bay, where they could hide out amongst a maze of small islands. The fleet was commanded by an Irish noble woman called Gràinne ni Mhàille, or Grace O'Malley. In 1593 she negotiated a pardon from Elizabeth I, in person.

Grace O'Malley's pirate galleys attacked English and Irish ships. In 1557 she repelled an English attack on her stronghold.

UNWELCOME SETTLERS

Mary I may have been a Roman Catholic, but she supported an English policy of colonization or 'plantation' in Ireland. English settlers were 'planted' in Laois and Offaly, which were now to be known as Queen's County and King's County. Under Elizabeth I, Irish colonization became a religious drive, with Protestant nobles eager to grab land from the Catholic Irish. Elizabeth I 'planted' Ulster, in the north. Most early plantation attempts failed, but they started a process which proved to be disastrous for Ireland.

In 1607 Hugh O'Neill fled to the Netherlands, which were at that time ruled by Spain. He died in Rome in 1616.

REBELLION AND FLIGHT

The most serious Irish rebellion broke out in Ulster, in 1595. It was led by Hugh O'Neill, Earl of Tyrone. In 1598 he led a victory over the English at the battle of the Yellow Ford, but was himself defeated by 1601. By the Treaty of Mellifont, signed in 1603, vast areas of land were seized from the Irish. By 1607 the Irish nobles were in despair. Many cut their losses and fled to mainland Europe – the 'Flight of the Earls'.

⊠ 1504
James IV marries Margaret Tudor

⊠ 1505
James IV starts to build a Scottish navy

⊠ 1513
James IV killed by English at the battle of Flodden

⊠ 1538
James V marries Mary of Guise, a French Catholic

⊠ 1542
James V dies. He is followed by his infant daughter Mary

MARY, QUEEN ⋅ OF ⋅ SCOTS

THE Stewart family ruled Scotland for over 340 years. Many of their early kings came to the throne in their childhood, and this allowed powerful Lowlands families, highland chieftains and Lords of the Isles to grasp power for themselves. There were court plots, royal murders and endless wars with the English. Scotland's closest links were with France, which kept to the 'auld alliance'.

THE STEWART COURT

The greatest of the Stewart kings was James IV, who became king in 1488. He married Margaret Tudor, sister of Henry VIII. His court attracted poets and musical composers such William Dunbar and Robert Carver. James IV built new palaces and a fleet of warships. Tragically, he was killed at the Battle of Flodden in 1513. He was the last Scottish king to speak the Gaelic language.

James V, son of James IV, inherited the Scottish throne as a baby. He died in 1542, shortly after the Scots were defeated by the English at Solway Moss. His daughter was Mary, Queen of Scots.

Edinburgh's castle towers over the Scottish capital. In it visitors can still see the rooms of Mary of Guise and Mary, Queen of Scots, as well as the room in which James VI was born.

SCOTTISH RULERS
House of Stewart

✤ Robert II	1371–1390
✤ Robert III	1390–1406
✤ James I	1406–1437
✤ James II	1437–1460
✤ James III	1460–1488
✤ James IV	1488–1513
✤ James V	1513–1542
✤ Mary (Stuart)	1542–1567
✤ James VI (I of England)	1567–1625

HOLYROODHOUSE

James IV and James V built a royal palace called Holyroodhouse in Edinburgh. It was here, in Queen Mary's apartments, that secretary David Rizzio was horribly murdered in 1566. His killers included William Ruthven and James Douglas, Earl of Morton.

Holyroodhouse was built on the site of a medieval abbey founded by David I. The palace was repeatedly destroyed by the English. Much of it was rebuilt after the 1650s.

A QUEEN RETURNS

James V's widow, Mary of Guise, ruled as regent, for her daughter Mary was still a baby. A French Catholic, she soon clashed with the Protestants. The young queen was sent to the French court and raised as a Catholic. In 1558 she married the heir to the French throne, but her husband – and her mother – both died in 1560. Mary Stuart (as the family name was now spelt) returned to Scotland. In 1565 Mary married her cousin, Henry Darnley. It was a disastrous mistake.

IMPRISONED IN ENGLAND

Darnley became involved in a plot to murder Mary's Italian secretary, and was then murdered himself. Mary then married the suspected murderer, the Earl of Bothwell. Mary was forced off the throne and imprisoned. Her baby son James VI became king. Mary escaped and fled to her cousin, Elizabeth I. In England, however, she was held prisoner for 19 years. Elizabeth feared that Catholics would plot to put Mary on the English throne.

The life of Mary, Queen of Scots ended tragically. The English secret service uncovered a Catholic plot and claimed that Mary was involved. She was beheaded at Fotheringay Castle in February 1587.

124

⊠ **1585**
England enters war between the Dutch and Spanish

⊠ **1585**
Spanish ports attacked by Francis Drake

⊠ **1585**
Spain confiscates English ships in Spanish ports

⊠ **1586**
English and Dutch defeat Spanish at battle of Zutphen

⊠ **1587**
Francis Drake raids Spanish port of Cadiz

THE SPANISH ARMADA

I N May 1588 a massive invasion fleet or 'Armada' sailed from the port of Lisbon. It was made up of 130 ships fitted with 2,500 guns. They carried 30,000 soldiers and sailors. The ships included large warships called galleons, armed merchant ships, galleys (which used oars as well as sails) and supply vessels. This great war fleet was bound for the English Channel.

When the English sea captain Francis Drake carried out illegal raids on Spanish shipping in the Americas, Elizabeth I ignored complaints from Spain. In 1587 Drake set fire to the Spanish port of Cadiz. The raid was described as 'singeing the King of Spain's beard'.

DRAKE'S DRUM

This drum was beaten during the Armada crisis, when Sir Francis Drake called his crew to action on the deck of the *Revenge*.

WHY DID THE ARMADA SAIL?
Spain had become the richest and most powerful country in Europe. It was still ruled by King Philip II, former husband of Mary I of England. From 1580 he was also king of Portugal. The Netherlands too were under Spanish rule, as were vast, newly discovered regions of the Americas. When Dutch Protestants rose up against rule by Catholic Spain, English armies were sent to help them. And across the Atlantic Ocean, the English were fiercely competing with the Spanish to grab the riches of the Americas.

SEA DOGS FROM DEVON
Most of the great Elizabethan seafarers spoke English with strong west-country accents. Francis Drake, John Hawkyns, Humphrey Gilbert, Walter Raleigh and Richard Grenville were all from Devon, in the southwest of England. Francis Drake was a hero to the English and was knighted by Elizabeth I. To the Spanish, who called him *El Draco*, he was a common pirate.

The Spanish fleet was devastated by fireships, small boats which were packed with timber, pitch and explosives. It was then the victim of storms. Spanish ships were wrecked off Norway, blown around Scotland and driven ashore in Ireland. Only 70 battered ships returned to Spain.

IN PLYMOUTH AND TILBURY

As the Armada approached Cornwall, naval squadrons were stationed along the Channel coast, under the command of Lord Howard of Effingham. Drake's ships lay in Plymouth harbour. An army of 20,000 men was drawn up at Tilbury, on the River Thames, as a Spanish army from the Netherlands was expected to invade the southeast. Elizabeth I rode out to speak to the troops and steady nerves.

SCATTERED BY STORMS

The English ships sailed out to meet the Armada. They had long-range guns and chased the big galleons as they wallowed in high seas, driven by westerly winds. Fighting off Portland Bill and the Isle of Wight was followed by an eight-hour sea battle off Gravelines. The Armada was badly damaged. It was now driven northwards and scattered by roaring gales.

The English sea captain John Hawkyns was responsible for the navy's new ship designs.

BUILDING A FLEET

Elizabeth I's new navy was built at the royal dockyards in Chatham, Kent. The navy was still small, having only 34 ships – although merchant vessels could also be used in warfare.

The old ships of the Middle Ages, which were really floating troop carriers, were replaced by new ships of oak. These were nippier than the big Spanish galleons – sleeker and lower in the water.

126

🗙 **1562**
John Hawkyns ships slaves from Africa to the New World

🗙 **1576**
Martin Frobisher seeks 'Northwest Passage' round Canada to Asia

🗙 **1580**
Francis Drake sails around the world

🗙 **1607**
John Smith settles Jamestown, Virginia

🗙 **1612**
East India Company's first trading port, Surat

In 1577 Francis Drake sailed to the Strait of Magellan, in South America. He crossed into the Pacific Ocean, sailed north to Vancouver and then returned home via Asia and Africa. His ship, the Golden Hind, became the first English vessel to sail round the world.

ΠEW WORLDS

EUROPEAN seafarers had begun to discover the world beyond their own shores in the 1400s, as they searched for new trading routes. Portugal and Spain led the way, exploring the coasts of Africa, Asia and the 'New World' of the Americas. English exploration began in the reign of Henry VII, who sent Italian-born navigator John Cabot to find a northwestern route to Asia. In 1497 Cabot sailed as far as Nova Scotia, Canada, and discovered rich fishing grounds off Newfoundland.

In the medieval world, little was known of the world beyond Europe, North Africa and Western Asia. After the 1500s, horizons suddenly expanded.

EXPLORERS AND COMPANIES

Many more English seafarers sailed off into the unknown. Martin Frobisher reached Labrador, Canada, in 1577. Francis Drake completed his voyage around the world in 1580. In 1595 Walter Raleigh explored the coasts of Trinidad and sailed up the River Orinoco, in South America. Following the explorers, came the merchants. Companies were set up to organize control foreign trade. The British East India Company opened its first trading post in India at Surat in 1612.

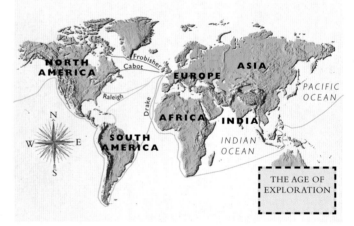

THE AGE OF EXPLORATION

ALL-AMERICAN CROPS

It is easy for us to forget that many of the foods we take for granted today were unknown in Europe before the 1500s and 1600s. New food plants from the Americas included maize, tomatoes, pineapples and potatoes. Spain was probably the first European country to grow potatoes. Legend has it that it was Sir Walter Raleigh who first introduced them into the British Isles, in 1585.

Sir Walter Raleigh was one of the favourite courtiers of Elizabeth I. In 1585 he sent settlers to Roanoke Island, off North Carolina. Their colony failed, as did his first attempts to colonize Virginia.

COLONIES IN THE AMERICAS

The Spanish controlled most of Central and South America, but Britain did gain Caribbean islands such as St Kitts (1623), Barbados (1625) and Jamaica (1665) as well as the mainland territory now called Belize (1638). Scottish merchants tried to found a colony in Darién, Panama, in the 1690s, but it failed. Britain's most successful settlements were on the Atlantic coast of North America. The first of these was Jamestown, Virginia (1607). Plymouth Colony was founded in Massachussetts in 1620, by a group of religious exiles from England, known as the 'Pilgrims'.

THE STORY OF POCAHONTAS

Matoaka, or Pocahontas, was born in 1595, the daughter of a Native American chief called Powhatan. She became a Christian and married a Virginian settler called John Rolfe. In 1616 she went with him to England and was received at the royal court. Sadly, she died of smallpox in 1617, at Gravesend. Her ship had been preparing to sail down the River Thames for the return voyage to America.

Pocahontas kept the peace between her people and the settlers. In 1607 she saved the life of John Smith, the founder of Jamestown.

THE SLAVE TRADE

The first Europeans came to Africa's Guinea Coast in search of ivory and gold dust, but they soon were dealing in another commodity – human misery. The first Englishman to trade in slaves was John Hawkyns, in 1562. Slave-traders took on board West African men, women and children, who had been captured and put in chains. The slaves were then shipped to the Caribbean and North American colonies and sold into a wretched life of toil on the plantations.

West African slaves were packed below decks, like animals. Many of them perished during the sea voyage, and their bodies were thrown overboard.

128

🔲 **1603**
Union of English and Scottish thrones

🔲 **1604**
The first English dictionary is published

🔲 **1605**
Guy Fawkes arrested at the English parliament

🔲 **1606**
Guy Fawkes and seven others are executed

🔲 **1606**
The first version of the Union Flag is flown

TREASON AND GUNPOWDER

I N her old age Elizabeth I was still riding, dancing and hunting, but her face was drawn and haggard. She died of pneumonia, at Richmond palace, in 1603. The throne now passed to James VI of Scotland, the protestant son of Mary, Queen of Scots, and descendant of Margaret Tudor. He was crowned James I of England.

This silver coin, minted in 1603-1604, was called a 'crown'. It shows James I on horseback and gives his name in Latin – Jacobus.

The first version of the Union Flag was flown from 1606 until 1801. It combined the English flag (a St George's cross, red on a white field) with the Scottish flag of St Andrew (a saltire or diagonal cross, white on a blue field).

AT THE COURT OF KING JAMES

The thrones of Scotland and England were now united, but in 1607 the English parliament rejected a full union of the two countries. James remained absent from Scotland for 14 years. He brought in harsh anti-Catholic laws, but they were never enough to satisfy the growing number of extreme protestants, or Puritans. People also resented the favours he gave his personal friends at court, such as Robert Carr, Earl of Somerset, and George Villiers, Duke of Buckingham.

Lancashire had major witch trials in 1612 and 1633.

A WITCH HUNT

Laws against witchcraft were passed in 1563 and 1604. There was public hysteria about so-called pacts with the devil and many poor, innocent women were accused of being witches. They were thrown into ponds, tortured and hanged. In 1645 a lawyer called Matthew Hopkins turned 'witchfinder', prowling East Anglia in search of people he could send to the gallows.

IN A COUNTRY COTTAGE

Life for working people in the countryside had improved since the Middle Ages. Even so, it was far from easy. Most cottages now had some furniture and some pots and pans. Bedsteads had sheets of coarse hemp, occasionally of linen. Fuel was hard to come by, as woodland was fast disappearing. Poor people often burnt peat or bracken in the hearth, for only the rich could afford coal.

ANTI-SMOKING CAMPAIGN

The Spanish were the first Europeans to bring back tobacco from the Americas. In 1586 Francis Drake and Ralph Lane (the first governor of Virginia) presented Walter Raleigh with tobacco and a pipe. Soon it became the fashion to puff on a long pipe made of clay – much to the disgust of King James, who campaigned against this new tobacco habit.

King James failed in his bid to stop people smoking tobacco

RULERS OF GREAT BRITAIN AND IRELAND

House of Stuart

✤ James I of England (VI of Scotland)	1603-1625
✤ Charles I	1625-1649

Commonwealth and Protectorate

✤ Council of State	1649-1653
✤ Oliver Cromwell	1653-1658
✤ Richard Cromwell	1658-1659

House of Stuart

✤ Charles II	1660-1685
✤ James II of England (VII of Scotland)	1685-1688
✤ William III of Orange	1689-1702
✤ Mary II	1689-1694
✤ Anne	1702-1714

THE GUNPOWDER PLOT

On the night of 4 November 1605, a search party was sent to Parliament buildings in London. A suspicious letter had been discovered. Was there a Catholic plot to blow up King James there, the following day? In the cellars, lantern light revealed barrels of gunpowder and one of the conspirators, Guy Fawkes. He was arrested, tortured and executed for treason along with seven others. His death is still celebrated each year on 5 November, with dummy 'guys' being burnt on bonfires. However some historians argue that the conspirators were set up – in order to discredit the Catholics.

Guy (or Guido) Fawkes was just one of the people accused of the murder plot. The leader was said to be Robert Catesby.

130

1628	1629	1634	1637	1638
Petition of Right increases power of English Parliament	Charles I starts rule without Parliament (until 1640)	Charles I brings in a tax called ship money to fund the navy	Attempt to force Scots to use English form of worship	The Covenant is signed in Scotland

CAVALIERS AND ROUNDHEADS

O N 22 August 1642, King Charles I raised his standard at Nottingham. His enemy was not a foreign power, but forces loyal to the parliament of his own country. This was a Civil War, which would rage across England, Wales, Scotland and Ireland, dividing communities and even families.

Charles I reigned for 24 years. He married Princess Henrietta Maria of France and had six children. However his failure to come to terms with Parliament put the future of the monarchy at risk and cost him his life.

CHANGING TIMES

King James I of England (VI of Scotland) died in 1625. His son, Charles I, came to the throne of a country which was going through many changes. The power of the extreme Protestants, or Puritans, was growing and they were suspicious of his marriage with a Roman Catholic. The middle and lower classes of society were beginning to have more economic power. The country squires and landowners who were members of the House of Commons were demanding more say in running the country. Charles I treated them with disdain.

Civil War armies fought with swords, pikes, muskets and pistols. Royalist commanders, who often wore fancy clothes and long hair, were known as Cavaliers ('knights'). Supporters of Parliament were often Puritans, who wore plain clothes and cropped their heads. They were known as Roundheads.

COVENANTERS IN SCOTLAND

Charles I had little understanding of Scotland. The Scottish Church was Presbyterian – it was against having bishops. Charles I tried to force the Scots to follow English forms of worship. In 1638 the Scots drew up a petition, the National Covenant, rejecting his demands. Charles I went to war with the Covenanters in 1639 and 1640, but was forced to make peace. He had made enemies which, in the end, would cost him dearly.

☒ **1642**
Charles I fails in bid to arrest 5 Members of Parliament

☒ **1642**
Start of the first phase of the Civil War

☒ **1645**
Royalist defeat at Battle of Naseby

☒ **1646**
Charles I surrenders to the Scots at Newark

☒ **1648**
A second phase of Civil War. Charles I is seized by the army

131

A GROWING CRISIS

From 1629 to 1640 Charles I summoned no parliaments at all. He brought in unpopular taxes, which caused protests and unrest. In 1641 Parliament demanded that the king replace his ministers and bring in religious reforms. In 1642 Charles I forced his way into the House of Commons and attempted to arrest five Members of Parliament. He failed, and so went to war.

THE FIRST CIVIL WAR

The first battle took place at Edgehill in 1642. Both sides claimed to have won. In 1643 Parliament allied with the Scottish Covenanters and defeated the Royalists at Marston Moor in the following year. They were crushed again at Naseby, near Leicester, in 1645. In 1646, Charles I surrendered to the Scots.

ROADS AND COACHES

The roads tramped by Civil War armies were still muddy and potholed, but attempts were now being made to map them, improve them and carry out repairs.

The first stage coach service began in 1640.

THE SECOND CIVIL WAR

Charles I now tried to come to an agreement with the English Parliament, but failed. In 1647 he fled to the Isle of Wight. He made a secret deal with his former enemies in Scotland, promising them the reforms they desired. The Scots marched on England and there were Royalist risings in Wales, too. However all were defeated and by 1649 Charles was imprisoned.

Weapons are brandished and horses whinny as a battle of the Civil War is re-enacted. In 1645 a commander called Oliver Cromwell reorganized Parliament's forces. His New Model Army was efficient, ruthless and very successful.

132

⊠ 1649
Charles I is executed in
London

⊠ 1649
A republic, or
'Commonwealth' is declared

⊠ 1649
Government is by a Council
of State

⊠ 1649
The Levellers are defeated at
Burford

⊠ 1651
Scots crown Charles II king,
but are defeated at Worcester

COMMONWEALTH

O N 30 January 1649, Charles I was marched from St James's Palace to Whitehall. It was a bitterly cold day in London, with flurries of snow. At one o'clock the king stepped to the scaffold, or execution platform. When the axe had fallen, his head was shown to the ranks of soldiers and the crowd.

THE KING IS DEAD

It was reported that although Charles I had been an unpopular king, a groan passed through the London crowd when he died. Ever since the Middle Ages, people had believed that kings ruled by the will of God. Charles I himself believed in this 'divine right' of kings. He kept silent throughout his trial. News of the king's death spread like wildfire through the British Isles and mainland Europe. To many people, it was simply unbelievable.

A LORD PROTECTOR

The nation was now a republic, or 'Commonwealth'. Parliament ruled the land instead of a king or queen. It governed through a Council of State, made up of 40 members. However as far as the army was concerned, Parliament was much too cautious in its reforms. In 1653 power was handed over to one man, Oliver Cromwell, who was appointed Lord Protector. His rule was harsh but effective. He attempted to bring in military rule, and in 1556 he was even offered the crown.

Charles I died bravely, within sight of the Parliament he despised.

George Fox believed that all people were equal and that nobody should fight wars.

THE QUAKERS

In 1646 a Puritan called George Fox preached a new kind of faith. He called upon his followers to 'quake at the word of the Lord'. They became known as 'Quakers', or The Society of Friends. The Friends worshipped God in silence, with no priests or prayers or churches. Many of them were imprisoned for their beliefs or forced to flee the country.

Oliver Cromwell was a squire from the Huntingdon countryside. He made sure that no ruler could ever again afford to ignore the wishes of Parliament.

NO MORE FUN!

Many of Cromwell's supporters were Puritans. The only joy that they could accept was through religious worship. Dancing and theatre were banned. Meat or ale could not be consumed on a Sunday, and even Christmas Day was no longer to be celebrated with plum puddings and merry-making.

Playing cards were believed to be the work of the Devil.

WHAT KIND OF REVOLUTION?

The English revolution was controlled by landowners and wealthy merchants, but its footsoldiers were poor people, craft workers, small farmers and tradesmen. Some of these formed a political movement called the Levellers. They demanded true democracy (rule by the people), but were quickly crushed by Cromwell in 1649. In 1650 an even more radical group was broken up. These True Levellers or 'Diggers' demanded equality for all and the common ownership of land.

TUMBLEDOWN DICK

Warfare did not come to an end with the Common-wealth. In 1651 Charles I's son was crowned Charles II in Scotland. The Scots marched south, but were defeated and Charles II fled abroad. From 1652-1654 Britain fought the Netherlands (now a free and increasingly wealthy nation) over trade. Oliver Cromwell died on a stormy night in 1658. His son Richard (known as 'Tumbledown Dick') was made Lord Protector, but had little taste for power. The revolution was over.

1609
Plantation of six counties of Ulster

1626
Charles I unofficially accepts Catholic worship in Ireland

1633
Wentworth (later Earl of Strafford) becomes Governor

1641
Strafford executed for treason. Rising in Ulster

1647
Dublin yields to Parliament in the Civil War

DROGHEDA AND AFTER

MORE and more lands belonging to Irish Catholics were seized and given over to Protestant English and Scottish settlers. This continuing policy of 'plantation' was supported by the Dublin parliament. In 1628 Charles I decided to allow Roman Catholic worship to continue alongside the Protestant Church, but this infuriated Ireland's Protestants.

WENTWORTH AND ULSTER

In 1633 Charles I appointed a new man to govern Ireland. He was Thomas Wentworth, who later became Earl of Strafford. Wentworth's only aim was to increase royal power in Ireland. He managed to earn the hatred of Catholics and Protestants alike. He drew up plans for further plantation. As a result, violence broke out in Ulster in 1641 and soon spread far and wide. Perhaps 2,000 Protestants were killed and many more were stripped and chased naked from their homes.

Charles I sent Thomas Wentworth, Earl of Strafford, to fight the Scots in 1639-1640. Defeated, he was taken back to London and executed.

A ROMAN LIFELINE

Irish Catholics were supported by the Church in Rome, which trained priests for work in Ireland. Political support also came from Roman Catholic countries in Europe. When Oliver Cromwell came to Ireland, he blamed Catholic priests for all the country's problems. Many of them were murdered by his troops.

Luke Wadding was a monk who founded St Isidore's College in Rome in 1625. He worked tirelessly to keep the Roman Catholic faith alive in Ireland.

FROM WAR TO WAR

The tragic fate of the Protestant settlers in Ulster was used to whip up extreme anti-Catholic feelings in Britain. In 1642 an army of Scottish Covenanters arrived in Ulster to defend the Scottish Protestants who had settled there. A Catholic army was formed too by Owen Roe O'Neill. An alliance was made between Old English royalists and Irish Catholics, but there were bitter divisions.

CROMWELL INVADES

Events were overtaken by the Civil War in Britain. Oliver Cromwell invaded Ireland in August 1649, with a battle-hardened army of Puritan troops. They hated all Roman Catholics and wanted revenge for the events of 1641. Cromwell besieged and sacked Drogheda, killing no fewer than 2,500 people. A massacre at Wexford claimed a further 2,000 lives. Perhaps a quarter of all Irish Catholics were killed during this savage campaign. Cromwell followed it up in 1652 by seizing Catholic lands and granting them to his soldiers and followers. He sowed seeds of hatred which still bear fruit today.

The River Shannon became a new frontier after Oliver Cromwell's invasion. Irish Catholic landowners were told that they had until 1 May 1654 to resettle west of the Shannon.

Oliver Cromwell sacked Drogheda in September 1649. Some of the defenders were burnt alive in a church he set on fire. Cromwell's official report called the massacre 'a righteous judgement of God upon these barbarous wretches'.

136

| 1660 | 1660 | 1661 | 1662 | 1665 |
| Samuel Pepys starts to write his diary | The monarchy is restored. Charles II returns | The Church of England is established | Tea drinking becomes fashionable | The Second Anglo-Dutch War (until 1667) |

THE RESTORATION

GREAT Britain and Ireland had a king again, Charles II. In 1660 Parliament had finally asked him to return from exile and be crowned. In return, Charles had to agree to recognize Parliament and the limits of his power. There was great rejoicing as he entered London on his thirtieth birthday. Oliver Cromwell's remains were seized from his tomb in Westminster Abbey and publicly hanged from the gallows at Tyburn.

THE WORLD OF POLITICS

During the reign of Charles II, the way in which the British political system was organized became rather more like the one in use today. From 1667–1673, Charles II began to consult with a group of ministers instead of just one. These were rather like the Cabinet in modern times. They were known as the 'Cabal', because of their initials (Clifford, Ashley, Buckingham, Arlington, Lauderdale). The world 'cabal' is still used to describe a small, powerful group of people. The first political parties were formed in the 1680s. They were known as Tories and Whigs.

THE DIARY OF SAMUEL PEPYS

Samuel Pepys wrote freely about his private life and everyday pastimes.

In January 1660 a Londoner called Samuel Pepys began to write a diary. It was written in a secret code. Pepys offers us a lively look at how people lived in the 1660s. He knew many famous people and was mixed up in all sorts intrigues at the court. He describes the news stories of his day, as when Dutch warships sailed up the River Thames.

◀ *Nell Gwyn began her career as an orange-seller. She became a famous actress, much admired by Samuel Pepys, and was a lover of the king himself.*

◀ *Charles II is chiefly remembered as a pleasure-loving king, the 'merry monarch'. He married a Portuguese Catholic, Catherine of Braganza, but he was never faithful to her.*

RELIGIOUS FREEDOM?

In 1662 the Church of England was recognized as the official Church. In the following year Charles II declared that both Catholics and Puritans would be free to worship in their own way. However, he was forced to end this offer in 1673, when Parliament ruled that Catholics could not hold public office.

A MERRY DANCE

After the Restoration, the English began to enjoy life again. Theatres re-opened in 1660. Female parts in plays were now taken by actresses, who became as popular as film stars would be 300 years later. Dancing was never more popular, from the royal court to the village maypole. Women wore make-up and fancy dresses. Fashionable men wore long, curled wigs. There were river trips, fireworks, processions and fairs. In the 1660s and 1670s it became fashionable to drink new beverages – coffee and tea.

THE PLOT THAT NEVER WAS

There was growing anti-Catholic hysteria in England. In 1678 an English spy called Titus Oates claimed that Catholics were plotting to kill the king. He had actually made the whole story up, but 35 Catholics were executed because of this 'Popish Plot'.

This painting shows Charles II at a ball in the Hague, in the Netherlands. His dancing partner is his sister Mary, Princess of Orange (1631-1660), whose son came to the British throne as William III in 1688.

During Stuart times, the climate was colder than today. Often, the River Thames froze solid. 'Frost Fairs' were held on the ice and people practised ice-skating – a sport recently brought in from the Netherlands.

138

⊠ **1628**
William Harvey's theories on
blood circulation

⊠ **1631**
Death of the poet John
Donne

⊠ **1631**
Anthony van Dyck is court
painter to Charles I

⊠ **1651**
Thomas Hobbes writes about
politics and philosophy

⊠ **1662**
Chemist Robert Boyle's
research into gases

GREAT MINDS

THE 1600s was an age of exploration and discovery. The old ways were challenged and knocked down. This exciting new world was reflected in literature, the arts, in philosophy and especially in science. In 1660 the Royal Society of London was founded to encourage learning. Leading members included Robert Boyle, Samuel Pepys and Isaac Newton.

Paradise Lost, *one of the greatest works of English literature, was published by the English poet John Milton in 1667. During the Civil War, Milton was a keen supporter of Parliament. He became blind in middle age.*

METAPHYSICAL POETS

In the 1600s many English poets broke away from the forms of poetry which had been popular in Elizabethan times. These 'metaphysical' poets included John Donne, George Herbert, Richard Crashaw and Andrew Marvell. They used unusual and sometimes complicated images, some of them taken from new discoveries in science and geography.

COURT MUSICIANS AND PAINTERS

In the 1630s the great Flemish painters Peter Paul Rubens and Anthony van Dyck came to the court of Charles I, as did the Dutch painter Peter Lely in the 1640s. The English musical composer Henry Purcell wrote the first English opera in 1689 and music for the coronations of James II of England (VII of Scotland).

THE PHILOSOPHERS

Thomas Hobbes (1588-1679) was a keen royalist. He wrote about politics and the human mind. John Locke (1632-1704) argued that governments ruled only with the agreement of the people. If they broke faith, they deserved to be overthrown.

The English scientist Robert Hooke used the newly invented microscope to study the structure of plants and chemicals. His Micrographia was published in 1665.

⊠ 1665
Robert Hooke describes experiments with microscope

⊠ 1668
John Dryden is made first Poet Laureate

⊠ 1670
Aphra Behn is first woman playwright in English

⊠ 1680
Musical composer Henry Purcell's *Dido and Aeneas*

⊠ 1684
Isaac Newton's theories of gravity

139

Isaac Newton experimented with the first reflecting telescopes.

William Harvey was doctor to Charles I. His theories on blood circulation were ridiculed by many scientists of his day.

GRAVITY AND LIGHT

Isaac Newton was born in Lincolnshire in 1642 and studied at Cambridge University. He was a brilliant mathematician and became one of the greatest scientists the world has ever known. Newton studied the nature of light. He also described how the forces of gravity work – legend has it, after watching an apple fall from a tree.

GREENWICH OBSERVATORY

In 1675 King Charles II founded a Royal Observatory at Greenwich, overlooking the River Thames. It was built by Christopher Wren and its first director was an astronomer from Derbyshire, called John Flamsteed. Its purpose was to observe the Sun, Moon, stars and planets, in order to help ships navigate across the oceans.

Today, the Royal Greenwich Observatory is a museum. However its work continues at Herstmonceux, Sussex, and at Cambridge.

SCIENCE, MEDICINE, ASTRONOMY

The new science was based on careful observation and experiments. In 1628 an English doctor called William Harvey became the first person to describe how the heart pumps blood around the body through arteries and veins. In 1654 the Irish scientist Robert Boyle came to Oxford University to study gases, vacuums and the burning process. An English mathematician called Edmond Halley became a great astronomer. The most famous comet is named after him, for in 1680 he accurately predicted that it would return to the Earth's skies every 76 years.

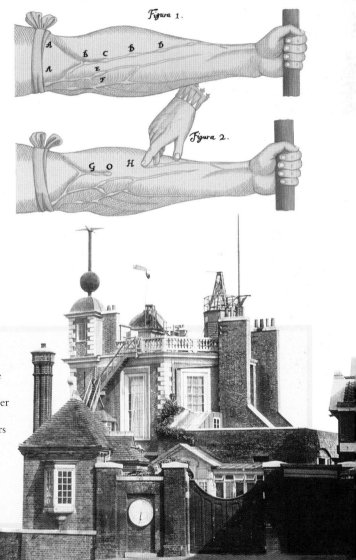

⊠ **1665** June:
first reports of Great Plague
in London

⊠ **1665** October:
death toll from plague reaches
70,000

⊠ **1666** September:
fire breaks out in London

⊠ **1666** December:
end of the Great Plague

⊠ **1669**
Christopher Wren is
appointed Surveyor-General

·OUT ·OF THE ASHES

LONDON, by now a city of about half a million people, was hot and stifling on 6 June 1665. That was the day on which an outbreak of plague was reported in London. It caused little fuss at the time. Since the Black Death of the Middle Ages, the plague had returned time after time.

THE GREAT PLAGUE

This time, though, it was different. The bubonic plague, marked by foul swellings on the body, claimed 70,000 lives in just the first few months. As Londoners fled to the country, they brought the dreaded disease to villages and market towns. Survivors clutched bunches of sweet-smelling flowers to ward off the stench. The air itself seemed poisoned. An old nursery rhyme recalls plagues past: *Ring-a-ring o' roses, A pocket full of posies, Atishoo! Atishoo! We all fall down.*

The cobbled streets and alleys of London had changed little since medieval times. They still swarmed with rats and their deadly fleas.

Crosses were painted on the doors of houses stricken by plague. Carts rumbled down the streets, collecting corpses.

⊠ 1675	⊠ 1677	⊠ 1694	⊠ 1698	⊠ 1710	141
Work starts on the rebuilding of St Paul's Cathedral, London	The Monument is completed in memory of the Great Fire	Christopher Wren builds new wings at Hampton Court	Work starts on the Royal Naval Hospital, Greenwich	The new St Paul's Cathedral is completed	

Many people took to the river to escape the heat and flames. After the fire, the old city with all its familiar landmarks was gone forever.

LONDON BURNS

After more than a year of plague, another disaster struck London. In the early hours of 2 September 1666, a fire started at a baker's in Pudding Lane. The flames were soon blazing over a wide area and continued to do so for five whole days, driven by the wind. Timber houses had to be blown up to stop the fire spreading. By the time it was over, the Great Fire had burnt down 13,200 houses, the old city gates, the Guildhall, 89 churches and the great cathedral of the City of London, St Paul's.

ASYLUM SEEKERS

The British Isles were not the only part of Europe to experience religious hatred and conflict in the 1500s and 1600s. In France there were terrible wars between Roman Catholics and the Protestant followers of John Calvin, who were known as Huguenots. After 1598 Protestant rights were protected by the Edict of Nantes, but during the reign of King Louis XIV many Huguenots were persecuted or forced to become Catholics. In 1685 the Edict of Nantes was cancelled, and 400,000 Huguenots fled the country. Many of these sought refuge in London. France's loss was England's gain, for many were hard-working weavers and skilled workers.

REBUILT IN STONE

Perhaps the Great Fire was a blessing in disguise. The old, rat-infested wooden houses were burnt to the ground. An architect was chosen to rebuild the capital. His name was Christopher Wren. Soon the streets were being widened and fine new houses were being built of stone. Wren built 52 new churches, of which 24 may still be seen today.

Wren's masterpiece was the new St Paul's Cathedral. Its great dome remained the chief landmark of London for 300 years.

142

⊠ **1685**
James VII of Scotland (II of England) becomes king

⊠ **1685**
The Monmouth rebellion and the Bloody Assizes

⊠ **1688** July:
William of Orange invited to become king

⊠ **1688** December:
James is overthrown

⊠ **1689**
William III and Mary II rule jointly

JAMES, WILLIAM AND MARY

CHARLES II died in February 1685. He was followed as king by his brother, who became James VII of Scotland and II of England. James was a Roman Catholic and this dismayed the Protestants. Many of these belonged to the more radical political party, the Whigs. They had had enough of Stuart kings who showed little regard for the wishes of the people.

LILLIBULERO

The dramatic events of the Glorious Revolution of 1688 were played out to a popular political song of the day. It was called *Lillibulero*. The music was a march by Henry Purcell while the words, written by Thomas Wharton in 1686, mocked King James and the Catholics of Ireland. The song was sung as violent anti-Catholic mobs celebrated James's downfall in London.

Rebel fighters gathered at Sedgemore, Somerset, in support of Monmouth's rebellion. They were defeated by forces loyal to King James.

BLOODY ASSIZES

In June 1685 the Protestant James, Duke of Monmouth, a son of Charles II born outside marriage, landed in Lyme Regis, in southern England. He claimed the throne, but was defeated in July at Sedgemoor and executed. His followers were dealt with savagely by a judge called George Jeffreys, in a series of trials called the Bloody Assizes. A death sentence was passed on 320 people and 840 more were sold into slavery. It was a bitter start to the reign.

THE GLORIOUS REVOLUTION

By 1688 leading politicans had decided on a drastic plan. They invited the Dutch ruler, William of Orange, to become king. He was a Protestant and married to Mary, the king's daughter. William landed at Torbay in Devon and gained rapid support. James fled to France and it was agreed that William III and Mary II would rule jointly. This change of power became known as the Glorious Revolution.

A BILL OF RIGHTS

The most important outcome of the revolution was a Bill of Rights, passed in December 1689. This made it very clear that Parliament was now the chief governing body in the land, and that the power of kings and queens was strictly limited.

⊠ **1689** March:
James lands in Ireland

⊠ **1689** May:
Highland Scots rebel in
support of James

⊠ **1689** December:
The Bill of Rights

⊠ **1690**
Battle of the Boyne in Ireland.
James is defeated.

⊠ **1694**
Mary II dies of smallpox.
William III rules on his own.

143

ENGINEERS AND BUILDERS

Engineering works began to change the face of many parts of Britain in the 1600s and early 1700s. The wetlands of East Anglia were drained and channelled by experts from the Netherlands. Harbours were rebuilt and new lighthouses guarded rocky shores. Gates called turnpikes were set up along the highways to collect money from travellers for repairs and road-building.

The first Eddystone lighthouse was built off Cornwall between 1695 and 1699, but was destroyed by severe autumn gales in 1703.

James's attempt to regain his throne finally ended in a pitched battle with William of Orange on the south bank of the River Boyne, on 1 July 1690. 'King Billy's' victory is still celebrated by the Protestant 'Orangemen' of Northern Ireland today, who see it as an important turning point in the history of the Union.

SCOTLAND AND IRELAND

William and Mary did not enjoy an easy reign. The Highland Scots rose up in support of James. Their leader was John Graham of Claverhouse, Viscount Dundee, a persecutor of the Covenanters. They won the battle of Killiecrankie in May 1689, but Dundee was killed and the rising failed. James now landed with French troops in Ireland, trying to regain the throne. William too led an army into Ireland, reinforced with Ulster Protestants. They met at the battle of the Boyne in 1690 and James was defeated.

MASSACRE AT GLENCOE

At this bleak spot, Glencoe in Stratchclyde, 37 members of the MacDonald clan were massacred in 1692. William III demanded that all the clans in the Scottish Highlands swear an oath of loyalty. They obeyed, but MacIan MacDonald of Glencoe signed late, due to a misunderstanding. Troops sealed off the ends of the glen, while others, billeted in MacDonald homes, carried out a brutal attack. They were commanded by Campbells, old enemies of the Macdonalds.

☒ **1668**
Henry Morgan leads
buccaneer army on Spanish
Main

☒ **1671**
Irish adventurer Thomas Blood
tries to steal Crown Jewels

☒ **1684**
Highwayman John Nevison
hanged in York

☒ **1695**
Pirate Henry Avery captures
flagship of the Moghul
emperor

☒ **1700s**
Increase in taxes leads to
smuggling around coasts of
British Isles

A ROGUES' GALLERY

G ALLOWS were a familiar sight to travellers through the British Isles in the 1600s and 1700s. The corpses of those who had been hanged were left to rot, swinging in the wind. Their eyes were pecked out by crows. Gallows often stood at crossroads, as a warning to highway robbers or sheep-stealers. They were erected at Tilbury docks, in London, too, as a grim reminder to would-be pirates as they sailed down the River Thames and out to sea.

SMUGGLERS ON THE COAST

People who lived in fishing villages around the coasts of the British Isles had always raided shipwrecks for cargoes and timber. About three hundred years ago they found a new source of income – smuggling. In order to pay for foreign wars being fought at that time, the government greatly increased the taxes on imported goods. Smugglers would meet up with merchant ships out at sea and run untaxed cargoes ashore in small boats, hiding them in caves or cellars. The illegal brandy, tobacco or silk was often sold on to the local squire – or even to the parson – at a handsome profit.

MARY READ AND ANNE BONNY

Mary Read was an English girl who dressed herself up as a young man in order to join the English army. She married a Flemish soldier. When he died, she sailed off to the Caribbean, where she was captured by pirates. She joined forces with them, only to find an Irish woman, Anne Bonny, was already serving in the crew. The two fought fiercely under the command of Captain 'Calico' Jack Rackham, sailing out of the Bahamas. In 1720 Rackham and his crew were captured and hanged in Jamaica. The women were expecting babies and so they escaped the gallows, but Mary Read soon died anyway, of a fever.

While Anne Bonny and Mary Read fought for their lives, Calico Jack hid below decks.

⊠ **1701**
Captain William Kidd hanged in London for piracy

⊠ **1718**
Pirate Edward Teach (Blackbeard) killed

⊠ **1719**
Howell Davis and Bart Roberts raid West African coast

⊠ **1720**
Anne Bonny, Mary Read and Jack Rackham on trial

⊠ **1729**
Dick Turpin takes up highway robbery

145

ON THE HIGH SEAS

Piracy greatly increased between the 1630s and the 1720s. As European nations grabbed land and plunder around the world, independent adventurers, escaped slaves, mutineers and murderers were washed up on foreign shores. At first, the British were quite happy to leave the Caribbean pirates or 'buccaneers' alone – as long as they attacked the ships of their enemies. In 1668 a Welsh adventurer called Henry Morgan was commissioned to lead a buccaneer army against the Spanish. He ended up as deputy governor of a British colony, Jamaica. Bristol-born Edward Teach, the dreaded 'Blackbeard', had the governor of another British colony, North Carolina, in his pay. Once pirates began to prey upon British trade, many were hunted down and executed. Blackbeard was shot and beheaded in 1718 and his head displayed on a pole.

◑ Highwaymen lurked in woods and on lonely heaths such as Hounslow, to the west of London.

◐ European pirates sailed all over the world. Two Welsh pirates, Howell Davis and Bartholomew Roberts ('Black Bart') raided West Africa's Guinea Coast in 1719.

GENTLEMEN OF THE ROAD

Highwaymen held up stage coaches and robbed the travellers. A former soldier called John Nevison (known as 'Swift Nicks') only robbed the rich. He was sent to the gallows in York in 1684. The most famous highway robber of all was Dick Turpin, also hanged in York in 1739. He was a burglar, murderer, smuggler and horse-thief. The public loved to watch hangings and read the popular ballads written about the dreadful crimes that had been committed.

◀ Stage coach guards carried heavy firearms called blunderbusses to protect their passengers.

146

⊠ **1701**
Act of Settlement decides the royal succession

⊠ **1702**
William III falls from horse and dies. Anne becomes queen

⊠ **1704**
Duke of Marlborough wins the Battle of Blenheim

⊠ **1706**
Marlborough's victory at the Battle of Ramillies

⊠ **1707**
Union of English and Scottish parliaments

QUEEN ANNE

QUEEN Anne came to the throne in 1702, after William III died in a fall from his horse. She was a Protestant, the daughter of James VII of Scotland (II of England) and the sister of Mary II. It was during her reign, in 1707, that the Scottish and English parliaments united. Great Britain, for the first time, was a single political unit rather than a union of kingdoms.

Queen Anne had married Prince George of Denmark in 1683, but all their 17 children died, mostly in infancy.

LAST OF THE STUARTS

Anne was the last Stuart monarch. In 1701 she had agreed that on her death, the throne would pass to the royal house of Hanover, in Germany. Anne was easily influenced by her circle of friends. Her closest companion was Sarah, wife of a brilliant soldier called John Churchill. Anne made him Duke of Marlborough in 1702. After 1710 Anne quarrelled with the Churchills and fell under the spell of Sarah's cousin, Abigail Masham.

THE WAR OF SPANISH SUCCESSION

In 1701 a wrangle broke out between the great powers of Europe. Who would inherit the throne of Spain? On the one side was Louis XIV's France, the south German kingdom of Bavaria and Spain. On the other was the Grand Alliance – Britain, Austria, the Netherlands, Denmark and Portugal. The Duke of Marlborough commanded the Dutch and English armies and won spectacular victories at Blenheim in Bavaria, and Ramillies and Oudenaarde in what is now Belgium. Peace was made at the treaties of Utrecht (1713) and Rastatt (1714).

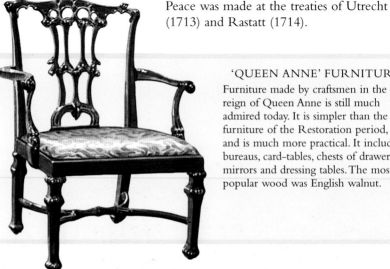

The finest pieces of the period are chairs which are comfortable and solid. By the end of Anne's reign, more ornamental styles were coming back into fashion.

'QUEEN ANNE' FURNITURE

Furniture made by craftsmen in the reign of Queen Anne is still much admired today. It is simpler than the furniture of the Restoration period, and is much more practical. It includes bureaus, card-tables, chests of drawers, mirrors and dressing tables. The most popular wood was English walnut.

WHIGS AND TORIES

In the days of Queen Anne, society was rigidly divided between the two political parties of the day. The Whigs were supporters of the Bill of Rights and of the Hanoverian succession. Many of them were merchants and business men with radical Protestant views. The Tories were conservative and royalist, and included many churchmen. Queen Anne disliked the Whigs and was determined to use all her personal powers to control British politics.

● British troops commanded by John Churchill, the first Duke of Marlborough, took part in the struggles between European powers in the 1700s. Casualties were very high on all sides.

◑ The grand buildings of Blenheim Palace surrounded three sides of a great courtyard. Winston Churchill, a descendant of the first duke, was born at Blenheim in 1874.

BLENHEIM PALACE

The Duke of Marlborough was rewarded for his victories with a splendid palace in Oxfordshire, named after the battle of Blenheim. Built from 1705-1722 by Sir John Vanbrugh, it was decorated by the best craftsmen of the day and surrounded by beautiful gardens.

6

A WORLD POWER

1714–1901

THE WORLD AT A GLANCE

ELSEWHERE IN EUROPE

1720
Russia defeats Sweden in the Great Northern War, gains Estonia

1740
Frederick II ('the Great') becomes King of Prussia, Maria Theresa becomes Empress of Austria

1789
Outbreak of the French Revolution in Paris. King Louis XVI is executed in 1793

1804
Napoleon Bonaparte is crowned Emperor of France. Draws up new code of laws

1815
The Congress of Vienna redraws the map of Europe. Poland is united with Russia

1821
Greeks rise against Turkish rule. Greece is recognized as independent in 1832

1871
Germany unites as a single empire under the rule of Wilhelm I, King of Prussia

1871
Rome becomes capital of a united Italy for the first time since the Roman empire

ASIA

1739
Persia (Iran) invades India and captures the city of Delhi

1750
The French gain control of southern India

1819
British empire-builder Stamford Raffles founds modern port at Singapore

1858
Rule of India passes from the East India Company to the British government

1867
The Meiji Restoration: Japan modernizes under the rule of emperor Mutsuhito

1883
One of the world's worst ever volcanic eruptions destroys Krakatoa island

1891
Work begins on the Trans-Siberian Railway (from Moscow to the Pacific)

1900
Defeat of nationalists ('Boxers') rebelling against foreign influence in China

AFRICA

1720
Sultan of Zanzibâr takes control of the East African coast

1730
Revival of the Bornu empire, south of the Sahara desert

1806
Britain gains control of Cape Colony, South Africa, from the Dutch

1818
Shaka founds the Zulu kingdom in South Africa

1822
Liberia is founded in West Africa, as a colony for liberated slaves

1869
Suez Canal opens, European powers have growing influence in Egypt

1896
Emperor Menelik II of Ethiopia defeats an Italian army at Adowa

1899
Boer War begins between British and Afrikaners in South Africa

"A British empire is founded on cotton, coal and toil..."

the Portland Vase

NORTH AMERICA

1718
French found the port of New Orleans, Louisiana

1759
Britain defeats France to capture the Canadian city of Quebec

1776
American colonists declare their independence from Britain

1823
Mexico becomes an independent republic

1838
Slavery ended in Jamaica and other British Caribbean colonies

1861
Civil war in the United States (until 1865, abolition of slavery)

1867
Canada becomes a self-governing Dominion within British empire

1876
Native Americans defeat US Cavalry at the Battle of Little Bighorn

SOUTH AMERICA

1763
Rio de Janeiro becomes capital of Spanish Brazil

1780
Uprising of indigenous peoples in Peru under Tupac Amaru II

1816
Argentina declares its independence from Spain

1818
Chile becomes independent from Spain, under Bernardo O'Higgins

1819
New Granada (Colombia, Venezuela, Ecuador) independent under Simon Bolívar

1822
Brazil proclaims its independence from Spain under Pedro I

1826
Peru gains its independence from Spain

1888
Slavery is finally abolished in Brazil

OCEANIA

1768
British navigator James Cook visits Tahiti, New Zealand and Australia (to 1771)

1788
British convicts and settlers arrive at Botany Bay, southeast Australia

1840
Treaty of Waitangi: Maori chiefs cede New Zealand to British

1843
First Maori War, start of many conflicts with the British colonists (into the 1860s)

1850
Self-government granted to Britain's Australian colonies (New Zealand 1856)

1851
A Gold Rush begins in Australia

1884
Northeastern New Guinea taken over by Germany. Britain claims the southeast

1901
Australian colonies unite within a federal Commonwealth

150

᠗ 1714
Start of rule by the House of
Hanover

᠗ 1739
Trade dispute with Spain, the
War of Jenkins's Ear

᠗ 1740
War of the Austrian
Succession begins

᠗ 1743
George II, last king to
command forces in battle

᠗ 1751
The Prince of Wales is killed
by a cricket ball

THE HOUSE OF HANOVER

GEORGE I, ruler of Hanover in Germany, came to the throne as a distant descendant of James VI of Scotland (I of England). He was 54 years old, a dull and uninspiring man. His kept his divorced wife, Sophia Dorothea, imprisoned in a German castle from 1694 until her death in 1726. George I cared little for life in Britain and never learned to speak English.

This medal was made in memory of the coronation of George I, the first Hanoverian ruler of Britain, in October 1714.

Men wore a coat and waistcoat, breeches, stockings and buckled shoes. Wigs were still worn, but it became the fashion to tie them at the neck. Hats were three-cornered and made of felt.

RULERS OF GREAT BRITAIN AND IRELAND	
House of Hanover	
♣ George I Elector of Hanover	1714-1727
♣ George II	1727-1760
♣ George III	1760-1820
♣ George IV	1820-1830
♣ William IV	1830-1837
♣ Victoria	1837-1901

THE NEW DYNASTY

George I was unpopular, but he was supported by the Whigs simply because he offered the best chance of stopping a return to Stuart rule. In return, he supported the Whigs against the Tories.

His son came to the throne in 1727. In 1743 George II became the last British king ever to lead his troops on to the field of battle – at Dettingen, in Bavaria, against a French army. Under his rule, the British began to build up a large overseas empire.

THE MADNESS OF GEORGE III

George III, grandson of George II, came to the throne in 1760 and ruled for 60 years. He was an energetic but obstinate ruler, often clashing with the politicians of his day. His reign saw Britain lose its colonies in North America. In 1810 George became mentally ill, probably as a result of a body disorder called porphyria.

〜 **1752**
Public protests when the calendar is revised by removing 11 days

〜 **1756**
Seven Years' War: European powers fight over their empires

〜 **1756**
Britain allied with powerful German kingdom of Prussia

〜 **1760**
George III is crowned king of the United Kingdom

〜 **1810**
George III becomes mentally ill

151

THE EAR THAT STARTED A WAR

The great powers of Europe were almost continuously at war in a pattern of shifting alliances. Wars were caused by disputes over trade and territory and rival claims to thrones. In 1739 a British sea captain claimed that his ear had been cut off by Spanish customs officials, so Britain went to war with Spain in the 'War of Jenkins's Ear'. This was followed by the War of the Austrian Succession (1740-1748) and the Seven Years' War (1756-1763).

Women wore dresses with full skirts, often made of cotton or silk. Court dresses were stretched out over wooden hoops and decorated with frills. Women too now wore high, powdered white wigs.

A MAN OF MUSIC

Händel liked to write music for public festivities. His *Music for the Royal Fireworks* was first performed in Green Park, London, on 27 April 1749.

George Friedrich Händel was from Saxony, in Germany. In 1710 he was appointed court musician to the Elector of Hanover, but irritated his employer by spending more and more time in London. When that ruler was crowned King George I in England, Händel made his peace by composing his *Water Music*, for a royal procession on the River Thames. Händel wrote 46 operas, but his best loved piece of music was *The Messiah*, first performed in Dublin in 1742. He died and was buried in Westminster Abbey in 1759.

152

☙ **1708**
The Old Pretender lands in
Scotland. but rising fails

☙ **1715**
The Old Pretender
joins Jacobite rising, which
again fails

☙ **1716**
Execution of Jacobite
supporters in Scotland

☙ **1719**
Spanish troops defeated in
Scotland at Glenshiel

☙ **1722**
The Atterbury Plot –
Jacobites plan to seize the king

BOΠΠIE PRIΠCE CHARLIE

S UPPORT for the exiled Stuarts did not
suddenly disappear. People who wished
them to return to rule Britain and
Ireland were called Jacobites (from *Jacobus*, the
Latin for 'James'). They presented a serious
threat to the House of Hanover, for they had
supporters all over the British Isles. However
their most loyal supporters were to be found in
the Highlands of Scotland.

> ### THE OUTLAW ROB ROY
> Robert MacGregor, known as Rob
> 'Roy' (meaning the 'red-headed') was
> born at Buchanan in Stirlingshire in
> 1671. He raised a private army which
> supported the Jacobites. In 1712 his
> lands were seized by the Duke of
> Montrose and he became an outlaw. A
> raider and rustler, he became famous
> for his daring exploits and his help for
> the poor and needy. He died in 1734.

THE OLD PRETENDER
Someone who claims to be king or queen is
called a 'pretender' to the throne. James
Francis Edward Stuart became known as the
Old Pretender. A Roman Catholic, he was
the son of James VII/II and had been taken
away to France as a baby. He landed in
Scotland in 1708, but the French fleet sent in
his support was defeated. In 1715 the Earl of
Mar launched a Jacobite rising and James
landed once more at Peterhead.

*To the Jacobites, the Old Pretender was
James VIII of Scotland (III of England).
However he failed to win back his father's kingdom.*

THE '15 RISING FAILS
The rising, known as the '15, came to grief at
Preston and Sherrifmuir. James fled to exile in
Rome and his followers were executed. The
Jacobite cause had many supporters in Catholic
Europe, and in 1719 Spanish troops invaded
Scotland, but were defeated at Glenshiel. The
Old Pretender married a Polish princess,
Clementina Sobieski, and died in 1766.

⚓ **1744**	⚓ **1745**	⚓ **1745**	⚓ **1746**	⚓ **1746**	153
Charles Edward Stuart plans invasion. French fleet is scattered	July: Charles raises battle standard in Glenfinnan	Battle of Prestonpans: Jacobite victory	Battle of Culloden: Jacobites defeated by Duke of Cumberland	Highlanders disarmed and persecuted	

BONNIE PRINCE CHARLIE

The Young Pretender was James's son, Charles Edward Stuart. He landed at Eriskay in the Hebrides in 1745 and raised his father's standard at Glenfinnan. The '45 rising very nearly succeeded. 'Bonnie Prince Charlie' won a victory at Prestonpans, captured Carlisle and reached Derby. London was in a state of panic, and Jacobites were planning to rise in Wales. Then, Charles's support began to falter and he turned back to Scotland.

◀ Jacobite forces at Culloden included massed ranks of clansmen from the Scottish Highlands. They were gunned down and bayoneted without mercy. Charles became a fugitive with a price in his head.

◀ Flora Macdonald disguised Bonnie Prince Charlie as her maid and spirited him out of Scotland. A ship carried him from the island of Benbecula into a life of exile.

CULLODEN AND AFTER

In 1746 Charles won another battle at Falkirk, but his Jacobites soon received a crushing defeat on Culloden moor, Inverness, at the hands of William, Duke of Cumberland – 'the Butcher'. In England a flower was named 'sweet william' in honour of Cumberland, but Scottish Jacobites called it 'stinking billy'. Highland clansmen were ruthlessly hunted down. The carrying of weapons, even the wearing of the kilt and the playing of bagpipes were banned. Scotland's future now lay in the growing towns of Lowlands, where manufacturers and merchants were becoming wealthy.

AULD LANG SYNE

Scotland's greatest poet was born in 1759 in Alloway, near Ayr. Robert Burns created simple, bold verse in the language of the Lowlands Scots. He wrote about country life, nature and love. His most popular poems include *A Red, Red Rose*; *Scots, Wha Hae*; *John Anderson, my Jo*; *Tam O'Shanter* and *Auld Lang Syne*.

◀ Burns died in 1796, but his birthday is still honoured around the world each 25 January.

154

〰 **1694**
The Bank of England is founded in London

〰 **1715**
The Riot Act is passed, controlling public order

〰 **1720**
The 'South Sea Bubble': financial crash

〰 **1721**
Robert Walpole is first British Prime Minister

〰 **1731**
No 10 Downing Street is residence of Prime Minister

MONEY AND POLITICS

THE gap between rich and poor people in the British Isles was growing ever wider. London society in the 1730s and 40s is shown up in the paintings and engravings of William Hogarth. Poor families brawl, desperate young mothers drink cheap gin on the street until they fall into a stupor. Adventurers are on the make, climbing their way up the all too corrupt social scale, only to fall back down and end their days in a debtors' prison.

Dealers in shares, or stockjobbers, drove up the trading price far beyond the real value.

The 'South Sea Bubble' crash provided a wealth of material for the newspapers of the day and for political cartoonists.

BANKS AND MONEY

Paper bank notes were first issued in Britain in 1695. There was a growing view of wealth as an abstract idea, of deals made on paper rather than as chests full of gold coins. New companies, many of them founded in order to make money in distant colonies overseas, issued shares. At first these were bought and sold in coffee shops. A Stock Exchange was founded in the City of London in 1773.

THE SOUTH SEA BUBBLE

Trading shares in the hope of making a profit is called speculation. It is a form of gambling, and can lead to reward or ruin. Britain's first great financial crash happened in 1720. Shares in the South Sea Company, founded in 1711 to trade with South America, rose to a ridiculous value, driven up by feverish speculation and crooked government dealings. When this South Sea 'bubble' burst, thousands of people were ruined. Many committed suicide.

1735
Pitt the Elder enters
Parliament

1765
Edmund Burke enters
Parliament

1773
Founding of the London
Stock Exchange

1776
Adam Smith argues that
government should not
interfere in trade

1783
Pitt the Younger becomes
Prime Minister

155

PRIME MINISTERS AT NO 10

Because George I spoke no English and was
often away in Hanover, government affairs began
to be dealt with by his chief ('prime') minister,
who chose a working committee of ministers
(the 'cabinet'). From 1721 the first – unofficial –
Prime Minister was a formidable Whig politician,
Sir Robert Walpole. The use of Number 10
Downing Street as the London residence of
British Prime Ministers dates back to 1731.

The few men who were allowed to vote did so in public. There was opportunity for bullying and corruption. Drunken crowds, in the pay of one party or another, often rioted at election time.

THE GREAT DEBATERS

Powerful debaters could be heard in the House
of Commons. William Pitt the Elder entered
politics in 1735, part of a group within the
Whigs who were opposed to Walpole. He was
a great supporter of Britain's overseas wars. His
popular son, William Pitt the Younger, served
over 17 years as Prime Minister. His great
opponent was Charles Fox, who became a
Member of Parliament at the age of just 19.

PRIME MINISTERS OF GREAT BRITAIN

✦ Sir Robert Walpole (Whig)	1721-1742
✦ Earl of Wilmington (Whig)	1742-1743
✦ Henry Pelham (Whig)	1743-1754
✦ Duke of Newcastle (Whig)	1754-1756
✦ Duke of Devonshire (Whig)	1756-1757
✦ Duke of Newcastle (Whig)	1757-1762
✦ Earl of Bute (Tory)	1762-1763
✦ George Grenville (Whig)	1763-1765
✦ Marquess of Rockingham (Whig)	1782
✦ Earl of Shelburne (Whig)	1782-1783
✦ Duke of Portland (coalition)	1783
✦ William Pitt the Younger (Tory)	1783-1801

Robert Walpole entered politics in the reign of Queen Anne and was made Chancellor of the Exchequer by George I, in 1715. He died in 1745.

WHO GETS TO VOTE?

New industries were growing fast. To make a
profit, they needed a large workforce but low
wages. Economic forces were driving politics
along, but the workforce was not represented
in Parliament at all. Only a few men with land
and money had the vote. In 1789 a revolution
broke out in France. British politicians eyed the
dramatic events in mainland Europe nervously.
Could they happen here?

156

〰 1746
French capture Madras, British base in India

〰 1750
British capture Arcot, gain control of southern India

〰 1757
Battle of Plassey, Britain gains Bengal, India

〰 1759
Britain captures Quebec, Canada, from France

〰 1763
Treaty of Paris. Britain gains Canada and Caribbean islands

'BROWN BESS'

To fire a musket, the cock first had to be set at the safety position. The metal pan was opened, filled with a small amount of gunpowder and closed. The main charge of gunpowder and a ball were then rammed down the muzzle. When the trigger was pressed, it released a hammer containing a flint. This struck against the raised pan cover, dropping sparks into the gunpowder. When this ignited, the shot was fired.

Ramrod
Each new charge had to be rammed down the muzzle. The iron ramrod could be fitted under the barrel.

Long barrel
The great length of the musket's barrel was meant to help it fire straight, but it was not very efficient. Later gun barrels were 'rifled', having spiral grooves that made the bullet spin.

Bayonet
A long dagger could be fitted to the barrel for hand-to-hand fighting.

The flintlock
The flintlock mechanism was slow to use and unreliable. Gunpowder had to be kept dry.

British troops carried a type of flintlock musket known as 'Brown Bess'.

FARAWAY LANDS

B Y THE 1740s, Europe's most powerful countries were warring with each other around the world. The stakes were high – rich trade and new lands. The first overseas colonies were often founded by commercial companies, which had their own armies and fleets of ships. Local people were powerless in the face of heavily armed European troops.

THE EAST INDIA COMPANY

As India's mighty Moghul empire fell into decline in the 1740s and 50s, the British East India Company seized land from local rulers. It ended up controlling much of the country, fighting its French rivals every step of the way. British success was largely due to a brilliant general called Robert Clive. By fair means or foul, Company officials became hugely rich. When they returned to Britain, they found themselves not only envied but mocked for their new-found wealth. They were nicknamed 'nabobs' (from the Hindi word *nawab*, 'governor').

1768
James Cook explores the Pacific Ocean (to 1771)

1770
James Cook claims New South Wales, Australia for Britain

1779
James Cook is killed by Hawaiians

1789
Crew of HMS Bounty mutiny on Pacific voyage

157

ACROSS THE ATLANTIC

In Canada, the story was similar. The French had a colony on the St Lawrence River, while the British Hudson's Bay Company controlled land to the north. In 1759 British troops captured Quebec. By the Treaty of Paris, which ended the Seven Years' War in 1763, Britain gained Canada and also some of France's Caribbean islands – Tobago, St Vincent, Grenada, and Dominica.

To capture Quebec in 1759, British troops climbed up cliffs to take the French by surprise. Both commanders – James Wolf and the Marquis de Montcalm – died in the battle.

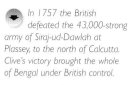

In 1757 the British defeated the 43,000-strong army of Siraj-ud-Dawlah at Plassey, to the north of Calcutta. Clive's victory brought the whole of Bengal under British control.

FROM AFRICA TO ENGLAND

In about 1760 a 10 year-old Nigerian boy called Olaudah Equiano was kidnapped from his West African home and sold to slave traders. He was transported to the Caribbean, but ended up buying his freedom from his master. He became a sailor and took ship to London, where he campaigned against slavery until his death in 1797. He wrote about his experiences in a book published in 1789.

AUSTRALIA AND THE PACIFIC

In 1761, a naval captain called James Cook sailed to explore the Pacific Ocean. He mapped the coast of New Zealand and landed in Australia, claiming New South Wales for Britain. On later voyages, Cook explored the coasts of Antarctica and discovered many Pacific islands. He also sailed along the North America's west coast as far as the Bering Strait. He was killed in Hawaii in 1779.

James Cook was a Yorkshireman, the son of a farm worker. He captained British ships to the far ends of the Earth. A brilliant navigator, he was well liked by his crews.

∽ 1732
Colony of Georgia is founded,
named after George II

∽ 1763
Treaty of Paris gives
Britain territory west
to the Mississippi

∽ 1765
Britain attempts to tax North
American colonists

∽ 1773
'Boston Tea Party':
colonists throw tea
into the harbour

∽ 1774
British close Boston harbour
and send in troops

THE LOSS OF AMERICA

B Y 1763, Britain had
gained control of North
America from the Atlantic
shore to the Mississippi River.
Their lands were divided into
13 colonies. The colonists were
independently minded. Many
of them were descended from
people who had come to America
to escape injustice – Puritans,
Quakers, political rebels. They
resented the British government's
strict controls on shipping and
trade across the Atlantic Ocean.
They were furious when the
British demanded that they pay
for the wars against the French
– through taxation.

Native American
warriors were
used by the British in
their colonial wars
with the French.

In 1776 Britain
recruited about
29,000 Hessian troops
(German mercenaries)
to fight for them in
North America.

A colonist militia,
the Green
Mountain Boys were
formed in Vermont as
early as 1770.

In 1773 colonists disguised themselves as
Native Americans and boarded British ships
anchored in Boston harbour. They threw the cargoes
of tea into the sea. This protest against taxation was
jokingly called the 'Boston Tea Party'.

TAXES – BUT NO VOTES

Britain first attempted to tax its American
colonies in 1765. A costly tax was placed on all
legal documents. This was soon withdrawn, but
it was replaced by other taxes. Customs duties
had to be paid on European goods. The
colonists declared that it was unfair for them to
pay taxes to a government in which they were
not represented. Britain responded by sending
in troops and in 1770 they massacred protestors
in Boston.

The prosperous port of Charles Town or Charleston,
in South Carolina, had been founded in 1670. Its
inhabitants included people of English, Irish, Scottish,
Dutch, German, French and African descent.

AN AMERICAN REVOLUTION

The American War of Independence broke out in April 1775 when George Washington defeated the British at Lexington. In 1776 the American colonists declared their independence from Britain. One of them, a Scot called John Paul Jones, sailed across the Atlantic to attack British shipping. In 1778 both France and the Netherlands joined the American side against Britain. The fighting continued until 1781, when the British surrendered at Yorktown, in Virginia. Britain had lost its richest prize.

BATTLES IN AMERICA
American War of Independence

- ✤ Bunker Hill   1775
  British victory
- ✤ Lexington   1775
  American victory
- ✤ Saratoga Springs   1777
  American victory
- ✤ Brandywine Creek   1777
  British victory
- ✤ Yorktown   1781
  American victory

THE RIGHTS OF MAN

Thomas Paine was an English political thinker. He went to live in Philadelphia in 1774 and became a keen supporter of American independence. In England in 1791, he started to write *The Rights of Man*, supporting the French Revolution and calling for an end to monarchy in Britain. Accused of treason, Paine fled to France. His last years were spent in America, but his refusal to believe in God made him few friends in his old age.

THE WAR OF 1812

In 1783 Britain finally recognised the United States of America as an independent country. However in 1812, when Britain was at war with France, it tried to prevent the free movement of American shipping. War broke out again. In 1814 British troops occupied Washington and burned down government buildings. Peace was made, but before news of it reached America, General Andrew Jackson defeated the British at New Orleans. Within a hundred years, the USA would have become the world's most powerful nation.

160

⚬⚬ **1728**
First performance of *The Beggars' Opera* by John Gay

⚬⚬ **1732**
Vauxhall pleasure gardens are developed and improved

⚬⚬ **1738**
Preacher Charles Wesley founds the Methodist movement

⚬⚬ **1740**
Earliest known score for a game of cricket

⚬⚬ **1753**
The British Museum is started in London

TOWN AND COUNTRY

I N THE 1700s, a new kind of story became popular with English readers. It was called the novel. Famous novelists included Daniel Defoe and Henry Fielding. Some novels told tales of the rich and the poor, of adventures in foreign lands or of young men who came from the country to seek their fortune in the city. Witty plays were popular, too. Those by the Irish writer Richard Brinsley Sheridan mocked the world of high fashion.

In the Georgian period red-brick houses were built in the cities (below), as well as elegant mansions in the countryside (below right).

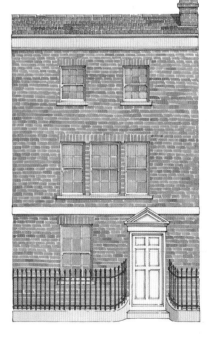

TASTE AND FASHION
Lords and ladies liked to put their wealth and good taste on display. Inside their houses were cabinets in the Chinese-style by Thomas Chippendale or elegant chairs designed by George Hepplewhite. On the walls, paintings by Joshua Reynolds or Thomas Gainsborough flattered the beauty of the lady of the house or showed off the family's estates. Outside, formal gardens were now being replaced by more natural looking landscapes, often planned by the great gardener Lancelot 'Capability' Brown.

Pleasure gardens were laid out at Vauxhall on the south bank of the River Thames. Fashionable Londoners would parade and dance by the light of lanterns, or listen to music.

≪≫ **1755**
Dr Johnson's *Dictionary of the English Language*

≪≫ **1768**
Joshua Reynolds is the Royal Academy's first president

≪≫ **1773**
She Stoops to Conquer, a play by Oliver Goldsmith

≪≫ **1779**
School for Scandal, a play by Richard Brinsley Sheridan

≪≫ **1780**
The 'Derby' horse race is first run at Epsom, Surrey

161

COUNTRY SQUIRES

In country districts, the most important person was the squire, who lived in the manor house. He would keep a watchful eye on the parson and the teacher, on land improvement and law and order. Many squires enjoyed shooting or fox-hunting with horse and hounds. A few had enquiring minds, following politics or reading the latest work of scientists, geographers and the French and English philosophers. In Wales, squires took over from the old nobility as patrons of poets and musicians.

◗ *Along stage coach routes inns provided stables for horses as well as accommodation. A coach journey from London to Holyhead, the seaport for Ireland, took about 48 hours. Mail was carried by horseback riders called Post Boys until 1785, when coaches began to carry mail as well as passengers.*

◗ *In the inns of Fleet Street, in London, groups of friends met to discuss literature, language, art and politics. Their leader was Dr Samuel Johnson, who in 1747 started to write his* Dictionary of the English Language.

SERVANTS AND LABOURERS

Big country estates and town houses employed many servants and cooks. The men wore a uniform, called livery. Maids ran up and down the stairs, carrying boiling water for the bath tub or long-handled warming pans for the beds. Servants slept in attic bedrooms. At least they escaped the misery of living in city slums or run-down country cottages. Housing for farm workers may have looked pretty, but it was mostly damp and draughty. Poor living conditions brought on all kinds of medical problems.

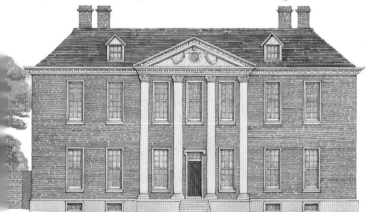

CHAPELS AND PREACHERS

Country labourers, craft workers and many city dwellers too preferred a more direct kind of Christianity than that offered by the Church of England. They were called Nonconformists, because they did not conform to standard worship.

Preachers toured the country and gained huge support in Wales, Cornwall and northern England. They addressed vast crowds at open-air sites such as Gwennap Pit, which can still be seen near Redruth, in Cornwall. Nonconformist chapels were built in many villages and towns.

John Wesley, who founded the Methodist movement in 1738, preached over 40,000 sermons in his lifetime. His brother Charles wrote many famous hymns.

162

㏒ **1709**
Abraham Darby uses coke instead of charcoal to smelt iron

㏒ **1712**
Thomas Newcomen's piston-operated steam engine

㏒ **1730**
Charles Townshend's theories on the rotation of crops

㏒ **1733**
John Kay's flying shuttle for the weaving industry

㏒ **1733**
Jethro Tull publishes farming guide: *Horse-Hoeing Husbandry*

NEW TECHNOLOGIES

B RITAIN was rich in coal and its overseas empire could provide valuable raw materials such as cotton or jute. These new lands also offered a huge market for manufactured goods such as textiles. Clever inventions made it possible to produce goods more quickly and cheaply than ever before. A new system of canals made it much easier to move goods from cities to ports. An 'industrial revolution' had begun.

Tin and copper had been mined in Cornwall since ancient times. By 1800 this industry was being transformed, with steam engines pumping out the mines, and with new roads and foundries being constructed. Soon the Cornish mines were employing 50,000 workers.

MILLS AND MINES

Britain became the world's first industrial country. By 1757 glowing furnaces rose from the heads of the South Wales valleys. The great ironworks at Carron brought industry to the Scottish Lowlands in 1759. The world's first iron bridge spanned the River Severn in Shropshire, England, by 1779. Factories and mills spread through Yorkshire, Lancashire, the English Midlands. Tin was mined in Cornwall, lead in Derbyshire, copper in Wales. The poet William Blake wrote of 'dark, satanic mills' appearing in a 'green and pleasant land'.

From the 1760s, a network of canals was dug by gangs of labourers called navigators, or 'navvies'. Pottery and other manufactured goods were transported in horse-drawn boats.

STEAM AND COAL

Steam power was developed in 1712 by two Devonshire engineers, Thomas Savery and Thomas Newcomen, to pump out water from mines. In the 1770s the steam engine was perfected by a Scottish engineering genius called James Watt. His successful steam pumps allowed deep mine shafts to be bored into the Northumberland and Durham coalfields.

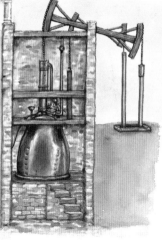

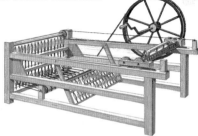

Massive, hissing steam engines provided the power for Britain's industrial revolution.

The spinning-jenny of 1768 was a machine which operated several spindles at once. It was developed in Lancashire, England, by James Hargreaves and mechanic Thomas Higgs, who named it after his daughter.

THE POTTERIES

Staffordshire, in the northwest of England, became the centre of pottery manufacture. The leading producer was Josiah Wedgwood, who set up the famous Etruria works in 1769. He produced black and cream-coloured wares, but his most famous design was of an unglazed blue decorated with a raised white pattern.

Wedgwood was inspired by classical designs. He made a copy of the Portland Vase, a fine piece of Roman glassware.

A TEXTILE REVOLUTION

Few industries changed so much in the 1750s and 60s as spinning and weaving. Output soared as new spinning frames and shuttles were invented by pioneers such as Richard Arkwright, James Hargreaves and Samuel Crompton. Work once carried out in the home was transferred to big textile mills powered by water or, later, by steam. By the 1800s, the industrial revolution was gaining speed. It would change the world forever.

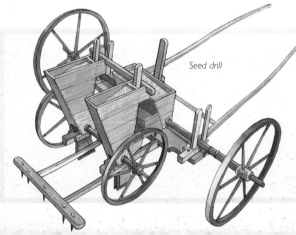

Seed drill

SCIENCE AND TURNIPS

Science and technology were beginning to change farming as well as manufacture. In 1701 Jethro Tull invented a drill which dropped seeds in rows instead of scattering them across the field. In 1730 a retired politician called Charles Townshed (nicknamed 'Turnip') developed a new system of improving the soil by switching ('rotating') crops, using wheat, grass and turnips.

164

∾∾ **1726**
Jonathan Swift publishes
Gulliver's Travels

∾∾ **1728**
Irish Catholics no longer
allowed to vote

∾∾ **1791**
Foundation of the United
Irishmen organization

∾∾ **1793**
Relief Act restores vote to
Irish Catholics

∾∾ **1795**
Foundation of the Orange
Order by Irish Protestants

İRİSH REBELLİON AND UNİON

I N THE 50 years after the Battle of the
Boyne, the Irish economy improved.
Trade passed along rivers, canals and much
improved roads to the the seaports of the east
and south. Farms prospered on the more fertile
lands, although the Irish-speaking peasant
farmers of the west struggled along on the
verge of famine. The Protestant ruling class
built splendid country homes. From the 1750s
onwards, Dublin was laid out with broad streets
of fine brick town houses and bridges over the
River Liffey. The population of Ireland rose to
about 5 million.

GULLIVER'S TRAVELS

Jonathan Swift was born in Dublin, of
English parents. He became known for
his poetry. He was appointed Dean of
St Patrick's Cathedral, in Dublin, and
campaigned against British restrictions
on Irish trade. In 1726 Swift wrote
Gulliver's Travels, in which the hero
describes his visits to various fantastic
worlds. The result is a bitter but
humorous look at the foolishness
of mankind.

*Swift uses the experiences of Gulliver
to point out human follies.*

DUBLIN AND LONDON

At the beginning of the 1700s,
Catholics made up 90 percent of the
Irish population, but owned only 14
percent of the land. The British
attitude to Ireland was that of a
colonial power. When Irish exports in
woollen cloth and cattle were so
successful that they threatened trade in
England, they were simply banned.
Catholics were not allowed to worship
freely or even to vote. Ireland still had
its own parliament in Dublin, but real
power lay in London.

*The production of linen cloth from flax was
a major industry among the Protestants of
Ulster. Much of the work was home-based.*

WHO HOLDS POWER?

More and more people in Ireland, Protestant as well as Catholic, wanted to see political reform. One leader of opinion was a member of the Irish Parliament called Henry Grattan. Many of his supporters were inspired by the American War of Independence and the calls for freedom grew louder. When the French Revolution took place in 1789, the British decided it might be best if they went along with Grattan's demands.

UNITED IRISHMEN

After 1791 a Protestant from Kildare called Theobald Wolfe Tone recruited many Irish people to a society called the United Irishmen. It called for equal religious rights and Irish independence. At first it had support both from Protestant militias called the Volunteers and from Irish Catholics. It soon became linked with more radical groups and sought help from the revolutionary government in France. In 1796 a French revolutionary fleet appeared off Bantry Bay in the south, but was scattered by storms.

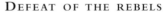 Politician Henry Grattan speaks to the Irish Parliament in 1780. He campaigned tirelessly for Ireland to be allowed to make its own laws.

DEFEAT OF THE REBELS

In May 1798 the Irish rebellion began in Wexford, and in August the French landed troops in support. It was too late. Both were defeated and many Irish rebels were hanged. Grattan's reforms were thrown out. A new Act of Union, in force from 1 January 1801, abolished the Irish parliament. A United Irishman called Robert Emmet attempted one more rising, in 1803. It failed and he too was hanged.

The 1798 rebellion came to an end at Vinegar Hill, near Wexford, on 21 June. That September, Wolfe Tone was captured. He committed suicide in prison.

166

∾ **1791**
Start of wars with revolutionary
France

∾ **1798**
Battle of the Nile. Nelson
defeats French off Egypt

∾ **1801**
Battle of Copenhagen. Nelson
defeats Danish fleet.

∾ **1802**
Peace of Amiens closes
French Revolutionary Wars

∾ **1803**
Start of Napoleonic Wars
with France

THE ΠAPOLEOΠIC WARS

G EORGE III's Britain and the revolutionary government in France were bitter enemies. They hated each other's politics and they were rivals for power. They went to war in 1791. Two remarkable characters made their name in the 11 years that followed. One was a popular British naval commander called Horatio Nelson. He defeated the French fleet at Aboukir Bay, Egypt, in 1798. The other was a brilliant French soldier called Napoleon Bonaparte. Napoleon had political ambitions.

Napoleon was a military genius, great law-maker and a ruthless politician.

A NEW EMPEROR IN EUROPE

A peace made between Britain and France in 1802 did not last. By 1804 the two countries were at war again – only by now Napoleon Bonaparte had crowned himself emperor of France and was planning to invade Britain. Round forts called 'Martello towers' were built to defend the Channel coast. The English anxiously peered through telescopes across the Straits of Dover. Mothers threatened naughty children that 'Boney' would come for them in the night if they did not behave – but the bogeyman did not invade.

The regiment of the Gordon Highlanders was raised in 1794 and was famed for its bravery. It took part in the ordeal of La Coruña, in the Peninsular War.

Napoleon's invasion of Russia was a step too far. His troops were defeated by the harsh winter conditions.

LAND AND SEA

In 1805 a French–Spanish fleet was defeated by Nelson off Cape Trafalgar, in Spain. Britain's navy ruled the seas. On land, however, Napoleon won stunning victories against the great powers of the day – Austria, Prussia, Russia. His empire soon stretched across Europe. In 1812 Napoleon invaded Russia, but his troops were caught in the winter snows and many perished. By 1814 France's enemies were in Paris. Napoleon was forced from power and exiled to the Mediterranean island of Elba.

The hugely popular admiral Horatio Nelson was killed in battle at Trafalga on the deck of HMS Victory.

🌊 1805	🌊 1806	🌊 1808	🌊 1814	🌊 1815	167
British defeat French and Spanish at Trafalgar. Nelson is killed	Napoleon attempts blockade of Britain	Peninsular War. British fight French in Spain	End of war in Spain. Napoleon exiled to island of Elba.	Napoleon escapes. Defeated by British and Prussians at Waterloo.	

THE PENINSULAR WAR

In 1808 Napoleon invaded the Iberian peninsula (Portugal and Spain). He made his brother Joseph King of Spain. The British sent a force under Sir Arthur Wellesley (the later Duke of Wellington) to help Spanish and Portuguese resistance fighters. The British suffered setbacks during the campaign, with a desperate retreat to La Coruña in 1809. They won a great victory at Salamanca (1812) and also at Vittoria (1814).

The Duke of Wellington went into politics after Waterloo and became Prime Minister in 1828. He was opposed to the reform of Parliament.

WATERLOO

Napoleon slipped away from Elba and on 1 March 1815 he landed in France. Loyal troops rallied to him as he marched through the land. On 18 June they reached Waterloo, near Brussels, for a final and terrible battle. They were defeated by Prussian, Dutch and British troops under the command of the Duke of Wellington. The victors met in Vienna in 1815 to re-draw the map of Europe. Napoleon was sent to the remote Atlantic island of St Helena, where he died in 1821.

The British fleet at Trafalgar was made up of 27 war ships carrying over 2,000 cannon. Britain remained the world's leading naval power for more than 100 years after the battle.

BELOW DECKS

A sailor's life was tough during the 1700s and 1800s. Naval discipline was severe and punishment included floggings. Voyages were long, with hammocks slung between the decks for sleeping. Hard biscuits and salted-down meat were eaten, and a ration of rum was allowed. Battle conditions were terrifying, as cannon balls splintered masts and brought down rigging. In 1797 there were major mutinies by British sailors at Spithead and the Nore.

Press gangs were groups of sailors armed with cudgels. They roamed the ports, searching for new recruits. Young men were beaten up and forced to join the navy.

≈ 1805
The artist JMW Turner paints
The Shipwreck

≈ 1811
George becomes Prince
Regent. His father is unfit
to rule

≈ 1812
The waltz becomes the most
popular dance in Britain

≈ 1820
Prince Regent becomes
George IV on the death of
his father

≈ 1820
The artist John Constable
paints *Flatford Mill*

THE REGENCY

EORGE III was getting old and increasingly insane. His son George was eager for power and in 1811 he was made Prince Regent, to rule in his father's place. The years until his father's death in 1820 are known as the Regency period. For noble ladies and gentlemen, this was a time of high fashion and society scandals. Horse-drawn carriages bowled through newly laid out green parks. Elegant, candle-lit balls were held at Bath or at the Prince's new palace beside the sea at Brighton, Sussex.

George III was increasingly confused and was unable to rule effectively. This resulted in the declaration of a regency.

THE DANDIES

Some Regency fashions for men were extreme. 'Dandies' squeezed themselves into corsets and wore wide trousers and frock coats which flared from the hips. Extraordinary hair styles peeked out from top hats. They were a source of amusement to many people. The leader of the dandies and self-appointed judge of all that was fashionable was George 'Beau' Brummell. He fell out with 'Prinny' (the Prince Regent) in 1813. Ruined by his gambling debts, he fled to France, where he died in the madhouse in 1840.

Standard dress for a Regency gentleman included trousers rather than breeches, a frock coat and a waistcoat.

CARTOONS — AND CAROLINE

The Prince Regent was a well-meaning, intelligent and witty man, a lover of art, literature and fine architecture. However, he was savagely mocked by the cartoonists of his day. He was despised for his lavish, extravagant way of life. Dinner guests at his Brighton Pavilion could be offered a choice of 116 dishes, at a time when large sections of society were desperately poor and hungry. When George tried to divorce his second wife, Caroline of Brunswick, his treatment of her outraged the public.

Women looked to Paris for the latest fashions. Dresses were loose flowing and high-waisted, tied with a bow at the back. Bonnets were worn, tied with ribbon under the chin.

〰 **1822**
Completion of the Royal
Pavilion in Brighton, Sussex

〰 **1826**
Royal Zoological Society
founded in London

〰 **1830**
George IV dies. His brother
becomes William IV

〰 **1834**
The Palace of Westminster is
destroyed by fire

〰 **1835**
The new Houses of
Parliament are built

169

PEN TO PAPER

The 1800s was an exciting time for writers. Jane Austen's novels tell us just what it was like to live in Regency England, describing courtship, marriage and money. The Romantic poets were fired by imagination and emotion. William Wordsworth and John Keats praised the power of nature. The poets George Byron and Percy Bysshe Shelley led wild lives. Lord Byron went to fight in the Greek war of independence, but died of fever in 1824.

Shelley was drowned in a storm off Italy in 1822.

Byron's most popular work was Childe Harold, *which he completed in 1817.*

PRIME MINISTERS OF THE UNITED KINGDOM

✤ Henry Addington (Tory)	1801–1804
✤ William Pitt the Younger (Tory)	1804–1808
✤ Lord Grenville (coalition)	1806–1807
✤ Duke of Portland (Tory)	1807–1809
✤ Spencer Perceval (Tory)	1809–1812
✤ Earl of Liverpool (Tory)	1812–1827
✤ George Canning (coalition)	1827
✤ Viscount Goderich (Tory)	1827–1828
✤ Duke of Wellington (Tory)	1828–1830
✤ Earl Grey (Tory)	1830–1834

A TIME OF CHANGE

The Prince Regent escaped an assassination attempt in 1817 and was crowned George IV in 1821. He had always been pro-Whig, but as ruler he gave his support to the Tories, who opposed political reform. When his brother William came to the throne nine years later, he opposed the Reform Act of 1832. However democratic reform could not be held back for long. All over Europe old empires were breaking up. New nations were being created and their citizens were calling for freedom.

By 1822 the Brighton Pavilion had been transformed into a splendid eastern-style palace by the architect John Nash.

170

≫≫ **1804**
World's first steam locomotive
built by Richard Trevithick

≫≫ **1813**
Puffing Billy in use at Wylam
Colliery, Newcastle

≫≫ **1819**
Paddle-steamer *Savannah*
arrives in Liverpool from USA

≫≫ **1825**
Stephenson opens Stockton
to Darlington railway

≫≫ **1829**
Stephenson's *Rocket* wins the
Rainhill trials

PUFFING BILLIES

THE COUNTRYSIDE of Britain and Ireland had been quiet and unspoiled throughout its history. In the 1800s, that peace was shattered. First came railway engineers, laying track, digging cuttings and building bridges. Then came clanking, steam-powered locomotives, huffing and puffing through the fields. Horses bolted in fright. Landowners cursed the infernal machines and sold their land to the railway companies to make a quick profit. The age of rail had arrived.

Puffing Billy, now in London's Science Museum, is the oldest steam locomotive still in existence.

THE RAINHILL TRIALS

In October 1829 the Manchester to Liverpool railway company offered a prize for the most reliable steam locomotive. Huge crowds gathered to see the locomotives battle it out on a length of track near Liverpool. *Perseverance* was much too slow. *Novelty* could travel at 30 mph (48 kph), but kept breaking down. *Sans Pareil* burned too much coal. The winner was the *Rocket*, built by George and Robert Stephenson.

The Stephensons' Rocket could average a speed of 15 mph (24 kph) and it did not break down once.

BIRTH OF THE RAILWAYS

The railway age began in 1804. A Cornish engineer called Richard Trevithick was working at Penydarren, near Merthyr Tydfil in South Wales. He mounted a steam engine on a wagon and created the world's first locomotive. He proved it could haul a heavy industrial load – and passengers too. By 1813 William Hedley's famous *Puffing Billy* was steaming away at Wylam Colliery, near Newcastle. Wylam was the birthplace of engineering genius George Stephenson. He greatly improved the design of locomotives and rails and between 1821 and 1825 he built the Stockton and Darlington Railway. His son Robert was also an engineer and in the 1840s and 50s he constructed magnificent railway bridges across the Menai Strait and the Conwy, Tyne and Tweed rivers.

ভি **1830**
Passenger service opens, Liverpool to Manchester railway

ভি **1833**
IK Brunel appointed chief engineer of the Great Western Railway

ভি **1837**
Euston Station opens, first major London terminus

ভি **1843**
IK Brunel launches the iron steamship *Great Britain*

ভি **1863**
World's first underground railway opens in London

171

THE AGE OF STEAM

William Huskisson, Member of Parliament for Liverpool, was run over and killed at the opening of the Liverpool to Manchester passenger service in 1830. However people were not put off. Rail travel gave ordinary people freedom of movement. They could travel to work in other towns. They could have holidays by the sea. Industry was transformed too, as coal and iron and products could be moved from one end of the country to the other at ever higher speeds.

In 1879, the rail bridge over the River Tay in Scotland collapsed during a storm. A train fell into the waters below, killing 75 people. The scene is here recreated with models.

ISAMBARD KINGDOM BRUNEL

The son of an engineer, IK Brunel was born in Portsmouth, England, in 1806. He was a great builder of bridges, tunnels and docks and in 1833 became chief engineer of the Great Western Railway. He also designed great steamships for the Atlantic crossing. *Great Britain* (1845) was driven by propeller screws, and *Great Eastern* (1858) held the record of the world's biggest ever vessel for over 40 years.

ACROSS THE OCEAN

In 1819 an American paddle steamer docked in Liverpool, and in 1821 the British steamer *Rising Star* left Gravesend for South America. These early ships used sail as well as steam, but by the 1830s steam-only crossings of the Atlantic Ocean were also being made. The master of building the new iron ships was the engineer IK Brunel. Tall sailing ships were at this time reaching perfection in their design, and it would be another 100 years before they disappeared from the seas.

The British empire relied on the profitable shipping of goods and passengers around the world. After the 1820s, steam power was an added bonus.

〰 **1837**
Start of the Victorian age

〰 **1837**
Buckingham House in London
becomes official royal palace

〰 **1838**
Grace Darling is heroine of
Northumbrian shipwreck rescue

〰 **1840**
Victoria marries Prince Albert
of Saxe-Coburg

〰 **1842**
Victoria escapes assassination
attempt

LONG MAY SHE REIGN

IN JUNE 1837 Princess Victoria, niece of
William IV, was woken to be told she was
queen. She was only 18 years old. Victoria
ruled the United Kingdom at a time when
it was the world's most powerful nation,
with a vast overseas empire. In 1840
Victoria married a German prince, Albert
of Saxe-Coburg and Gotha. They had four
sons and five daughters, who married into
many of Europe's royal families.

◀ The Great Exhibition of 1851 was planned
by Prince Albert. It was staged in Hyde Park,
London, in a huge glass building called the Crystal
Palace. It showed off produce and craft work from
all over Britain's growing empire.

◀ Victoria ruled
for 63 years,
becoming the United
Kingdom's longest-
reigning monarch.

⚙ 1851	⚙ 1852	⚙ 1861	⚙ 1868	⚙ 1901
The Great Exhibition opens in Hyde Park, London	Balmoral Castle becomes Victoria's Scottish residence	Prince Albert dies of typhoid. Victoria retires to Windsor	Election of Disraeli, Victoria's favourite Prime Minister	Victoria dies at Osborne House, on the Isle of Wight

173

THE PENNY POST

A modern postal service using stamps paid for by the sender was introduced by Rowland Hill, the Postmaster General, in 1840. The first stamps were called 'Penny Blacks' and 'Twopence Blues'.

VICTORIAN MORALITY

In 1861 Albert died of typhoid fever. Victoria was grief-stricken and disappeared from public view for many years. People began to grumble about this, but towards the end of her reign she did regain her popularity.

Victoria was not known for her sense of humour or fun. She believed in strict religious morality and in duty to one's country. These values were shared by many of her subjects. The Victorian upper and middle classes preached of progress, of doing good and improving society. Improvements were certainly needed. Living conditions for the poor in both cities and countryside were very harsh.

THE QUEEN AND POLITICS

In the 1830s the old political parties changed their names. The Tories became known as the Conservatives and the Whigs as the Liberals. Queen Victoria took a great interest in politics. Viscount Melbourne, the first Prime Minister of her reign, was her personal friend and advisor. She did not take so well to Sir Robert Peel or Viscount Palmerston. Later in her reign, Victoria clearly preferred the charming, conservative Benjamin Disraeli to William Gladstone, his more radical rival.

The Peelers worked 12 hours a day, seven days a week. At first they were treated with little respect by the public.

THE PEELERS

The first uniformed police went on parade in London in 1829. The force was founded by Sir Robert Peel and so the constables became known as 'Peelers' or 'Bobbies'. They wore blue-frock coats and top hats reinforced with metal. Helmets and tunics were worn as from 1864.

PRIME MINISTERS OF THE UNITED KINGDOM

✤ Viscount Melbourne (Whig)	1834
✤ Sir Robert Peel (Conservative)	1834–1835
✤ Viscount Melbourne (Whig)	1835–1841
✤ Sir Robert Peel (Conservative)	1841–1846
✤ Lord Russell (Liberal)	1846–1852
✤ Earl of Derby (Conservative)	1852
✤ Lord Aberdeen (Peelite)	1852–1855
✤ Viscount Palmerston (Liberal)	1855–1858
✤ Earl of Derby (Conservative)	1858–1859
✤ Viscount Palmerston (Liberal)	1859–1865
✤ Lord Russell (Liberal)	1865–1866
✤ Earl of Derby (Conservative)	1866–1868

From about 1855, women wore a dress called a crinoline, whose bell-shaped skirt stretched out over hoops of whalebone and steel. Hair was worn in ringlets. By 1875 dresses were narrower, with a bottom pad called a bustle. Underwear included tightly-laced corsets.

෴ **1834**
Poor, elderly, orphans and
disabled moved into 'workhouses'

෴ **1837**
Population of United Kingdom
is about 15 million

෴ **1842**
It becomes illegal for women
and children to work down
mines

෴ **1848**
Health of Towns Act, to improve
water supply and drainage

෴ **1851**
Over half the British
population now lives in towns

THE FACTORY AGE

FAMILIES were leaving the countryside to seek work in the new factories and mines. They left a hard life for an even harder one. They toiled in the cotton mills of Manchester, in the steel mills of Sheffield, on the docksides of Liverpool, Glasgow and Newcastle-upon-Tyne. Industry depended on steam and steam depended on coal. The number of miners in Britain's coalfields doubled between 1851 and 1881.

Children worked underground in the mines, hauling coal waggons with chains or opening trap doors in the tunnels.

WORKING CONDITIONS

Many factory owners put profit above the health and safety of their workers. Children and young women were employed in wretched conditions in textile mills and mines. Small boys worked as sweeps, being made to crawl up tall, narrow chimneys in houses and factories until they bled. Furnaces were operated without proper safety checks. Workers in factories and mills were deafened by steam hammers and machinery. Hours were long and there were no holidays.

THE DAVY LAMP

Mining disasters killed hundreds of people in Victorian times. Deep underground, just one spark amongst the coal dust could set off an explosion, causing fires to rage or shafts to collapse. One invention which saved the lives of many miners was a safety lamp, developed by Cornish scientist Humphry Davy in 1815.

The Davy lamp was first tested in 1816, at Hebburn Colliery.

LAWS TO PROTECT WORKERS

Many Victorians were shocked by the conditions in which working people were now forced to live. In the 1840s and 50s, Lord Shaftesbury pushed new laws through Parliament which stopped women and children from working down the mines, and which limited the working day to 10 hours. Other laws followed in which factory conditions were brought under control. They were bitterly opposed by employers.

∽∾ **1864**
New law stops children being used as chimney sweeps

∽∾ **1868**
The Salvation Army carries out Christian work in London slums

∽∾ **1870**
Education Act sets out requirements for schooling

∽∾ **1875**
A Public Health Act is passed by Parliament

∽∾ **1900**
Population of United Kingdom reaches 37 million

175

THE GROWING CITIES

New cities were eating their way into the surrounding countryside. Terraces of red-brick houses sprawled back-to-back, as far as the eye could see. In big cities, families were packed into slums and children ran barefoot in the streets. There would be a pump in the yard and an outdoor toilet, both serving many families. Many toilets were still not flushed by water. Deadly diseases such as typhoid and cholera spread quickly in these unhealthy conditions. Gradually drainage was improved and new sewers were built under the cities.

SOOT AND SMOKE

In London, the Thames had become a foul-smelling, polluted river, deserted by its fish. In northern English cities the air was filled with smuts from factory chimneys. Buildings were covered in black soot. In winter, smoke and fog made it hard to find one's way. Gas lamps, which first appeared on streets during the Regency period, became common in the Victorian period.

VICTORIAN SCHOOLING

Children from poor homes received little education at all. 'Ragged schools' were set up to teach children from the factories and slums in the 1820s and 30s. From 1870 onwards, all children were sent to state-run primary schools for the first time. For the first time in the nation's history, poor people were receiving an education.

Smoking chimneys rise into the sky at Sheffield, centre of world steel production, in 1879. Drovers herded sheep and cattle from the countryside into cities. There they were slaughtered to feed the growing population.

176

〰 **1799**
Socialist pioneer Robert Owen purchases New Lanark Mills, Scotland

〰 **1811**
'Luddites' destroy industrial machinery in north of England

〰 **1819**
Demonstrators killed in Manchester: the 'Peterloo' Massacre

〰 **1833**
Slavery abolished in British empire

〰 **1834**
'Tolpuddle Martyrs' – farm workers arrested for joining trade union

CHANGING SOCIETY

THE INDUSTRIAL age which was now spreading rapidly through Europe and North America, completely changed society. However old methods of government stayed in place. Some people campaigned against injustice and tried to reform society. Many called for greater democracy. Some revolutionaries wanted the workers to seize power for themselves.

◐ *Prisoners are exercised in the yard. Political protest and petty crimes were met with harsh sentences. Many convicts were transported to prison colonies in Australia.*

DICKENSIAN LONDON

Charles Dickens, born in 1812, had a hard childhood. His father was imprisoned for debt and he had to work in a factory making boot blacking. In 1828 he became a journalist and from the 1830s onwards began to write popular novels, many of them serialised in magazines. They tell us how the Victorians lived. *Oliver Twist* (finished in 1839) shows us life in the workhouse and the beggars and thieves of the London slums. Such tales shocked many people and encouraged social reform. Dickens died in 1870.

◐ *The poverty, violence, humour and humanity of Victorian London was recorded by Charles Dickens.*

FIGHTERS AGAINST INJUSTICE

William Wilberforce, Member of Parliament for Hull, led a long campaign against the slave trade in the colonies. In 1807 British ships were banned from carrying slaves and in 1833, one month after Wilberforce died, slavery was finally abolished throughout the British empire.

Another great reformer was a Quaker called Elizabeth Fry, who from 1813 campaigned against terrible conditions in the prisons. Changes were made to the system, but Victorian prisons remained grim.

VIOLENT PROTEST

New machines meant fewer jobs. In 1811, laid-off Nottingham workers began to smash machinery. In the five years that followed, protests spread across northern England. The protestors claimed their leader was a 'General Ludd', so they were called 'Luddites'. Many were hanged or transported. New machines were replacing labourers on the farms, too. In 1830 farm workers in southern England destroyed threshing machines and set fire to haystacks. Their leader was commonly known as 'Captain Swing'.

⚡ 1839	⚡ 1844	⚡ 1846	⚡ 1877	⚡ 1888	177
First National Convention of the Chartist Movement	Cooperative movement set up in Rochdale for mutual help in trade and housing	Corn Laws, which kept the price of bread high, abolished by Robert Peel	Government takes central control of all prisons	Local Government Act – first County Council elections	

A PEOPLE'S CHARTER

The Reform Act of 1832 gave the vote to more people and representation to the new cities. Between 1838 and 1848, working people campaigned for further reforms. They were called Chartists, because they presented a 'People's Charter' to Parliament. This demanded that all adult men should have the vote, that ballots should be secret and that anyone could become a Member of Parliament (MP). Parliament rejected the Charter, in 1840 and 1842. Mass protests and armed risings followed, but were put down by troops. However laws passed in 1867 and 1884 did bring in many democratic reforms.

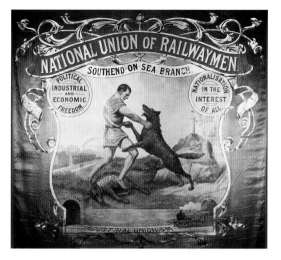

Trade unions campaigned for justice in the workplace. Sometimes members withdrew their labour, striking until their demands were met. Each union had its own embroidered banner.

THE COMMUNIST MANIFESTO

The writings of Marx (left) and Engels had a great influence on world history.

Karl Marx was a German writer on economics who moved to London. Friedrich Engels, another German, came to Manchester to work for his family's textile business. In 1848 Marx and Engels wrote the *Communist Manifesto*. They described how economic systems had developed through history and the conflict between social classes. They called upon workers all over the world to overthrow capitalism and create a society in which classes would exist no more.

TRADE UNIONS AND SOCIALISTS

Many working people organized trade unions, to fight for better conditions. Six Dorsetshire farm workers did this in 1834. Transported to Australia for this 'crime', they became known as the 'Tolpuddle Martyrs'. The richest people in Victorian society did not work. They used their money ('capital') to speculate, buying and selling shares. Socialists believed that the profits made by capitalists belonged rightfully to the workers who actually produced the goods.

In 1819, reformists meeting in St Peter's Fields, Manchester, were charged by mounted troops and volunteers. Eleven of the crowd were killed and 500 injured. Just 4 years after the Battle of Waterloo, the event became known as the Peterloo Massacre.

178

≫≋ 1796	≫≋ 1821	≫≋ 1834	≫≋ 1841	≫≋ 1855
Edward Jenner pioneers vaccination	Michael Faraday invents the electric motor	Charles Babbage designs his calculating machine	WH Fox Talbot pioneers negative process for photographs	Alfred Russel Wallace publishes theories of evolution

ΠATURE, SCIEΠCE AΠD TECHΠOLOGY

THE VICTORIANS were fascinated by the natural world and how it worked. There were breakthroughs in the human understanding of physics, chemistry, botany, zoology and geology. Science was now studied at universities, and introduced to the public in splendid new museums, botanical gardens and zoos.

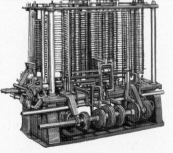

LIFE ON EARTH

Many people were becoming interested in the fossil remains of animals and plants. The scientists Alfred Russel Wallace and Charles Darwin both travelled the world, studying wildlife. They came to believe that life forms on our planet had evolved, or gradually developed, over many millions of years. Their ideas were opposed by many Christians, who believed that the world was only a few thousand years old and that all existing creatures had been created by God in their present form.

From 1831-1836 the crew of HMS Beagle carried out a scientific survey of South American waters. The chief scientist on board was a young naturalist called Charles Darwin. He collected and studied fossils, animals and plants.

INVENTIONS OF THE 1800s

Scientific discoveries were soon applied to technology. New inventions in Western Europe and North America transformed industry, transport, medicine, commerce and home life. Inventions in Great Britain and Ireland included waterproofing of cloth (Charles Macintosh, 1832) and cellulose (a form of plastic patented by Alexander Parkes in 1855).

calculating machine
This mechanical calculator was one of several designed by Charles Babbage from the 1820s to 1840s. It may be seen as an early attempt at making a computer.

bicycle power
The first bicycle to be powered by pedals was made by Scottish blacksmith Kirkpatrick Macmillan in 1840. Pneumatic (air-filled) tyres were first tried out in 1887 by John Boyd Dunlop.

～ 1856
Henry Bessemer develops
new method of making steel

～ 1856
William Perkin develops
chemical dyes

～ 1859
Charles Darwin publishes
The Origin of Species

～ 1865
Joseph Lister develops
antiseptic medical treatments

～ 1865
Natural History Museum opens
in Kensington, London

179

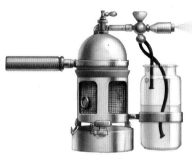

Joseph Lister's antiseptic
spray was used in
hospital wards and operating
theatres from 1867 onwards.

MEDICAL RESEARCH

Great medical advances were made in Western Europe in the 1800s. An English doctor called Edward Jenner had carried out the first successful vaccination against smallpox in 1796. Vaccination against disease became widely accepted in Victorian hospitals, as did the antiseptic treatment of surgical instruments to kill germs. This change, brought in by the surgeon Joseph Lister in the 1860s, saved countless lives.

THE FOSSIL COLLECTOR

Mary Anning was born in Lyme Regis, Dorset in 1799. She was already a first-rate fossil collector as a child, discovering the first fossil skeleton of an *ichthyosaur* in 1810. In 1821 she found the first fossilized *plesiosaur* and in 1828 the first *pteranadon*.

By studying Mary Anning's fossil ichthyosaur, scientists could work out how such creatures lived in prehistoric times.

SCIENCE AND ELECTRICITY

Michael Faraday's discoveries about electricity and magnetism in the 1830s changed the way in which people lived. In 1878 Joseph Swan demonstrated an electric light bulb in Newcastle upon Tyne. The first electric telegraph was developed by WF Cooke and Charles Wheatstone in the 1830s. The telephone was first demonstrated in the USA in 1876, by Scottish-born inventor Alexander Graham Bell. The 'wireless telegraph' or radio was invented by the Italian scientist Guglielmo Marconi. He sent the first radio signal across the Atlantic Ocean, from Cornwall to Newfoundland, in 1901.

The Royal Botanical Gardens at Kew, to the west of London, became a world centre of research into plants and seeds. A fine palm house, built of glass and iron, was completed there in 1848.

180

☙ 1831
The Merthyr Rising – a workers'
uprising in South Wales

☙ 1839
The Rebecca Riots in West
Wales (until 1844)

☙ 1839
The Chartists march on
Newport, in South Wales

☙ 1855
The first coal mine is
opened in the Rhondda
valley, South Wales

☙ 1858
The eisteddfod is revived as
a yearly festival of music
and poetry

VICTORIAN WALES

WALES HAD known peace since the Civil War, apart from a brief landing by French revolutionary troops at Fishguard in 1797. However the 1800s were less peaceful. There were no more wars or foreign invasions, but there was a period of violent social unrest brought about by rapid economic change.

LAND AND SEA

Most of Wales remained a land of small farms, where sheep grazed the green hillsides. In mid-Wales, the rivers were still fished from small wickerwork boats called coracles, as they had been since ancient times. Coastal dwellers caught herring and built ships and boats. In Victorian times, Welsh-built vessels sailed around the world. Among their cargoes was slate, shipped from the quarries of North Wales to roof the cities of the British empire. Another cargo was coal, exported through the growing port of Cardiff. For 130 years from 1855, coal would rule the economy of Wales.

THE MERTHYR RISING

In 1829 there was widespread unemployment in South Wales and wages were cut. The troubles came to a climax in 1831. Prisoners were broken out of jail and a series of marches and riots turned into a full-scale uprising. In Merthyr Tydfil, troops were brought in to face a crowd of some 10,000 people. The soldiers opened fire, killing about 24 and wounding many more. A young miner called Richard Lewis, nicknamed 'Dic Penderyn' was later hanged for wounding a soldier, despite his innocence. The Merthyr rising was followed by ten years of bitter political protest.

REBECCA'S DAUGHTERS

A verse of the Bible says: '...they blessed Rebekah and said unto her, Let they seed (descendants) possess the gates of those which hate thee'. The poor people of West Wales knew all about gates – the hated toll gates where they had to pay taxes each time they transported goods along the highway. From 1839 onwards, groups of farmers attacked the gates and smashed them. Leaders of these protests took the name 'Rebecca' from the Bible.

The 'Rebecca' rioters jokingly disguised themselves as women, so that nobody would know their true identity. The riots lasted until 1844.

Coal miners led a hard life. Many suffered from illnesses caused by the coal dust they breathed in underground.

1865
A Welsh colony is founded in Patagonia, South America

1872
University College of Wales opens at Aberystwyth

1886
The Young Wales movement (Cymru Fydd) is founded

1886
The 'Tithe War' – protests against tax paid to Church

1890
David Lloyd George becomes MP for Caernarfon

181

CHAPEL AND SCHOOLHOUSE

In the 1700s and 1800s, more and more Welsh people turned away from the Church of England to follow 'non-conformist' forms of worship. Chapels with names from the Bible, such as Bethesda or Jerusalem, now dotted the map of Wales. Whatever their beliefs, people still had to pay taxes, called tithes, to the Church of England. This led to many protests in the 1880s. It was the Chapels and their Sunday schools which helped to keep the Welsh language alive, for children were often punished for speaking their own language at the village school.

Cockle gatherers southwest Wales 1890s.

Spinning and knitting were the Welsh cottage industries. The 'national costume' was mostly a Victorian invention.

WALES IN PATAGONIA

In 1865 a group of Welsh settlers sailed to Argentina, in South America. They founded a colony in the Chubut valley, in the remote region of Patagonia. Another colony was later founded at Cwm Hyfryd, at the foot of the Andes mountains. The settlements prospered and the colonists built their own farms, chapels and law-courts. During the 1900s they became outnumbered by new Spanish and Italian settlers, but the Welsh language can still be heard in Patagonia to this day.

OLD AND NEW

The ancient poetry festivals called *eisteddfodau* were reinvented in the 1790s. After the 1850s, these annual meetings became a focus for Welsh cultural – and often political – life. Young Wales (*Cymru Fydd*), a movement for Welsh self-government, was started in 1886. It was soon eclipsed by support for a rising star in the world of politics, a young Liberal called David Lloyd George. He became MP for Caernarfon in 1890. By 1916 he would be Prime Minister.

The Menai Suspension Bridge, an engineering marvel of its age, was built by Thomas Telford and opened in 1826. It lay on a new road built from London to Holyhead, the port for Ireland.

182

〰 1820
Political protests end in harsh reprisals

〰 1832
The death of Sir Walter Scott, historical novelist

〰 1843
Disruption – Free Church breaks with Church of Scotland

〰 1848
Scotland linked with England by rail

〰 1850
The birth of Robert Louis Stevenson

VICTORIAN SCOTLAND

QUEEN Victoria liked to visit Scotland. Her family would hunt the moors and fish for salmon. They made popular a romantic view of Scotland which was quite at odds with the harsh reality. In the Highlands, poor people were being forced from their cottages. In the industrial Lowlands, fortunes were being made while children starved in the sprawling slums of Glasgow.

The 'clearance' of the Highlands caused great hardship. In the 1830s and 40s things were made even worse by food shortages and starvation.

ROMANTIC TALES

In the 1820s, readers across Europe were thrilled by the tales of adventure written by Sir Walter Scott. Many of his novels, such as *Rob Roy*, were rooted in exciting periods in Scottish history. Robert Louis Stevenson, who wrote from the 1870s to 90s, travelled far from his native Scotland. However he set several exciting tales such as *Kidnapped* in his homeland. He is remembered around the world for his story about the pirate Long John Silver, *Treasure Island*.

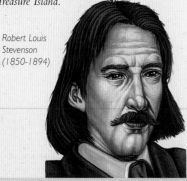

Robert Louis Stevenson (1850-1894)

HIGHLAND CLEARANCES

Between the 1750s and the 1860s, landowners in the Scottish Highlands reorganized their estates along more commercial lines. They brought in sheep, which were more profitable than cattle. In the Victorian age, they encouraged deer hunting and fishing. A large workforce was no longer needed and tenants simply stood in the way of the landowners' profits.

Families were evicted by force and their cottages were destroyed. By the 1860s the Highlands had become largely depopulated and the Gaelic language spoken there was under threat. It was the 1880s before the rights of remaining tenants were protected by law.

LEAVING THE OLD COUNTRY

Many of the evicted Highlanders sought work in the Lowland cities. Others gave up and sailed off to foreign lands. Many emigrated to the coastal regions and cities of eastern Canada, to the United States and Australia.

SCOTLAND AT WORK

The eastern ports of Scotland were home to large fleets of sailing ships, which trawled the North Sea for herring. Women worked on shore gutting and cleaning the fish. Textiles and iron were the major industries around Lanark and Glasgow, and the River Clyde became a great centre for shipbuilding and shipping. Dundee grew wealthy processing jute imported from the lands of the British empire. By the time of Queen Victoria's death in 1901, one in three Scots lived in the cities – in Edinburgh, Glasgow, Dundee or Aberdeen.

THE DISRUPTION

In 1843 there was a major crisis in the Church of Scotland. In this 'Disruption', large numbers of people left the established Church. They were unhappy with the way in which it was influenced by the state, so they set up their own Free Church. In an age when Churches were deeply involved in education and social welfare, this had a great effect on everyday life.

The tartan cloth of the Scottish Highlands, which had been banned after the Jacobite rebellion of 1745, was made fashionable once more by the novels of Sir Walter Scott and by the royal family.

RADICAL POLITICS

The economic changes in Scotland encouraged calls for political change. In the early 1800s a Welsh socialist called Robert Owen set up the New Lanark Mills, with the aim of benefiting the workers. In 1819-1820 there was widespread rioting and three Scottish radicals, James Wilson, Andrew Hardie and John Baird were hanged. Scotland remained a centre of Chartist and Liberal politics and in 1893 a former Scottish miner called Keir Hardie founded the Independent Labour Party, the forerunner of the modern Labour Party.

In the early days of the Industrial Revolution, few factory owners cared about working conditions. Robert Owen was an exception. The cotton mills he purchased from his father-in-law David Dale at New Lanark, in 1799, were designed to be healthy and clean. Owen provided workers with housing, a school and leisure activities.

184

⚭ **1823**
Daniel O'Connell founds the
Catholic Association

⚭ **1829**
Catholics receive voting rights
– 'Emancipation'

⚭ **1842**
The Young Ireland movement
is founded

⚭ **1845**
Famine after potato crop fails
(until 1848)

⚭ **1858**
Growth of the Irish
Republican Brotherhood

FAMINE IN IRELAND

I N IRELAND, industry chiefly developed in the north. Belfast soon grew to be larger than the Irish capital, Dublin. Belfast's economy depended upon linen textiles, engineering and shipbuilding. At the same time, much of rural Ireland was suffering from poverty and hunger. Ireland may now have been part of the United Kingdom, but its citizens did not seem to be treated equally. The Union was challenged time after time.

O'CONNELL AND 'YOUNG IRELAND'

The fight for Irish Catholics to be able to vote was taken up by Daniel O'Connell, a popular lawyer known as 'the Liberator'. His campaign succeeded in 1829, but most Catholics did not own enough property to qualify for the vote. O'Connell went on to campaign against the Union with Great Britain. At first he was allied with a nationalist movement called 'Young Ireland', but its members soon disagreed with his policy of non-violence. They organized an armed uprising in 1848, but it was too small to succeed.

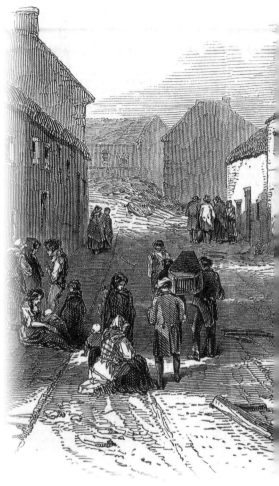

Daniel O'Connell, lawyer, politician and veteran campaigner for Irish rights, died in 1847, heartbroken by the tragedy of the famine.

THE IRISH FAMINE

The tenant farmers of rural Ireland lived a wretched life. The high rents they had to pay to landlords meant that they had to sell all the grain they could grow. For their own food, they relied on potatoes and little else. In 1845 the potato crop was struck by a blight, or mould. The people starved and began to die of fever and dysentery. The landlords never went hungry and crops that could have saved lives were exported to England. The blight continued and the famine lasted three years.

∾ 1875
Charles Stuart Parnell is
elected to Parliament

∾ 1879
Michael Davitt founds Irish
National Land League

∾ 1882
The Phoenix Park murders,
Dublin

∾ 1884
The National League replaces
the Land League

∾ 1886
Home Rule Bill defeated in
Parliament

185

LANDLORDS AND FENIANS

The famine left lasting bitterness. It was felt that
the government had done very little to prevent the
tragedy and that landlords had neglected their
tenants. New campaigns were now launched to
protect tenants, in a long 'land war'.

The Irish Republican Brotherhood grew up in
the late 1850s. Its members, known as Fenians
('warriors') organized unsuccessful risings in 1865
and 1867 and campaigns of violence in England.
Their aim was an independent Ireland.

IRISH AMERICANS

Many Fenians did not
live in Ireland, but in the
large Irish communities
that were growing up
overseas. The Irish who
had settled in the eastern
United States kept the
campaign for Irish
independence alive.

*In 1841 the population of
Ireland was about 8 million.
Perhaps 800,000 to a million of them
died during the years of famine.*

EMIGRATION

During the famine and the
years that followed, some 1½
million Irish people left their
homeland to seek a better life
overseas. Many ended up in
Glasgow, Liverpool or
London. Others sailed to seek
a new life in the United
States, Canada and Australia.
They left behind deserted
villages – and large areas
where the Irish language was
no longer heard.

*Generation after
generation left
Ireland to search for
work. Here crowds
gather on the dockside.
Conditions on the
Atlantic crossing were
often terrible, and in the
days of the famine
many people died
during the voyage.*

THE BOYCOTT

A new word entered the
English language in 1880: 'to
boycott'. It meant 'refusing to
deal with someone'. The
name came from Charles
Boycott, the land agent for
Lord Erne, who had an estate
in County Mayo. When
Boycott would not lower the
rents, the tenants protested by
refusing to speak or deal with
him in any way.

HOME RULE FOR IRELAND?

In the 1870s the campaign for Irish tenants'
rights was taken up by a Protestant politician
called Charles Stewart Parnell. He won the
support of many Fenians, but was cleared of
involvement in acts of terror such as the
murder of two English officials in Phoenix
Park, Dublin, in 1882. Parnell's constant
demands for 'home rule' by an Irish
parliament were at last supported in London
by the Liberal leader, William Gladstone.
New laws were brought in to protect
tenant's rights in the 1880s, but when Parnell
died in 1891, Parliament still had not agreed
to Irish home rule.

1819
Highland Games held in
Perthshire, Scotland

1829
Oxford wins the first
University Boat Race on the
River Thames

1841
Rugby football is invented at
Rugby School, England

1842
First ice-skating rink opens in
London

1863
The Football Association
(soccer) is founded in England

SPORTS AND ENTERTAINMENT

M ANY OF today's sports were first given proper rules in the nineteenth century. Some were developed at famous public schools. In the later Victorian period, improved working conditions gave middle-class and working-class families more leisure time and holidays, making sports such as association football massively popular. The oldest football club, Sheffield, was founded in 1857.

Christmas cards were first printed in London in 1843 and soon became highly popular.

A Bright and Happy Christmas.

Rugby was invented when a pupil at Rugby School, in England, picked up a football and ran with it. His name was William Webb Ellis and the year was 1823. The Rugby Football Union was founded in 1871.

A VICTORIAN CHRISTMAS

In 1832 young Princess Victoria was very excited by a Christmas tree put up at Kensington Palace, in London. The royal family had adopted this German custom as early as 1800, but it was not until the 1840s that Christmas trees became more commonly seen. It was then that the first Christmas crackers were made, too.

TEAM SPORTS

Some popular sports were updated versions of old favourites such as golf or cricket. The most successful Victorian cricketer was a bearded doctor called WG Grace, with whom few umpires dared to argue. Each year huge crowds would gather to watch the University Boat Race between Oxford and Cambridge, first rowed on the River Thames in 1829. In Ireland, sports such as hurling and Gaelic football were encouraged from the 1880s onwards.

▧ 1864	▧ 1868	▧ 1872	▧ 1884	▧ 1886	187
WG Grace starts playing cricket for Gloucestershire	British doctor James Moore wins first known cycle race, in Paris	A lawn tennis club is founded at Leamington, England	Founding of the Gaelic Athletic Association, Ireland	Founding of the Hockey Association in England	

◀ *Lawn tennis was adapted from the old indoor game of 'real' or 'royal' tennis. It became very popular in the 1870s.*

◀ *In an age when most people still travelled on horseback, rocking horses were popular toys in many nurseries.*

THE GREAT OUTDOORS

Tourists now began to visit areas once considered as wilderness, climbing the Welsh and Scottish mountains. Cyclists left the towns for the country, some wobbling on high 'penny-farthing' machines which had one large wheel and one little one. Active lives made standards of dressing more free and easy. For leisure pursuits, men would wear blazers and round straw hats called 'boaters'. Some women cyclists caused outrage by wearing baggy breeches instead of long dresses.

TOYS AND GAMES

Victorian children played with lead soldiers, cheap tin toys and trumpets, wooden bricks, jack-in-the-boxes and Noah's arks full of model animals. Children flew kites and bowled hoops in the street. Board games, card games and jigsaw puzzles were popular, too. Teddy bears did not appear in the shops until 1903.

◀ *Marie Lloyd started playing the music halls in 1885. She was a comedian and singer, and is still remembered for her hit songs 'Oh, Mr Porter' and 'My Old Man Said Follow the Van'.*

TREADING THE BOARDS

Popular Victorian entertainments included over-acted plays with sentimental story lines or plots based on dreadful murders. From the 1880s onwards, rowdy crowds packed into 'music halls' to watch comedians, singers and dancers. For more polite audiences, light operas were written in the 1870s and 80s by Sir WS Gilbert and Sir Arthur Sullivan. These were witty and light-hearted, poking fun at Victorian society.

1853
Russia occupies Moldavia and
Wallachia (Romania)

1854
March: British and French
enter Crimean War

1854
20 September: Battle of the
River Alma

1854
25 October: Battle of
Balaclava, Charge of the Light
Brigade

1854
5 November: Battle of
Inkerman, heavy casualties

THE GREAT POWERS

RUSSIA HAD grown into a huge empire, stretching from Central Europe into Asia. In 1853 it invaded the region now known as Romania. At that time, this was ruled by the powerful Ottoman empire of the Turks. Turkey went to war with Russia. Because the United Kingdom and France wanted to stop Russia gaining control of the Balkan region, they joined forces with the Turks.

THE CRIMEAN WAR

In 1854 France and Britain sent troops to the Black Sea, even though the Austrians had already forced the Russians out of Romania. The allies landed on the Crimean peninsula, part of the Russian empire, and laid siege to the Russian naval base of Sebastopol. They won victories on the River Alma, at Balaclava and Inkerman, but the war is chiefly remembered for a disastrous charge by the British cavalry. Ordered in error to launch a direct attack on Russian guns at Balaclava, the Light Brigade galloped to certain death. The war was won in 1855, when a French force finally burst through the defences of Sebastopol.

The charge of the 600-strong Light Brigade at Balaclava in 1854 was commemorated by the great Victorian poet Alfred, Lord Tennyson. He described them riding 'Into the jaws of Death, Into the mouth of Hell'.

THE LADY WITH THE LAMP

The blunder at Balaclava showed that the British army was run by ageing aristocrats who had little understanding of modern warfare. The troops were poorly dressed and equipped and died in their thousands from cholera and frostbite. One person did care for the wounded and dying. In 1854 an English woman called Florence Nightingale arrived at Scutari (Üsküdar) with 38 nurses. With her strict concern for hygiene, she saved countless lives. On return to England, Florence Nightingale started the training of professional nurses.

PRIME MINISTERS OF THE UNITED KINGDOM

✤ Benjamin Disraeli (Conservative)	1860
✤ William Gladstone (Liberal)	1868-1874
✤ Benjamin Disraeli (Conservative)	1874-1880
✤ William Gladstone (Liberal)	1880-1885
✤ Marquess of Salisbury (Conservative)	1885-1886
✤ William Gladstone (Liberal)	1886
✤ Marquess of Salisbury (Conservative)	1886-1892
✤ William Gladstone (Liberal)	1892-1894
✤ Earl of Rosebery (Liberal)	1894-1895
✤ Marquess of Salisbury (Conservative)	1895-1902

Florence Nightingale visited the sick and wounded by night, with a lantern. She became known as the 'lady with the lamp'.

REPORTS FROM THE BATTLEFIELD

Magazines such as the *Illustrated London News*, with its drawings of current events, were very popular with the Victorians. However reports of the Crimean War, published by *The Times* newspaper, shocked the public. They were sent directly from the war zone by an Irish journalist called William Howard Russell. It was during the Crimean War that the first war photographs were taken, too. For the first time in history people could read about distant battles and see the reality of warfare for themselves.

This van was used to process photographs taken during the Crimean War.

RIVAL NATIONS AND EMPIRES

New nation states were being founded across Europe. Italy united as a single kingdom in 1861. In 1867 the twin nation of Austria-Hungary was created. In 1871 Germany became a single country, for the first time. Its *Kaiser* (emperor) was Wilhelm I. He was followed onto the throne in 1888 by Wilhelm II, a grandson of Queen Victoria. This was an age of petty nationalism, or 'jingoism', in which each nation tried to outdo the others. By 1914, this would lead to the bloodiest war in history. In the meantime, European nations were building up vast empires overseas. The British empire now stretched around the world.

190

∾ 1819
Stamford Raffles founds modern
port at Singapore

∾ 1824
First Burmese War (Second
1852, Third 1885)

∾ 1838
First Afghan War
(Second 1878)

∾ 1839
The First Opium War with
China (Second in 1855)

∾ 1841
James Brooke becomes Rajah
of Sarawak

JEWELS IN THE CROWN

B Y 1869, ships could sail directly to Asia through the new Suez Canal. Passengers included troops and merchants, who were rapidly turning Asia's ancient empires into colonies from which they could reap rich rewards. Britain's Asian empire grew to take in the countries and ports now known as Aden, Pakistan, India, Bangladesh, Sri Lanka, Myanmar (Burma), Malaysia, Singapore, Brunei and Hong Kong.

BRITISH INDIA

British rule had a great influence on India, and India impressed the empire-builders in return. Generations of them came to know India's hot, dusty plains better than the distant islands of 'home'. They fought the Afghans along the Northwest Frontier, built railways, planted tea or played polo. Many of them were racists, who believed themselves to be superior to the Indians. Others worked hard for the country and its people, but British rule did not bring an end to poverty or starvation.

Indian brokers examine bales of cotton in Bombay. British cotton mills obtained about 20 percent of their cotton from India. However this changed when the civil war in the United States (1861-65) interrupted supplies from America. The result was a boom in Indian cotton.

THE JUNGLE BOOKS

Rudyard Kipling was an English writer born at Bombay, India in 1865. He was fascinated by India and wrote short stories and poems about common soldiers, officers and Indian life. For children he wrote the two classic *Jungle Books*. Although Kipling was inspired by the empire, he often criticized imperialism and realised that it must pass.

THE INDIAN MUTINY

In 1857 Indian soldiers (or 'sepoys') serving Britain's East India Company rose up against their commanders in northern India. In some regions this mutiny turned into a general uprising. The rebels captured Delhi and laid siege to Kanpur and Lucknow. They were defeated in 1858. From now on, however, India would be ruled not by the Company but by the British government itself. In 1877 Queen Victoria was declared Empress of India.

1842
Britain gains South China port of Hong Kong as colony

1857
The Indian Mutiny against the East India Company

1858
British government takes over the rule of India

1860
British and French troops sack Beijing, China

1877
Victoria is created Empress of India

191

THE CHINA TRADE

One crop grown in India was the opium poppy. It was made into a very addictive drug. Britain exported Indian opium to China. When the Chinese government tried to ban this deadly trade in 1839, Britain declared war. Britain won this shameful conflict and as a result gained the Chinese port of Hong Kong as a colony. The rest of China remained an independent empire, but was forced to grant more and more trading rights to Western nations. British and French troops sacked Beijing, the Chinese capital, in 1860.

IN SOUTHEAST ASIA

The British, French and Dutch all sought to control the rich Southeast Asian trade in spices, rubber, timber and minerals. An Englishman called Stamford Raffles founded Singapore in 1819, and in 1826 it joined Penang and Malacca as the Straits Settlements. In 1841 another Englishman, James Brooke, helped to defeat a rebellion against the Sultan of Brunei, on the island of Borneo. As a reward he was made the ruler, or Rajah, of Sarawak.

One of China's chief exports was tea. Fast merchant ships called clippers raced back to Britain with their cargo. Clippers were the finest sailing vessels ever built. One of them, the Cutty Sark, can still be seen beside the River Thames at Greenwich, London.

During the Indian Mutiny, the city of Delhi was held by the rebels for three months. British troops under the command of Sir Colin Campbell stormed its defences in September 1857.

192

≈≈ **1793**
Settlement of the first free
colonists in Australia

≈≈ **1840**
Treaty of Waitangi: Britain
claims New Zealand

≈≈ **1845**
Start of First Maori War, New
Zealand (Second War 1860)

≈≈ **1851**
Start of the gold rush in
Australia

≈≈ **1854**
Miners' revolt at Eureka, near
Ballarat, Australia

TO THE ENDS
OF THE EARTH

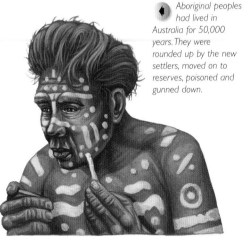

Aboriginal peoples had lived in Australia for 50,000 years. They were rounded up by the new settlers, moved on to reserves, poisoned and gunned down.

B RITAIN'S EMPIRE grew to take in the vast, unknown land of Australia, as well as New Zealand and many South Pacific islands. At first, the British only used as Australia as a place to send prisoners. Many convicts died on the outward voyage and life in the prison colonies was harsh. Some escaped and took ship to New Zealand.

BRITAIN'S AUSTRALIAN COLONIES

By 1793 the first free settlers had arrived in New South Wales, but it was 1868 before all transportation of convicts to Australia came to an end. Settlers gradually opened up the dry lands of the interior. New or breakaway colonies were founded – Van Diemen's Land (Tasmania) in 1804, Western Australia in 1829, South Australia in 1836, Victoria in 1851, Queensland in 1859. By 1861 an expedition led by Robert O'Hara Burke and William Wills had made the hazardous journey from Melbourne to the north coast.

GOLD NUGGETS, WOOLLY SHEEP

In 1851 gold was discovered in New South Wales. Settlers poured into Australia in search of a fortune. The miners, or 'diggers', had few legal rights and a major revolt took place at Eureka, near Ballarat in Victoria, in 1854. Thirty miners were killed by mounted police. Another great source of wealth was sheep farming. By 1890 there were 100 million sheep in Australia.

The discovery of gold in Australia led to further exploration and a rapid increase in the settler population, which reached a million in 1861.

∾ 1861
Burke and Wills cross the interior of Australia

∾ 1868
Last transportation of convicts to Australia

∾ 1874
Fiji becomes part of the British empire

∾ 1901
Australian colonies unite as a federal Commonwealth

∾ 1907
New Zealand becomes a Dominion of the British empire

193

WHOSE AUSTRALIA?

Between the 1823 and 1855 the Australian colonists gained increasing rights to govern their own affairs, and by 1901 the various colonies had come together to form a federation, the Commonwealth of Australia. There was a new Parliament – but the true Australians, the Aborigines, were denied the vote until 1967.

NED KELLY THE OUTLAW

Ned Kelly, the son of an Irish convict, was born in Victoria in 1855. He became an outlaw, or 'bushranger', whose gang robbed banks and stole cattle. After a train was held up at Glenrowan, three of the gang were killed. Ned Kelly was captured and hanged in1880.

▶ When Ned Kelly was finally captured he was dressed in home-made armour.

NEW ZEALAND AND THE MAORIS

New Zealand was inhabited by the Maoris, a Polynesian people, and by a small number of mostly British settlers. In 1840 the British signed a treaty with Maori chiefs at Waitangi and New Zealand became a British colony. The settlers failed to honour the treaty and Maoris fought them from 1845 to 1847 and again from 1860 to 1872. From 1856, the settlers had their own Parliament. Many gold miners and farmers now arrived in New Zealand. From the 1880s, advances in refrigeration meant that lamb could be shipped back to Britain.

ACROSS THE PACIFIC

European seafarers, planters and Christian missionaries were now spreading out through the islands of the South Pacific. Many islanders fell victim to kidnappers called 'blackbirders', and were shipped off illegally to forced labour in Australia. Fiji became British in 1874 and Britain claimed southeastern New Guinea (Papua) in 1884. By the end of the century, most Pacific islands were under foreign rule.

◀ This war canoe was made by Solomon Islanders. Britain gained control of these Pacific islands between 1893 and 1900.

194

⚘ **1806**
Cape Colony, South Africa, under British rule

⚘ **1873**
Ashanti Wars on the Gold Coast (Ghana) – to 1901

⚘ **1873**
David Livingstone dies in what is now Zambia

⚘ **1878**
The Zulu War in South Africa (to 1879)

⚘ **1881**
First South African ('Boer') War

İΠTO AFRICA

The map shows:
Spanish Morocco, Morocco, Ifni, Algeria, Libya, Egypt, Tunisia, Rio de Oro, French West Africa, Gambia, Port Guinea, Sierra Leone, Liberia, Gold Coast, Togo, São Tomé, Nigeria, Kamerun, French Equatorial Africa, Anglo-Egyptian Sudan, Eritrea, French Somalila, Ethiopia, British Somalila, Italian Somalila, Uganda, British East Africa, F.E.A, Belgian Congo, Cabinda, German East Africa, Angola, N.Rhodesia, Nysaland, German South West Africa, S.Rhodesia, Mozambique, Madagascar, Bechuanaland, Swaziland, Union of South Africa, Basutoland, Basutoland

Legend:
- Belgian
- British
- French
- German
- Italian
- Portuguese
- Spanish
- Independent

T HE BRITISH may have ended their part in the slave trade, but it remained a curse in many parts of Africa. European explorers and Christian missionaries were now braving lions, spears and tropical fevers as they led expeditions into the interior. They were followed by traders, prospectors, colonists. big-game hunters – and soldiers. By the end of Queen Victoria's reign, almost all of Africa was under European rule.

◄ The European powers competed with each other to control Africa. There were wars of resistance by peoples all over Africa, but they were helpless against troops armed with modern firearms. This map shows who ruled Africa in 1890.

SHARING THE SPOILS
Africans were now used as a labour force, but were often little better off than slaves. Their job was to extract the riches of the continent for their colonial rulers. In southern and eastern Africa the best farmland was seized by white settlers. At the Conference of Berlin in 1884-1885, whole regions of Africa were shared out between rival European powers. They knew almost nothing about the peoples living there and cared little for their needs.

EAST AFRICAN LANDS
In 1887 the British East African Company leased the Kenya coast from its ruler, the Sultan of Zanzibar. Eight years later, Britain claimed the interior, eventually creating a colony called Kenya. British rule extended into neighbouring Uganda and (after 1918) into Tanganyika (now the mainland of Tanzania). Railways were built by labourers brought in from India, while farmers seized the highlands and planted coffee.

◄ Explorers and traders led armed expeditions into the interior from the East African coast. They hired porters to carry their equipment.

DAVID LIVINGSTONE
When the Scottish explorer David Livingstone died of fever in what is now Zambia, in 1873, his African servants preserved his body and carried it all the way to the coast, a journey on foot which took them nine months. Livingstone was a Christian missionary and a tireless campaigner against slavery, who explored the lands around the River Zambezi.

◄ Livingstone was the first European to see the Victoria Falls and Lake Nyasa.

1885
General Charles Gordon
killed in Khartoum, Sudan

1886
Lagos, Nigeria, becomes British
colony

1895
East African Protectorate
(later colony of Kenya)

1898
British and Egyptian victory at
Omdurman, Sudan

1899
Second South African
('Boer') War (until 1902)

195

SUEZ TO SUDAN

In 1875 Britain became chief shareholder in the new, French-built Suez Canal, which cut through Egypt Britain soon became more powerful in Egypt than the government itself. It also took control of Sudan, to the south. In 1877 British General Charles Gordon became governor of Sudan. He was killed at Khartoum in 1885, after an uprising led by the fiery religious leader Muhammad Ahmed, known as the *Mahdi* ('saviour'). In 1898 the British avenged Gordon's death at Omdurman, killing 11,000 Sudanese warriors.

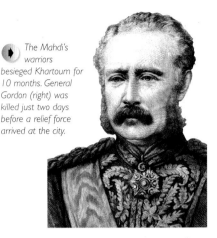

The Mahdi's warriors besieged Khartoum for 10 months. General Gordon (right) was killed just two days before a relief force arrived at the city.

ASHANTI GOLD

West Africa's Guinea Coast was also occupied by British empire builders. In 1874 they invaded Ashanti territory and destroyed the capital, Kumasi. In 1901 these lands became Gold Coast colony (modern Ghana), with an economy based on cocoa. Between 1861 and 1906 the huge colony of Nigeria was also created, out of various West African territories and trading posts.

This splendid leather helmet, decorated with gold and silver, was worn at the Ashanti royal court.

SOUTHERN AFRICA

In 1806 the British gained control of Cape Colony, South Africa. The Dutch had settled the area since the 1650s and resented British rule. In 1837 these 'Afrikaners' or 'Boers' ('farmers') left the Cape. They headed for the interior, where they founded independent republics. When rich reserves of diamonds and gold were discovered there, British empire builder and businessman Cecil Rhodes saw this as a great opportunity. His miners poured in the area, but Afrikaner president, Paul Kruger would not give these outsiders rights in his farmers' republic. In 1899 a bitter war broke out between the British and the Boers. Peace was made in 1902 and the Union of South Africa was formed in 1910.

In South Africa, the British clashed with highly disciplined armies of the Zulu nation. These inflicted a crushing defeat on British troops at Isandhlwana in 1879. Away from the main battlefield, a small British force at Rorke's Drift (right) fought off attacks by about 4,000 Zulus. British rule soon spread out from South Africa into the countries we now call Lesotho, Botswana, Swaziland, Malawi, Zambia and Zimbabwe.

⚡ **1831**
British Guiana (Guyana)
becomes a colony

⚡ **1833**
Falkland Islands (*Islas Malvinas*)
become a British colony

⚡ **1834**
Slavery ends in Britain's
Caribbean islands (to 1838)

⚡ **1840**
Act of Union between Lower
and Upper Canada

⚡ **1862**
British Honduras (Belize)
becomes British colony

NORTH AND
SOUTH ATLANTIC

The Inuit or Eskimo people
lived in scattered settlements
in the Canadian Arctic.

Q UEEN Victoria's empire took in remote
Atlantic outposts such as St Helena,
Tristan da Cunha and the Falkland
Islands. It governed Bermuda and
many Caribbean islands. On the American
mainland, the lands now known as Guyana and
Belize were all part of her empire, as well as
Canada's vast forests and prairies.

CANADA BECOMES A DOMINION

In 1791 Canada had been divided along the
Ottawa River. Lower Canada was the French-
speaking area, while Upper Canada was
English-speaking. These two were united in
1840, taking in the provinces of Ontario,
Quebec, Nova Scotia and New Brunswick.
A parliament was set up in 1849 and in 1858
Ottawa became the Canadian capital, the
personal choice of Queen Victoria. In 1867
Canada was made a self-governing Dominion
of the British empire. This was set up along
federal lines, with each province keeping its
own elected assembly.

PRAIRIES AND FORESTS

Canada continued to expand into lands occupied
by its First Peoples and by the Métis. They rose
up in rebellion in 1867, under the leadership of
Louis Riel, but were defeated. Manitoba joined
Canada (1870), British Columbia (1871), Prince
Edward Island (1873), Alberta and Saskatchewan
(1905). Poor farmers from all over Europe
arrived to settle the Canadian prairies, and
prospectors searching for gold arrived in the
remote Northwest in 1896. Canada prospered
from its timber, oil, mineral wealth and fisheries.
The last province to join the Canadian
federation was Newfoundland, in 1949.

The building of
railways encouraged
settlement of Canada's
prairie provinces and the
far west. The Canadian
Pacific Railway spanned
the country coast-to-coast
by 1885.

THE CARIBBEAN ISLANDS

In the 1830s, slavery was ended in Britain's Caribbean colonies, which were known as the 'West Indies'. Many freed slaves moved off the plantations and lived by farming small plots of land, or fishing. They remained desperately poor and there was an uprising against the British governor on Jamaica in 1865, led by George William Gordon and Paul Bogle. On Trinidad, contracted labourers were brought in from Asia to work on the sugar plantations, but the majority population throughout the Caribbean region was now of African descent.

CARIBBEAN CARNIVAL

Trinidad and some other Caribbean islands began to celebrate Carnival in the 1800s. This festival had been brought to the region from Catholic Europe. At first, slaves were not allowed to take part, but after they were freed they made it their own, with dancing, singing and drumming to African rhythms. From the Asian community came spectacular costumes and masks.

Carnival originally marked the beginning of Lent, the Christian period of fasting.

Slavery had dominated the culture and economy of the Caribbean for 300 years, when it was finally phased out in the 1830s.

IN CENTRAL AND SOUTH AMERICA

In 1862 a small region of the Central American coast, occupied by British loggers, was made into a colony called British Honduras (modern Belize). In South America, sugar-producing British Guiana (modern Guyana) had become a colony in 1834. British people played an important part in the development of other South American lands, too, building railways high into the Andes mountains.

Weathered wood, verandahs, shutters and porches are a reminder of the colonial age in Belize, formerly British Honduras.

7

THE
MODERN AGE

1902–2000

THE WORLD AT A GLANCE

ELSEWHERE IN EUROPE

1914
The First World War, fighting across Europe (until 1918)

1917
Revolutions in Russia, Bolsheviks (Communists) seize power

1933
The National Socialist (Nazi) party comes to power in Germany

1936
Civil War between Republicans and Nationalists in Spain (until 1939)

1939
Second World War, Germany overruns Europe (defeated 1945)

1948
Start of 'Cold War'. Europe divided into Communist East and Capitalist West.

1957
Treaty of Rome: the European Economic Community (later European Union)

1990
Communist governments fall in Eastern Europe, end of the Cold War

ASIA

1912
The last Chinese emperor, a young boy, is forced to give up the throne

1931
Japan invades Manchuria (northeastern China)

1940
Japan starts invasion of Southeast Asia in Second World War

1945
United States drops atomic bombs on Hiroshima and Nagasaki in Japan

1947
British India divided into two independent states, India and Pakistan

1948
Israel declares an independent state in Palestine, southwest Asia

1949
Communists defeat Nationalists in China, found a People's Republic

1979
An Islamist revolution in Iran, the Shah (emperor) is overthrown

AFRICA

1914
First World War: colonial powers fight in Africa, Germany loses empire (1918)

1942
Second World War: massive tank battles in North African desert

1953
Egypt becomes a republic (nationalises Suez Canal 1956)

1957
The Gold Coast becomes the independent nation of Ghana

1960
Nigeria gains independence from Britain

1960
Belgian Congo becomes independent, start of long civil war

1961
Tanganyika becomes independent (Uganda 1962, Kenya 1963)

1994
Democracy introduced in South Africa: Nelson Mandela first Black President

"World science, world wars and the search for world peace..."

first world war ambulance

NORTH AMERICA

1911
Revolution in Mexico: president overthrown, land reform

1914
Canada enters the First World War (United States, 1917)

1929
Wall Street 'crash' – US economic problems leads to Great Depression

1939
Canada enters the Second World War (United States, 1941). War ends 1945

1959
Revolution in Cuba, Fidel Castro seizes power

1961
USA becomes involved in Vietnam War, in Southeast Asia (until 1973)

1962
Jamaica and Trinidad gain independence from Britain

1963
US President John F Kennedy is assassinated in Dallas, Texas

SOUTH AMERICA

1910
Massive oil reserves discovered in Venezuela

1946
Juan Perón wins general election in Argentina

1949
Bitter civil war in Colombia, La Violencia

1960
Brasília replaces Rio de Janeiro as the capital of Brazil

1966
Guyana gains independence from Britain

1973
Chile's elected government is overthrown, Pinochet dictatorship

1975
Independence for Suriname, mass emigration to Netherlands

1982
Falklands War between Britain and Argentina in South Atlantic

OCEANIA

1907
New Zealand becomes a Dominion within the British empire

1914
Australia, New Zealand enter First World War (until 1918)

1918
Germany defeated, loses its Pacific island possessions

1931
Statute of Westminster confirms Australian independence

1939
Australia, New Zealand enter the Second World War (until 1945)

1941
Japan bombs Pearl Harbor (Hawaii), invades Pacific islands (until 1945)

1967
Aborigines granted citizenship rights in Australia

1968
Independence for Nauru (Fiji and Tonga 1970, Vanuatu 1980)

200

✝ **1902**
Coronation of Edward VII,
son of Queen Victoria

✝ **1902**
London's population reaches
6.5 million

✝ **1904**
The *Entente* ('Agreement')
is signed between France
and Britain

✝ **1906**
Germans and British compete
in building of battleships

✝ **1908**
Boy Scouts founded (Girl
Guides 1910)

THE EDWARDIAN AGE

Q UEEN Victoria's funeral was held
on 2 February 1902. It was
attended by rulers from all over
Europe, many of them her
relatives. The new king was Edward VII.
During his 60 years as Prince of Wales,
he had led a roguish life of pleasure.
How would he fare as a ruler?

UPSTAIRS, DOWNSTAIRS
The reign of Edward VII is often remembered as a
golden age, a brief period of peace before the tide
of war broke over Europe. For the aristocracy, it
was a time of lavish weekend house parties, of
balls, regattas and visits to the theatre.

The middle classes in the growing suburbs
worked in banks or businesses, played tennis and
sang songs around the piano. Even middle class
homes could afford servants and cooks. They
worked 'below stairs', polishing boots or cleaning
the silver. Upstairs were the halls, landings and
family rooms, often furnished with umbrella
stands, drapes and dark wooden furniture.

*Edward VII's reign would only last nine years, but
he was an active and effective ruler. His visit to
Paris in 1903 helped to prepare the ground for close
ties between Britain and France.*

*Edwardian ladies and gentlemen
enjoying the Henley Regatta*

✛ 1909
First old age pensions in
United Kingdom

✛ 1911
Coronation of
George V as Emperor
of India

✛ 1912
Robert Falcon Scott and his
team die on South Pole
expedition

✛ 1913
Senghenydd mining disaster,
South Wales: 439 miners die

✛ 1914
Two million British workers
are on strike

201

RULERS OF THE UNITED KINGDOM

House of Saxe-Coburg and Gotha

✤ Edward VII   1901–1910

House of Windsor (new name as from 1917)
✤ George V   1910–1936
✤ Edward VIII (abdicated)   1936
✤ George VI   1936–1952
✤ Elizabeth II   1952

Many working class women were
employed 'in service', as maids in
private homes. They wore neat uniforms.

POVERTY AND UNEMPLOYMENT

For the working class, this age was far from golden. By 1904
there were 800,000 people in England and Wales registered for
poor relief. In 1913, half a million school children were
reported suffering from disease or a poor diet. There were many
tragic mining accidents and industrial disasters – and an ever-
growing number of strikes, as trade unions campaigned for
fairer and safer working conditions. In 1909 the Liberal
government brought in the first old age pensions.

THE GROWING CRISIS

Europe was arming for war. The German *Kaiser* was building up
a naval fleet to challenge British rule of the seas. Britain made
alliances with France in 1904 and with Russia in 1907. In 1914,
these treaties were put to the test. The heir to the Austrian
throne, Archduke Franz Josef, was assassinated in Bosnia by a
young Serbian nationalist. Austria,
encouraged by Germany, went to war
with Serbia. Serbia was in turn
supported by Russia. Within just a
few weeks, almost the whole of
Europe was on the brink of war
– including the United
Kingdom.

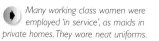

From 1900 to 1915 Labour
leader Keir Hardie, a Scot,
represented the Welsh town of
Merthyr Tydfil in Parliament. He was a
pacifist, strongly opposed to both the
Boer War and the First World War.

GOING SHOPPING

In Edwardian shop windows
there were elaborate displays
of goods or produce, and well
known advertisements for tea
or soap. Shop assistants were
formally dressed, with
starched white aprons and
cuffs. Goods could be
delivered to the home by
bicycle. Department stores,
which had first arrived in
Britain in the Victorian
period, were now popular in
cities. Here, clothes and
furnishings and other assorted
goods were all on sale under
the same roof.

202

✝ 1904
Mainline electric train runs
Liverpool to Southport

✝ 1904
First turbine-powered ocean
steamer launched in Belfast

✝ 1904
The Rolls Royce motor car
company is founded

✝ 1907
Brooklands motor racing
circuit opens in Surrey

✝ 1907
The first motorcycle TT race is
held on the Isle of Man

G.N.R.

SKEGNESS
IS SO BRACING

AN AGE OF SPEED

T HE NEW century saw a revolution in transport, even more extreme than the coming of the railways. Motor cars were on the road in ever greater numbers, along with motor omnibuses (buses), charabancs (open coaches), lorries and trams. Huge steamships called 'liners' – after the shipping lines that owned them – were powering their way across the oceans. Most amazingly, the sky itself was conquered, as the first airships and planes took to the air.

A poster for the Great Northern Railway advertises seaside holidays, which many families could now afford.

Steam locomotion had reached its peak by 1938, when Mallard *attained the speed of 126 mph (202 kph).*

BY LAND...

Steam locomotives were becoming ever more powerful and electric trains were in use in Britain as early as 1904. Some of the first cars were driven by steam too, or by electric batteries. The most successful were petrol-driven. Britain's early manufacturers included Charles Rolls and Frederick Henry Royce, who joined forces in 1904 to produce luxury cars, and W R Morris, who started production of more modest cars in Oxford, in 1913.

MALLARD

60022

ENGINES OF CHANGE

The motoring age gave people more freedom of movement than ever before in history. It seemed as if the distances across the British Isles were shrinking. Motor buses could now reach even remote country districts and traffic jams were still quite rare. Ambulances could take people to hospital – and away from battlefields, for motor transport would also change the nature of war.

Steam-powered omnibus, 1900s. Omnibus means 'for all' in Latin.

✝ 1919
John Alcock and Arthur Whitten Brown fly across the Atlantic Ocean

✝ 1919
Britain's first international airline service to Le Bourget, Paris, France

✝ 1919
British airship R34 flies across the Atlantic from Scotland to New York City

✝ 1928
The Morris Minor car brings in age of cheap family motoring

✝ 1930
Amy Johnson flies solo from England to Australia

203

By sea...

In 1897 an Irish engineer called Charles Parsons built a vessel called *Turbinia* at Heaton, in County Durham. Parsons had perfected the use of steam turbines (vanes rotated at high speed) in order to power ships at speeds of up to 35 knots (64 kph). By 1907 turbines enabled even the huge liner *SS Lusitania* to cross the Atlantic Ocean at an average speed of 23 knots (43 kph). Liners were fitted out with luxurious cabins, splendid dining rooms and ballrooms.

At the turn of the century steamships were ousting the last sailing vessels from coastal ports. These are Barry Docks in South Wales, which in 1906 exported over 9 million tonnes of coal.

Large aeroplanes designed to land on water were popular in the 1930s and 40s. They were called 'flying boats'. The Sunderland (right) saw service with the Royal Air Force.

THE TITANIC

In April 1912 the finest ocean liner ever built, pride of the White Star Line, was making its first voyage, across the North Atlantic. Although the *SS Titanic* weighed 46,329 tonnes, it was said to be unsinkable. However it hit an iceberg at high speed and sank to the sea bottom, drowning 1,513 passengers and crew in the freezing water. Some 700 escaped in lifeboats.

... And air

The first flight by an aeroplane took place in 1903, in the United States. Five years later, planes were flying in Britain, too. The first ones were fragile machines, often 'biplanes' (having twin wings). Flight developed rapidly during the First World War (1914-1918) and in the 1920s and 30s air races and flying shows became popular spectator sports. In the 1930s Imperial Airways were carrying small numbers of passengers to Africa, India and Australia. Airships – large gas-filled, cigar-shaped aircraft powered by engines – competed with aeroplanes until 1937, when a series of accidents made them unpopular.

Malcolm Campbell's Bluebird 1931.

204

✝ 1914
August: Germany invades Belgium, Britain declares war

✝ 1914
October: the First Battle of Ypres

✝ 1915
March: British fleet blockades German ports

✝ 1915
April: Australians, New Zealanders and British land at Gallipoli, in Turkey

✝ 1916
May: naval battle off Jutland

I N August 1914 the United Kingdom and Germany went to war. Most people believed it would all be over by Christmas, but this terrible conflict dragged on for over four years. It was known as the Great War. Today we call it the First World War, for it was fought in many different lands by armies from many nations.

FIRST WORLD WAR

⬤ Along the Western Front, the warring armies dug themselves into trenches defended by razor-sharp barbed wire.

NATIONS AT WAR

As well as British and Irish soldiers, empire troops included Indians, East Africans, South Africans, Canadians, Australians and New Zealanders. Their allies in the 'Entente' included France and its empire, Japan, Italy (from 1915), Russia (until 1918) and the United States (from 1917). Ranged against them were the 'Central Powers' – Germany, Austria–Hungary, Bulgaria and Turkey.

⬤ The area between the two enemy forces was called no-man's-land. It was a strip of stinking mud riddled with shell-holes and raked by machine-gun fire.

THE WAR POETS

B efore the First World War, poets used to celebrate victories and write of heroic deeds. Now many wrote of horror and anger at seeing so many young men being killed like cattle. Great poets who served as soldiers included Wilfred Owen (1893-1918) and Siegfried Sassoon (1886-1967).

✞ **1916**
July-November: First Battle of the Somme, 1,043, 896 killed

✞ **1917**
October: British victory at Passchendaele

✞ **1917**
The war now costs Britain £7 million every day

✞ **1918**
November: Armistice – Germany surrenders

✞ **1919**
Treaty of Versailles – peace terms agreed

205

THE PEOPLE'S WAR

In the 1800s, wars had been fought by professional soldiers, far from home. Now, warfare was coming home. Civilians found that they could be bombed in their houses by the new planes and airships, and that passenger liners as well as warships could be attacked by submarines. In 1916 the British government began to conscript members of the public, calling them up to serve in the armed forces.

Ambulances carried wounded men from the front line. Severe wounds meant a return to 'Blighty' – the British Isles.

The Royal Flying Corps (forerunner of the Royal Air Force) was founded in 1912. During the war, its pilots could expect to live for just two weeks of combat. The most famous British fighter plane was the Sopwith Camel, in production from 1916.

TRENCHES AND MUD

Fighting took place in the snowy forests of eastern Europe, in Turkey and the deserts of Arabia, on the plains of East Africa. There were great naval battles and beneath the waves, submarines stalked Atlantic shipping.

The bloodiest fighting was on the Western Front, a long line of defensive trenches which stretched from Belgium, through France, down to the Swiss border. Soldiers on both sides lived and died in wretched conditions. Any who fled were tried for desertion and then shot.

Deadly new weapons made their appearance – poison gas in 1915 and tanks (right) in 1916.

A LOST GENERATION

In 1914 the soldiers had marched off to war in a patriotic mood, singing the popular songs of the day. When the guns fell silent in 1918, some 10 million young men had been killed in all the armies. Countless more were left blinded, disabled, or in a state of severe stress called 'shell-shock'. The Allies had won the war, but at a terrible cost.

Troops are ordered 'over the top', leaving their trenches for a new assault. Thousands of lives were often sacrificed to gain just a few metres of land.

206

✝ **1905**
Sinn Féin founded, with aim
of a united Irish republic

✝ **1913**
Ulster protestors
threaten violence if Home
Rule is passed

✝ **1914**
Home Rule is passed, but
postponed because of the war

✝ **1916**
The Easter Rising suppressed
in Dublin. Fifteen executed

✝ **1918**
Sinn Féin wins support in
general election

EASTER 1916

THE question of Irish home rule had been a burning political issue for a hundred years. In 1912 the proposal returned to Parliament in London. In Protestant Ulster, supporters of the union with Britain were prepared to use violence to oppose the bill. Their leader was lawyer Sir Edward Carson. Would Ireland be divided? Would there be civil war? The bill was passed in 1914 but immediately postponed. The First World War had broken out.

WRITERS AND DREAMERS

The new century was an inspiring time for Irish writers. George Bernard Shaw (1856-1950) was writing challenging essays and plays about great social issues. The playwright JM Synge (1871-1909) was director of Dublin's Abbey Theatre. The beautiful poems of WB Yeats (1865-1939) took Ireland as their theme and were inspired by the events of 1916. In 1914 James Joyce published *Dubliners*, short stories about life in the Irish capital. His later work, in the 1920s and 30s, shocked the world with a new kind of language which reflected humans' rambling thoughts, fears and dreams.

A pall of smoke hangs over central Dublin at Easter 1916. The rising by the Irish Volunteers and the Irish Citizen Army resulted in the death of 418 people.

THE EASTER RISING

Many Irishmen were soon fighting in the war, but to others there was another priority – fighting against the union. Sir Roger Casement, a well known Irish diplomat, sought help from Germany for a rising – but was captured as he landed from a German submarine.

It was Easter 1916 and an uprising was taking place in Dublin. The rebels seized the large General Post Office and their leader, Pádraig Pearse, proclaimed a republic. After five days they were shelled into surrender by the British army. At first they had little widespread support, but when 15 of them were executed by the British, Irish public opinion changed. At the general election of 1917, the republican party Sinn Féin ('Ourselves Alone') won an historic victory.

✠ 1921
Anglo-Irish Treaty, civil war in Ireland

✠ 1922
Irish Free State established, excluding Northern Ireland

✠ 1937
Free State gains new constitution as Éire

✠ 1939
Second World War: Ireland remains neutral (to 1945)

✠ 1949
Ireland becomes a full independent republic

207

IRA AND THE 'BLACK AND TANS'

Sinn Féin, led by Éamon de Valera, did not take up its seats in Parliament. Instead, it set up its own Irish Assembly, or Dáil Éireann. In 1919 a ruthless guerrilla organization, the Irish Republican Army (IRA), was set up to fight the British. It was countered by special military units sent in from England to help the police. Known from their uniform colours as the 'Black and Tans', their tactics were often brutal. In 1920 Ireland was split in two. In the north, six out of Ulster's nine counties were given their own parliament, while the the rest of Ireland had theirs.

An impression of the Irish landscape by painter Jack B Yeats. The brother of the poet W B Yeats, he also produced portraits of Irish life and comic strips.

After 1919 the nationalist cause was fought by the IRA, which opposed the partition of Ireland. In 1969 a breakaway group was formed, the Provisional IRA.

AN IRISH FREE STATE?

In 1921, Sinn Féin sent delegates to London, including Arthur Griffith and Michael Collins. They agreed to the partition of Ireland, with the south becoming a Free State, similar to a self-governing Dominion of the British empire. Back in Ireland their decision was rejected by de Valera, who wanted nothing short of an independent republic. A bitter war broke out within Sinn Féin. Collins was set to be head of the new Irish Free State government when he was murdered by the IRA.

THE ROAD TO A REPUBLIC

Sinn Féin refused to recognize a Free State government, but in the end de Valera decided that it could be used as a step towards a full republic. In 1926 he founded a new political party, Fianna Fáil ('Soldiers of Destiny'), and in 1933 another party was founded, Fine Gael ('Tribes of the Gaels'). In 1938 the Irish Free State declared independence under the name of Éire. Éire remained neutral in the Second World War (1939-1945) and in 1949 became the fully independent Republic of Ireland.

ARAN ISLANDERS

The Irish nationalists came from many different backgrounds, but they were inspired by the Gaelic culture, language and way of life. Nowhere had this survived in a more traditional form than amongst the fishermen and farmers of the Aran Islands, in Galway Bay. The islanders inspired the writer J M Synge and were the subject of a famous documentary film, *Man of Aran*, in 1934.

208

✝ 1889
A Women's Franchise
League is founded by
Emmeline Pankhurst

✝ 1893
New Zealand is first country
in the world where women
can vote

✝ 1903
A Women's Social and
Political Union (WSPU) is
founded

✝ 1907
Women's Enfranchisement Bill
is defeated in Parliament

✝ 1912
Suffragettes smash shop
windows and protest at the
House of Commons

VOTES FOR WOMEN

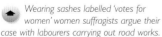 Wearing sashes labelled 'votes for women' women suffragists argue their case with labourers carrying out road works.

I N February 1913, the home of Chancellor David Lloyd George was destroyed by a bomb. In May of that year, a bomb was placed in St Paul's Cathedral, London. In June, during the Derby event at the Epsom races, a woman called Emily Davison dashed out and grasped the reins of a racehorse owned by the king. She was trampled beneath the hooves and died the next day.

A STRUGGLE FOR EQUALITY

The 1913 protests were all by women demanding suffrage – the right to vote. They were known as 'suffragettes' or 'suffragists'. Women had never been allowed to take a democratic part in choosing how the country was governed. Most men were shocked by the protests, for in those days women were expected to obey their husbands and raise children rather than take part in political campaigns. In 1889 a campaigner called Emmeline Pankhurst had founded the Women's Franchise League and in 1903 she and her daughter Christabel formed the Women's Social and Political Union (WSPU). The suffragists met with public ridicule and abuse, but they argued their case loud and long.

THE PANKHURSTS

Emmeline Pankhurst (1857-1928) campaigned for women's rights for forty years. She and her eldest daughter Christabel were often imprisoned. They stopped campaigning when the First World War broke out in 1914. Emmeline later joined the Conservative Party. Emmeline's other two daughters were also suffragists. Sylvia and Adela (who moved to Australia) actively opposed the war and became socialists.

 The Pankhursts all lived to see women gain equal voting rights with men.

☩ **1913**
Suffragettes bomb home of Chancellor, David Lloyd George

☩ **1913**
WSPU member Emily Davison dies in Derby protest

☩ **1918**
Votes granted to women over the age of 30

☩ **1919**
Nancy Astor is elected as Britain's first woman MP

☩ **1929**
Votes for women over 21 years of age

209

The sight of women brandishing placards and chaining themselves to railings infuriated many men in the Edwardian era.

PUBLIC PROTEST

The WSPU developed new forms of protest in order to gain publicity for their cause. They committed violent acts against property like smashing shop windows. When they raided the House of Commons, it resulted in 96 arrests. When they were sent to jail, they went on hunger strike, refusing to eat. The prison officers force-fed them through tubes. Under a special law, the authorities could keep releasing women hunger-strikers, only to send them back to prison again once they had recovered.

INTO THE WORKPLACE

During the First World War, men were needed to fight in the armed services and many were killed. Women took over jobs once done by men. They worked on the farms and in munitions factories, making shells and weapons for the front line. By the time the war was over, women had become more accepted as a part of the workforce. Public opinion was changing.

POLITICAL PROGRESS

In 1918, British women at last won the right vote in general elections, but only if they were aged over 30. It was not until 1929 that the voting age for men and women was equalized, at 21. During the 1920s more and more women found work as office secretaries, typists or telephone operators, but still received lower wages than men.

In 1919 American-born Nancy Astor became the first woman to be elected as a Member of Parliament, winning Plymouth for the Conservatives.

A woman bus conductor stands on the platform of a Number 19 double-decker bus. The twentieth century saw a revolution in women's role in society.

210

✝ **1896**
First cinema opens in United Kingdom

✝ **1914**
Charlie Chaplin goes to make films in Hollywood, USA

✝ **1919**
First jazz record to be released in United Kingdom

✝ **1922**
Fashion for wide trousers, known as 'Oxford bags', for men

✝ **1922**
British Broadcasting Company is set up (Corporation, 1927)

DANCE TO THE MUSIC

P EOPLE tried to forget the horrors of the First World War with dancing, popular songs and music, visits to the picture palace (cinema) or summer trips to the seaside. The stuffiness of the Edwardian era disappeared. Women wore shorter dresses. Their hair was now bobbed short, and was often curled into permanent waves ('perms'). They wore lipstick and face powder. They often smoked cigarettes – unaware of the risk to their health.

GOING TO THE PICTURES

The first films were silent, in black and white. A pianist played music to fit in with the story. The best known film star of all was Charlie Chaplin (1889-1977). During a childhood of poverty in south London, he performed on stage in the music halls. After 1914 he made comic films in Hollywood. In many of them he played a tramp. Chaplin hated social injustice and underlying the clowning there was often a serious message about the times he lived in.

JAZZ – AND JEEVES

The music of the new century was jazz, first played by African Americans in the USA. By 1919 this wild, free-flowing music was being heard in England. Wind-up record-players, or gramophones, now made it possible to play music and dance in the home. The good life of England in the 1920s and 30s was sent up by a witty writer called PG Wodehouse. His world was peopled by flappers, goofy young aristocrats and a butler named Jeeves – who was far wiser than his master.

✚ **1925**
Experimental television transmission, London

✚ **1927**
The first Ryder Cup golf match between Britain and the USA

✚ **1929**
First talking feature film made in UK: *Blackmail* by Alfred Hitchcock

✚ **1935**
First paperbacks published by Penguin Books

✚ **1936**
Edward VIII abdicates in favour of George VI

211

TUNING IN

The 'wireless' was all the rage. Schoolboys learned how to make very basic radio receivers, called 'crystal sets'. The British Broadcasting Company, established in 1922, was made into a Corporation (the BBC) in 1927. Soon people were listening to plays, music, sport, comedy shows and news, all in their own living room. King George V broadcast to the nation on Empire Day, 23 April 1924.

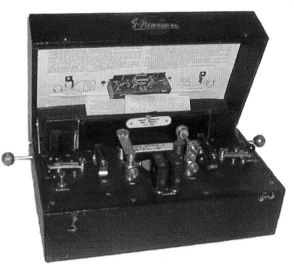

Fashionable, flighty young women were known as flappers. They shocked their parents with 'unladylike' American dances such as the Charleston.

The radio soon became a part of everyday life. News had once taken days to reach every corner of the British Isles. Now it could be broadcast as it happened.

Weekly visits to the cinema offered escape to the magical world of Hollywood stars.

A ROYAL CRISIS

In 1936 newspaper headlines reported a crisis in the royal family. George V had died and his eldest son Edward was due to follow him as king. However Edward intended to marry an American woman called Wallis Simpson, who was divorced. Divorce was considered to be scandalous in the 1930s. Public opinion forced Edward VIII to abdicate (resign) and his younger brother was crowned George VI in his place.

Edward VIII gave up the throne in order to marry Wallis Simpson. He became Duke of Windsor instead of king.

212

✛ **1920**
Limited financial aid provided
for the unemployed

✛ **1924**
Britain's first Labour
government

✛ **1926**
A General Strike brings
Britain to a halt

✛ **1929**
The Wall Street Crash: world
economic depression begins

✛ **1931**
Population of United Kingdom
is nearly 49 million

THE HUПGER YEARS

THE glitter of high society in the 1920s and 30s hid desperation and poverty. After 1922, the British economy slowed down and countless men who had fought for their country now found themselves jobless, while their families went hungry. Germany too faced economic chaos after the First World War, made worse by the harsh terms of the 1919 Treaty of Versailles. This dragged down the economy of the rest of Europe.

Armoured cars take to London streets during the General Strike. The government feared a Communist revolution, as had happened in Russia in 1917.

Life in Glasgow's Gorbals district was tough. It had some of the worst housing in Britain and a wretched record in public health.

✞ **1932**
Nearly 3 million people in Britain are unemployed

✞ **1934**
Nazi dictatorship in Germany under Adolf Hitler

✞ **1936**
Communists and Fascists fight in London's East End

✞ **1936**
Jarrow Crusade: protestors march from Tyneside to London

✞ **1936**
British and Irish volunteers fight in Spanish Civil War

213

THE GENERAL STRIKE

In 1926 a report on British coal mining called for wages to be lowered, yet the companies were demanding longer working hours. Miners went on strike and called on other workers to join them. Two million did and the country was paralysed. Middle-class volunteers tried to break the strike, driving buses and trains. The Trades Union Congress dropped their support within nine days, but it was another six months before the miners were defeated.

THE GREAT DEPRESSION

The United States now had the most powerful economy in the world. When it began to show signs of weakness in 1929, there was panic as people sold off their shares. The US economy crashed and European economies which depended on US credit came tumbling down too. Within a year, unemployment around the world had doubled. The crisis was so severe that British political parties joined together in a coalition government.

The dignity and endurance of the Jarrow marchers impressed many people. It brought home to them the desperate poverty in Britain's industrial regions.

PRIME MINISTERS OF THE UNITED KINGDOM	
✤ Arthur James Balfour (Conservative)	1902–1905
✤ Sir H Campbell Bannerman (Liberal)	1905–1908
✤ HH Asquith (Liberal)	1908–1915
✤ HH Asquith (coalition)	1915–1916
✤ David Lloyd George (coalition)	1916–1922
✤ Andrew Bonar-Law (Conservative)	1922–1923
✤ Stanley Baldwin (Conservative)	1923–1924
✤ Ramsay Macdonald (Labour)	1924
✤ Stanley Baldwin (Conservative)	1924–1929
✤ Ramsay Macdonald (Labour)	1929–1931
✤ Ramsay Macdonald (coalition)	1931–1935
✤ Stanley Baldwin (coalition)	1935–1937
✤ Neville Chamberlain (coalition)	1937–1940
✤ Sir Winston Churchill (coalition)	1940–1945

THE JARROW MARCH

During the 1930s, 'hunger marches' were held as workers from Wales, Scotland and the north of England marched on London to protest against unemployment. In 1936 two hundred men from Jarrow, on Tyneside, walked all the way to London on what they called a 'Crusade'. They were led by their Member of Parliament, Ellen Wilkinson, and were given food and sleeping places by supporters along the way.

THE RISE OF FASCISM

A new political system took root amidst Europe's economic chaos. Fascism first developed in Italy in 1921. It aimed to replace 'weak' democracies with thuggery, dicatorship and extreme nationalism. Fascists went under various names. Racist 'National Socialists' (Nazis) seized power in Germany in 1934. In 1936 'Falangists' attacked the democratic government in Spain. Fascist groups were formed in England and Ireland too. London's East Enders came out to stop them marching through the streets. Volunteers travelled to Spain to fight for or against Fascism in the Civil War.

214

✝ **1926**
John Logie Baird gives public demonstration of television

✝ **1928**
Penicillin is discovered by Alexander Fleming

✝ **1930**
Frank Whittle invents the jet engine

✝ **1935**
Robert Watson Watt perfects his radar system

✝ **1943**
A programmable electronic computer: Colossus

A BRAVE NEW WORLD

IN THE twentieth century, human understanding of life and the universe made rapid advances. New materials were invented, new technologies, new machines. The United Kingdom was often in the forefront of exciting new research and invention. However as science crossed new frontiers, it raised new fears. It could be used to save life and do good – but it could also be used to destroy life on a terrifying scale, in war.

TECHNOLOGY AND HOME DESIGN

In the 1920s and 30s many houses began to look less cluttered. Designers, inspired by German ideas, brought efficiency and hygiene to the kitchen. Electricity now powered all sorts of household gadgets, from refrigerators to washing machines. Such goods were still expensive, and it would be the 1950s before they became very common in the British Isles. New everyday materials included plastics – bakelite (1909), cellophane (1912), perspex (plastic glass,1930) and PVC (1943). Artificial fibres were developed too – nylon in 1935 and a British invention, terylene, in 1941.

A TELEVISION PIONEER

John Logie Baird (1888-1946) was a Scottish electrical engineer. In 1926 he gave the world's first public demonstration of television. The BBC used Baird's systems from 1929 to 1937. It was not until the 1950s that televisions became widely owned in Britain. Baird had experimented with colour television as early as 1928, but the BBC did not begin regular colour broadcasts until 1967.

John Logie Baird played a very important part in the invention and development of television.

Shining new buildings of glass, steel and concrete began to be built around British cities. The Hoover Building, at Perivale, West London, was constructed in 1935.

✠ **1948**
Manchester University's Mark I
stored-programme computer

✠ **1953**
The structure of DNA is
discovered at Cambridge

✠ **1955**
Christopher Cockerell
invents the hovercraft

✠ **1955**
First ultrasound scan used in
medicine

✠ **1957**
First large, mobile radio
telescope, Jodrell Bank

215

THE BOFFINS

In the 1940s and 50s, the slang word for inventors, scientists and engineers was 'boffins'. Frank Whittle was born in Coventry and joined the Royal Air Force. From 1930 onwards, he worked on theories of jet propulsion. The first jet aircraft was produced in Germany, but Whittle's engine was flight-tested by 1941, during the Second World War.

Radar (*R*adio *D*etecting *A*nd *R*anging) was also developed in various countries during the 1930s. It is a system which uses radio waves to detect objects such as aircraft. Britain's expert was a Scottish scientist called Robert Watson-Watt, who had an effective radar system up and running by 1935. It would play a crucial part in the coming war.

EARLY COMPUTERS

The most remarkable invention of the 1940s was the electronic computer. Colossus was the first programmable computer in Britain, built in 1943 to crack wartime codes. Manchester University's Mark I computer was built in 1948. The first computers were massive machines compared with today's, weighing many tonnes.

Frank Whittle's jet engine was the forerunner of those built in the United States and the Soviet Union during the 1940s and 50s.

LIFE AND THE LABORATORY

In 1928 a scientist called Alexander Fleming noticed mould growing on a culture dish in his laboratory. It contained an antibiotic – an organism which could destroy harmful bacteria in the human body. With the help of two Oxford research scientists, Ernst Chain and Howard Florey, it was developed into the drug penicillin.

It was in 1953 that one of life's great mysteries was finally solved – the structure of DNA. This is the chemical code that programmes all life, being passed on from one generation to the next. Research was carried out in London and Cambridge by Rosalind Franklin, Maurice Wilkins, Francis Crick and, American, James Watson.

Alexander Fleming's discovery saved countless lives.

The structure of DNA turned out to be a double spiral, or helix

✝ 1938
Munich Agreement
between Britain, France,
Germany and Italy

✝ 1939
Germany invades Poland,
Britain declares war on
Germany

✝ 1940
Rescue of British troops from
Dunkirk. Italy joins the war

✝ 1940
Germans invade the Channel
Islands. Battle of Britain fought
in the air.

✝ 1941
Germany invades Soviet
Union. Japan attacks USA at
Pearl Harbor

THE SECOND WORLD WAR

THE Nazi dictator of Germany, Adolf Hitler, was building up German military power. In 1938 British Prime Minister Neville Chamberlain made an agreement with Hitler at Munich, promising 'peace in our time'. It was soon broken. German tanks rolled into Czechoslovakia and Poland. By 1939 Britain and Germany were at war. The war spread around the globe like wildfire and claimed the lives of about 55 million troops and civilians, the bloodiest conflict in human history.

Fuselage
The body of the plane was still made of wood and fabric, around a steel tube.

In the late summer of 1940, the skies of Britain were filled with vapour trails and the sound of fighter aircraft. By the end of October, the Germans had lost 1733 planes, the Allies 915. The Battle of Britain had been won. The most common British fighter at this time was the Hawker Hurricane. It was mainly used for attacking German bombers.

Hawker Hurricane Mark I
Wingspan: 12.2m
Length: 9.59m
Height: 3.96m

St Paul's Cathedral rises above a blazing London skyline. German night-time bombing of Britain's major cities began on 7 September 1940. This 'Blitz' killed about 40,000 civilians and injured many more. Over a million homes were pounded into rubble.

V FOR VICTORY

In 1940 Winston Spencer Churchill (1874–1965) became British Prime Minister. As a young soldier, he had fought in the Sudan and he later served both as a Conservative and a Liberal MP. He was always a controversial politician, but in wartime he inspired people with his gritty personality, his brilliant speeches – delivered in a growling voice – and his shrewd judgement.

Winston Churchill gestures V – for 'Victory'

✛ 1942
Japan captures Singapore, taking 70,000 Allied prisoners

✛ 1942
Allied victory at El-Alamein, in the North African desert

✛ 1944
D-Day: Allies land on beaches of Normandy

✛ 1945
Hitler commits suicide, Germany surrenders to Allies

✛ 1945
Atomic bombs dropped on Japan. Japanese surrender

217

Cockpit
The *Hurricane* was a single-seater fighter.

Engine
The Rolls Royce Merlin III engine gave the plane a top speed of 520 kph.

Wings
The wings were armoured with metal and had an area of almost 24 square metres

Fuel tank
The *Hurricane* had a top range of 965 km.

Armament
The *Hurricane Mark I* had four 7.7mm machine guns built into each wing

The atomic bombs which brought the Second World War to an end utterly destroyed the Japanese cities of Hiroshima and Nagasaki.

BRITAIN STANDS ALONE

In 1940 Germany rapidly invaded Scandinavia, the Netherlands, Belgium and France. Fascist Italy entered the war on Germany's side, and the Balkans and Greece were invaded. Britain was isolated in Europe.

In 1941 Germany attacked its former ally, the Soviet Union (as Russia was then called), and Japan declared war on Britain and the United States. Japan had already invaded areas of China and it now advanced through Southeast Asia. Although Britain now had more enemies, it had also gained powerful allies.

Allied bombers pounded German cities.

THE TIDE TURNS

By 1943 the tide of the war was turning. The Soviet Red Army was pushing back the Germans in eastern Europe. The Allies had defeated them in North Africa and were advancing through Italy. On 6 June 1944, ('D-Day'), Allied troops landed in occupied France and began to battle their way eastwards. Germany was devastated by Allied bombing raids and surrendered in 1945.

After long and bitter fighting in the Pacific, the United States dropped two terrifying weapons of mass destruction on Japan – atomic bombs. Surrender was immediate.

HORROR OF THE CAMPS

The Nazis were racists. They blamed all the troubles of Europe on Jews, Slavs and Roma (Gypsies). They built secret 'concentration camps' where these peoples – alongside political opponents, disabled people and homosexuals – were forced into labour, shot, hanged or gassed to death. No fewer than six million Jews were murdered in this 'Holocaust'. As Allied troops invaded Germany and the lands that had been occupied, they were sickened to find starving prisoners and piles of corpses.

218

✝ 1945
Churchill defeated in General
Election, Labour takes power

✝ 1946
Nationalization of Bank
of England, coal mines
and railways

✝ 1947
Extremely severe winter
weather, snow and floods

✝ 1947
Education Act takes effect:
school leaving age raised
to 15 years

✝ 1948
The National Health Service is
founded in Britain

POST-WAR BRITAIN

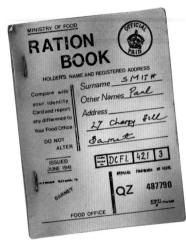

MINISTRY OF FOOD
OFFICIAL PAID
RATION BOOK
HOLDER'S NAME AND REGISTERED ADDRESS
Surname _SMITH_
Other Names _Paul_
Address
27 Cherry Hill
Barnet
ISSUED JUNE 1941
DCFL 421 3
QZ 487790
FOOD OFFICE

SOLDIERS returned to a Britain that was victorious but battered. In the cities there were bomb sites to be cleared. Barbed wire, concrete and mines had to be removed from British coasts. Shortages of food and other goods meant that these had to be strictly rationed – and the birth rate was suddenly rising as families looked forward to a safer, more peaceful world.

Ration books, brought in during the shortages of the Second World War, were still necessary in the post-war years. Certain goods could only be purchased with government-issued coupons.

The radical Welsh Labour politician Aneurin ('Nye') Bevan founded the National Health Service. Here, he is at a London health centre site in 1949.

GAMES AND FESTIVALS

Post-war life was far from easy, but the British people still had time for celebrations. London staged the first post-war Olympic Games in 1948, and in 1951 a Festival of Britain was held. It looked to the future and was marked by the construction of many very modern-looking public buildings.

The futuristic Skylon was the symbol of the Festival of Britain

THE WELFARE STATE

The Second World War had convinced many British people of the need for social change. In 1945 the wartime leader Sir Winston Churchill lost the election to the Labour Party under Clement Attlee. By 1950, 650,000 new publicly owned, low-rent 'council houses' had been built across the country. A National Health Service was founded in 1948, with free medicine for all. This 'welfare state', which aimed to provide care for all its citizens, was also supported by Conservative governments, from their re-election in 1951 until 1979.

✝ 1951
The Festival of Britain opens in London

✝ 1952
Air pollution creates heavy 'smogs' (smoke and fog) in cities

✝ 1951
Conservatives voted in under Sir Winston Churchill

✝ 1952
King George VI dies of cancer. Elizabeth II succeeds him

✝ 1954
Food rationing comes to an end in Britain

219

WHO RUNS INDUSTRY?

The Labour government of 1945 followed socialist policies, nationalizing privately owned industries. It believed that public ownership would bring about fairer working conditions and better serve the national interest. Coal mines, railways, road transport and public utilities such as gas, electricity and water were all brought under the control of national or local government. The Bank of England, too, was nationalized. The power of trade unions increased during the 1950s and 60s, and strikes became a common form of protest about pay or working conditions.

The post-war years saw the high point of spectator sports in Britain. Vast crowds gathered in the stands at football matches to see stars such as Stanley Matthews, who played for England 54 times and was named Footballer of the Year in 1948. Cricket too attracted its largest crowds ever, with 159,000 attending the 1948 England-Australia test match at Headingley, Leeds.

ON THE FARM

British farms aimed to increase production. Farms were mechanized, with milking machines being installed and electricity and piped water being brought to many remote country regions. New chemical sprays and fertilisers were used to improve crop yields, but these often proved to have a harmful effect on wildlife and the environment.

Everest was conquered by New Zealander Edmund Hillary and a Nepalese Sherpa called Tenzing Norgay.

Ploughs were now increasingly hauled by tractors instead of the big shire horses which had been used for centuries.

ON TOP OF THE WORLD

In 1953 the streets of the United Kingdom were decked out in red, white and blue for the coronation of Queen Elizabeth II. Some people watched the ceremony on newly purchased television sets.

Crowds lining the streets of London were thrilled by one news report that had just come in. Two members of a British-led expedition had become the first people to climb the world's highest peak, Mount Everest.

220

✝ 1947
British divide India into independent India and Pakistan

✝ 1948
Racist policy of apartheid introduced in South Africa

✝ 1949
The modern form of the Commonwealth replaces the old empire

✝ 1957
Independence for Gold Coast (Ghana) and Malaya

✝ 1960
Nigeria independent, South Africa leaves the Commonwealth

WINDS ⊙ OF CHANGE

SUN SETS ON THE BRITISH RAJ

The campaign for Indian freedom had begun as early as 1885, with the founding of the Indian National Congress. From the 1920s this movement was led by a former lawyer called Mohandas K Gandhi. He used non-violent methods to oppose the British, organising marches and fasts. He was often imprisoned.

Amidst bloody riots in 1947, Britain partitioned India into a mainly Hindu India and a mainly Moslem Pakistan. These two nations achieved independence, making the nationalists' dream come true. However Gandhi was dismayed by the religious hatred. He was assassinated by a Hindu fanatic in 1948.

Gandhi championed the poor and he himself led a very simple lifestyle. He became known as the Mahatma ('great soul').

I N 1960 the Conservative Prime Minister Harold Macmillan spoke in South Africa of a 'wind of change' blowing through the African continent. In reality this wind had been blowing throughout the world for some years. With the Second World War, the age of colonial empires had come to an end. In Africa, Asia and the Caribbean, people were demanding independence from Britain. At the same time, self-governing nations such as Canada, Australia and New Zealand were increasingly breaking ties with 'the mother country' and going their own way.

INDEPENDENCE STRUGGLES

Nationalist movements were founded in many parts of the British empire from the 1920s to the 1950s. Their leaders were often jailed and in some lands the independence campaigns turned violent. In Kenya, there was a bitter uprising from 1952, the Mau-Mau Rebellion. By the end of the 1950s, Britain was forced to realize that it no longer had the power to rule the world. Local political leaders were released from jail and became the leaders of independent nations.

During Kenya's Mau-Mau Rebellion, about 100 White settlers were killed. Many African Kenyans, mostly Kikuyu people, were also killed and tens of thousands were imprisoned in camps.

✛ 1961
Tanganyika becomes
independent (Tanzania 1964)

✛ 1962
Jamaica, Trinidad and Uganda
become independent

✛ 1963
Kenya becomes
independent

✛ 1965
White minority block path to
African rule in Rhodesia
(Zimbabwe)

✛ 1997
Hong Kong, Britain's last major
colony, is returned to China

221

A COMMONWEALTH OF NATIONS

In 1931 the lands of the British empire had been formally joined together within a 'British Commonwealth'. After 1947 this became a union of independent nations, most of which had formerly had links with Britain. 'British' was dropped from the title. While some newly independent nations kept the British monarch as their head of state, others became republics. The Commonwealth fostered economic and cultural links between its members.

In 1957 2000 Britons were emigrating to other Commonwealth countries each week. The Australian government encouraged many British people to settle in Australia.

Racial segregation in South Africa was called apartheid. It had a disastrous effect on the country for 46 years.

WHITE MINORITIES

In some parts of the former empire, the ruling Whites were not prepared to allow democracy or independence. In South Africa, governments refused to give the vote to people of African or Asian descent. South African society was cruelly segregated along racial lines until democratic government was introduced in 1994. In 1965 the White minority government in Rhodesia broke away from British rule, preventing independence (as Zimbabwe) until 1980.

AFTER THE EMPIRE

Many former colonies faced political strife in the years that followed independence. Their economies were still linked into colonial patterns and international powers still effectively controlled trade and industry. Local people had not been trained or educated. There was violence and corruption. In many places however, idealism and hard work did succeed in creating new and fairer societies.

222

✛ 1948
The *Empire Windrush* brings first Caribbean immigrants to Britain

✛ 1955
Increased immigration into Britain from Commonwealth lands

✛ 1958
White youths attack Black immigrants in Notting Hill, London

✛ 1965
Race Relations Act makes discrimination illegal (also in 1968)

✛ 1965
The first Caribbean carnival is staged in Notting Hill, London

ΠEW BRITOΠS

CHANGING TASTES

During the 1960s Indian and Chinese restaurants opened throughout the British Isles and were soon hugely popular. By the end of the century, it was claimed that chicken *tikka masala* was the British people's favourite meal – ahead even of fish and chips.

Indian curries became firm favourites in restaurants, take-aways and homes.

T HE BRITISH Isles have been settled by many different groups of people throughout their history. Black people were in Britain as early as Roman times. In the 1950s a new wave of immigration began from the lands of the former British empire. Like others before them, these immigrants came either to find work or to escape persecution in their homelands.

THE NEWCOMERS

In the 1950s, British governments recruited many workers from the Caribbean region – where there was widespread unemployment – to staff National Health Service hospitals or to work in public transport. Others came in search of jobs and were joined by their families. Indians and Pakistanis arrived too during the 1960s. In 1972 Asians, including many who held British passports, were expelled from their homes in Uganda. Most of the new arrivals settled in large industrial cities such as London or Birmingham.

ARRIVING IN HOPE

The first Caribbean immigrants to arrive in Britain came on board the *Empire Windrush*, a ship which docked at Tilbury, London, on 22 June 1948. They numbered 500, many of them ex-servicemen hoping to make use of skills they had learned while fighting for Britain during the war. The group included a dozen women and one 13 year-old boy.

Young Caribbeans came to England in search of a decent wage, but found that there was little money left to save or send home.

✝ **1968**
Conservative politician Enoch Powell speaks against immigration

✝ **1972**
Asians expelled from Uganda, many settle in Britain

✝ **1976**
Commission for Racial Equality is founded by UK government

✝ **1976**
A further Race Relations Act (amended in 2000)

✝ **1999**
About 2 percent of Britons are of African, Caribbean or Asian descent

223

A COLD WELCOME

It was the ancestors of the 1950s and 60s immigrants who had created the wealth of the British empire. The new arrivals were often hard-working and enterprising. Some were trained as doctors, nurses or teachers.

However they often met with a lack of understanding and prejudice. They might be refused lodgings, passed over for jobs or even attacked in the streets. Some politicians stirred up trouble by exaggerating the scale of immigration and forecasting touble. Racist political parties were formed, but they remained small and were actively opposed by many British people.

BRITAIN OF MANY CULTURES

Racism had certainly not ended in Britain by the end of the century but many prejudices had been effectively challenged and public attitudes were changing. Laws had been passed against discrimination and many British people began to understand and respect the other cultures in their midst.

A Caribbean carnival, first held in London's Notting Hill district in 1965, soon developed into one of Europe's most popular street festivals. A love of Caribbean music and dance styles have forged links between young people for over 40 years.

The golden dome of a mosque rises above Regent's Park, in central London. Islam, Sikhism and Hinduism now played an important part in modern British life, alongside Judaism and Christianity.

224

✝ **1946**
Churchill warns of an 'Iron Curtain' dividing Europe

✝ **1948**
West Berlin is blockaded by Communists. Allies fly in vital supplies

✝ **1949**
China becomes a Communist republic under Mao Zedong

✝ **1949**
British troops fight Communist rebels in Malayan jungle

✝ **1950**
Korean War (to 1953). Multi-national force fights Communists

THE COLD WAR

THE PERIOD from 1945 to 1990 is often called the Cold War. This refers to the tension between Russia (the 'Soviet Union') and the countries of the West, led by the United States. The Soviet Union was still ruled by the Communist Party, although supporters of its ruthless leader Joseph Stalin (who died in 1953) had by now killed most of the idealists who had taken part in the revolution. The West remained capitalist. In the United States anti-Communist feelings reached fever pitch in the 1950s. The world teetered on the brink of war.

THE IRON CURTAIN

After the Second World War, Europe was divided into two power blocs. Winston Churchill said it was as if an 'iron curtain' had fallen across the continent. In 1949 Western Europe and North America joined in a military alliance, the North Atlantic Treaty Organization (NATO). Eastern and Central Europe were now in the hands of Communist governments and in 1955 they united within the Warsaw Pact. The rival blocs faced each other in Germany, which was divided in two. The former capital, Berlin, was itself divided and surrounded by Communist territory. British troops were stationed in the west.

Long-range targets
The first Polaris missile had a range of 2,200 kilometres. The final model, adopted by the United Kingdom in 1969, had a range of 4,800 kilometres.

NATIONAL SERVICE

During the Second World War, young men had been called up into the armed services. Conscription continued until 1962, even though the United Kingdom was no longer at war. Some said that this National Service was good for young people, teaching them discipline and a trade.

Many recruits felt that weapons drill and army routine served little use in peacetime.

The Polaris missile system was developed in the United States in the 1950s and came into service in 1960. By 1968 it was being used by Britain's Royal Navy. It was the first missile to be fired from submarines. In the 1990s the Royal Navy replaced Polaris with the Trident missile system.

Polaris missile
Each missile was 9.4 metres long and 1.4 metres thick. It carried a nuclear warhead.

✝ 1952
Britain's first atomic bomb is tested in Monte Bello islands, Australia

✝ 1958
Campaign for Nuclear Disarmament (CND) founded in London

✝ 1961
East Germans divide Berlin with fortified wall (until 1989)

✝ 1968
Massive protests in London against the US war in Vietnam

✝ 1990
The Cold War comes to an end, Soviet Union collapses

225

WHEN THE WAR TURNED HOT

In Asia the Cold War turned hot, especially after China too became ruled by Communists in 1949. The newly formed United Nations Organization sent a multi-national force, including many British troops, to fight a Communist invasion of Korea. This war lasted from 1950 to 1953. From 1965 the United States also fought a bitter war against Communists in Vietnam, but was defeated in 1973. Cold War tensions spread around the world, preventing peaceful development in Africa, Asia, Central and South America.

SPIES WHO CAME IN FROM THE COLD

Spies slip through Checkpoint Charlie on the Berlin Wall, in a scene from the film Funeral In Berlin, 1966.

Much of the conflict between the Cold War powers was secret, carried out by spies and undercover agents. Some Russian and Central European spies were secretly working for the west, while some members of the British secret service gave away secrets to the Soviet Union. These included Guy Burgess, Donald Maclean, Kim Philby and Anthony Blunt. British writers loved to create Cold War thrillers with spies as heroes, such as Ian Fleming's James Bond or Len Deighton's Harry Palmer.

Many British people thought that the Vietnam War was unjust and protested against it on the streets. British governments supported the United States' policy, but – unlike Australia – sent no troops.

BOMBS AND PROTESTS

The chief danger of the Cold War was the rapid increase in the number of nuclear bombs and missiles, just a few of which could destroy the world. Britain held nuclear weapons as a 'deterrent', so that no other country would risk an attack. The United States set up large air and naval bases in the United Kingdom. Many British people protested against nuclear weapons and a Campaign for Nuclear Disarmament (CND) was founded in 1958.

END OF THE COLD WAR

Many Western leaders believed that once one nation had turned Communist, its neighbour would soon follow, one falling after the other like so many dominoes. This did not happen, for the Communist nations were divided amongst themselves. The Soviet Union tried to bring in political reforms in the 1980s, but its economy finally collapsed. By 1991 the old Soviet Union was finished and the Cold War was over.

226

✝ **1952**
The first Top Ten pop music chart is published in Britain

✝ **1955**
Britain's first television commercial

✝ **1958**
First section of motorway opens in England, M6

✝ **1961**
The first contraceptive pills go on sale in Britain

✝ **1962**
First television link across the Atlantic via Telstar satellite

ROCKING AND ROLLING

IN THE second half of the 1950s, the European economy began to recover from the war years. More and more families watched television. Glossy magazine advertisements offered dreams of foreign travel or the ideal home. British car designer Alec Issigonis produced the classic Morris Minor in 1948 and the world famous Mini in 1959, the year in which England's M1 motorway opened. High-rise flats began to tower above Britain's cities in the 1960s.

TEENAGE REBELS

It was in the post-war years that teenagers began to be seen as a separate social group. For the first time they had money and leisure, which they devoted to pop music and outrageous fashion. In the 1950s came American rock'n'roll music, skiffle and modern jazz. Rebels were known as 'teddy boys', 'teddy girls' and 'beatniks'. They were followed in the 1960s by gangs of 'mods' and 'rockers', mini-skirted girls, long-haired 'hippies', and shaven-headed 'skinheads'. English popular music became famous all over the world.

Putting on the style... rock 'n' roll music took over dance halls in the years 1957-1959.

ANGRY YOUNG MEN

At the beginning of the 1950s, many people watched the witty, elegant plays of Noël Coward or read about the English upper classes in the novels of Evelyn Waugh. Then a new generation of writers came on the scene. They wrote about everyday life and despised snobbery. Many were from working class backgrounds. Writers such as John Osborne and Kingsley Amis became known as the 'Angry Young Men'.

✝ **1962**
First Beatles hit single, *Love me Do*

✝ **1965**
Mini-skirts are worn over 15cm above the knee

✝ **1966**
The England football team wins the World Cup

✝ **1968**
First decimal coins introduced into United Kingdom

✝ **1969**
Britain and France fly the supersonic *Concorde* jet airliner

227

CHANGING THE WORLD

To the older generation, it seemed that young people had lost all respect for authority. The old class system was ridiculed. In the 1940s and 50s, politicians had been listened to with deference. In the 1960s they were publicly mocked on satirical television shows such as *That Was The Week That Was*. By the late 1960s many young people were experimenting with drugs or exploring new religions.

A great social upheaval was taking place – but it was hardly a revolution. The working-class pop stars were soon living in splendid mansions, just like the aristocrats had before them. Many young people did turn to revolutionary politics, but capitalist economics remained firmly in place.

The 'punks' of the late 1970s despised the hippies for going soft. Punks listened to loud, discordant music. They pierced their bodies, dyed their hair in bright colours and wore torn clothes and metal chains.

WOMEN'S LIBERATION

By the late 1960s, feminists were calling for changes which went far beyond matters of voting rights and equal pay. They had a new vision of the roles of men and women in society, of how they should relate to each other and how girls and women should be empowered in a society dominated by men.

Four young lads from Liverpool formed a pop group in 1960. Paul McCartney, Ringo Starr, George Harrison and John Lennon made up The Beatles. During the 1960s they became the most successful band the world has ever known.

MODERN ART IN BRITAIN

In the 1950s British artists explored abstract shapes and new media. Sculptors such as Henry Moore and Barbara Hepworth produced rounded, flowing figures and forms with hollows and holes. In the 1960s, 'pop artists' such as painter Peter Blake drew their inspiration from advertising and comic strips, while 'op artist' Bridget Riley played with optical illusions in paintings that seemed to twist and turn before one's eyes. Later artists turned to video, photography and light and sound installations.

Tate Modern, a gallery given over to modern art, was opened on the south bank of the Thames, in London, in 2000. It was built in a former power station.

228

✛ 1945
The founding of the United
Nations (UN) Organization

✛ 1947
Britain hands rule of Palestine
over to UN, Israel is founded

✛ 1949
Britain and Ireland are
founder members of the
Council of Europe

✛ 1956
The Suez Crisis: Britain and
France invade Egypt

✛ 1957
The Treaty of Rome sets up
the European Economic
Community (EEC)

CONFLICT, PEACE AND TRADE

I N 1919 an international body called the League
of Nations was founded, in order to prevent the
outbreak of another world war. It failed
completely, so in 1945 a new organization was set
up, the United Nations (UN). Its aim was to
promote peace, health and human rights as well as
world economic and cultural co-operation.

WORKING FOR WORLD PEACE

The United Kingdom (from 1945) and the Republic of
Ireland (from 1955) played an important part in the
United Nations. Both committed troops to international
peacekeeping operations and to military task forces. The
blue berets of UN soldiers became a familiar sight in
trouble spots around the world.

  Individual citizens also began to play an important part
in tackling the world's problems. Volunteers from Britain
and Ireland were to be seen in some of the world's
poorest countries, teaching, building, distributing food,
caring for the sick.

A British teacher working for
Voluntary Service Overseas
(VSO) talks with pupils in Thailand.

Delegates from all over the world gather to
debate the issues of the day at United
Nations headquarters in New York City, USA.

✝ **1959**
UK is a founder member of the European Free Trade Association (EFTA)

✝ **1973**
UK, Ireland join EEC – known as European Union (EU) from 1993

✝ **1982**
Falklands War: UK recaptures Falkland Islands from Argentina

✝ **1991**
Gulf War: UK joins international force liberating Kuwait from Iraq

✝ **1992**
British troops start a series of actions with international forces in the Balkans (to 2000)

229

Argentineans had always claimed the Falkland or Malvinas Islands as their own. In 1982 they invaded this tiny British colony, which had a population of about 1900. British troops were sent to recapture the islands. The Falklands War cost £700 million and claimed the lives of 254 British troops and 750 Argentineans. It was probably Britain's last colonial war.

NO END TO THE FIGHTING

British troops served in many smaller conflicts after the Second World War. They were in strife-torn Palestine before the creation of the Israeli state in 1948. From 1954 they saw action in Cyprus. In 1956 Britain and France launched an invasion of Egypt, in a bid to stop Egypt nationalizing the Suez Canal. The affair was a disaster, which taught Britain that it could no longer take action without full international backing. In the 1990s Britain joined international forces fighting in the deserts of the Gulf and in the Balkan regions of Bosnia and Kosovo.

THE NEW EUROPE

After the Second World War, many people wanted to safeguard the future peace of Europe. As early as 1946, Sir Winston Churchill was calling for a United States of Europe. In 1949 Britain and Ireland joined the new Council of Europe, and in 1973 both countries finally joined the European Economic Community (EEC) – an economic and political alliance known since 1993 as the European Union (EU).

Many enjoyed the economic benefits of EU membership and the Irish economy was transformed. In Britain, critics nicknamed 'Eurosceptics' complained of bureaucracy and loss of national sovereignty. However supporters ('Europhiles') believed that the union was necessary in a world economy which was no longer based on nation states.

Unlike other international economic unions, the EU has its own directly elected parliament, based in Strasbourg and Luxembourg.

230

✝ 1966
Free Trade Agreement betwen
United Kingdom and Ireland

✝ 1967
Civil Rights Association
founded in Northern Ireland

✝ 1969
British troops sent to
Northern Ireland

✝ 1969
Provisional IRA breaks away
from Official IRA

✝ 1969
Start of terror bombing
campaigns (until 1990s)

İRELAND NORTH AND SOUTH

B Y 1949 most of Ireland was a republic, fully independent from the United Kingdom. However six counties of the northern province of Ulster remained part of the UK. The Irish Republic still claimed those counties, and the Irish Republican Army (IRA) continued its campaign of violence against Britain during the 1950s and 60s.

IN THE REPUBLIC

In the 1950s, Ireland remained a conservative, largely agricultural society. The Roman Catholic Church dominated public and political life. The Irish language, although taught in schools, was no longer widely spoken. The pockets where it survived were called *Gaeltachtaí*.

After the 1960s, the power of the Church began to lessen. Ireland opened up more to the world and tourists poured into the west. After Ireland joined the European Economic Community (EEC) in 1973, its economy began to grow rapidly and new industries were developed, such as computer assembly or food processing.

WORDS AND MUSIC

Great Irish playwrights of the 1950s included Brendan Behan and Samuel Beckett, who wrote bleak plays about the human condition. The 1960s and 70s saw a great revival in traditional Irish music. The sound of the *bodhrán* (hand-drum) and the Uilleann pipes were made popular around the world by groups such as the *Chieftains*. Their success was followed by many folk singers, rock bands and dance groups.

Mary Robinson, born in County Mayo in 1944, became Irish President in 1990. She was a popular head of state who worked hard to bring about peace in the north. She served as UN Human Rights Commissioner (1997-2001).

PRESIDENTS OF THE IRISH REPUBLIC	
✤ Douglas Hyde	1938-1945
✤ Séan O'Ceallaigh	1945-1959
✤ Éamon de Valera	1959-1973
✤ Erskine Childers	1973-1974
✤ Cearbhall ó Dálaigh	1974-1976
✤ Patrick Hillery	1976-1990
✤ Mary Robinson	1990-1997
✤ Mary McAleese	1997-

✠ 1971
Internment without trial in Northern Ireland (to 1980)

✠ 1972
Bloody Sunday: 13 civil rights protestors shot by British troops in Derry

✠ 1972
Northern Ireland under direct rule from London

✠ 1985
Anglo-Irish Agreement, Hillsborough, angers Loyalists

✠ 1998
Good Friday Agreement promises peace for Northern Ireland

231

After 1969, armed British troops became a familiar sight on the streets of Northern Ireland's cities. Between 1969 and 1996, 3,212 soldiers, police and civilians died as a result of the troubles.

PRIME MINISTERS OF THE IRISH REPUBLIC

✢ Éamon de Valera (Fianna Fáil)	1932–1948
✢ John Costello (Fine Gael)	1948–1951
✢ Éamon de Valera (Fianna Fáil)	1951–1954
✢ John Costello (Fine Gael)	1954–1957
✢ Éamon de Valera (Fianna Fáil)	1957–1959
✢ Sean Lemass (Fianna Fáil)	1959–1966
✢ Jack Lynch (Fianna Fáil)	1966–1973
✢ Liam Cosgrave (Fine Gael)	1973–1977
✢ Jack Lynch (Fianna Fáil)	1977–1979
✢ Charles Haughey (Fianna Fáil)	1979–1981
✢ Garret Fitzgerald (Fine Gael)	1981–1982
✢ Charles Haughey (Fianna Fáil)	1982
✢ Garret Fitzgerald (Fine Gael)	1982–1987
✢ Albert Reynolds (Fianna Fáil)	1987–1994
✢ John Bruton (Fine Gael)	1994–1997
✢ Bertie Ahern (Fianna Fáil)	1997–

NEW TROUBLES

A new round of 'troubles' broke out in Northern Ireland in 1969, as the minority supporting the Republic, mostly Catholics, clashed with the Protestant majority who supported the union with Britain. British troops were drafted in and the situation became worse after 'Bloody Sunday' in 1972, when 13 civil rights protestors were shot dead by British troops in Derry. New paramilitary groups were formed on both sides, engaging in murder and terrorist bombing, often in English cities. Direct rule from London was imposed and basic civil rights were suspended.

THE ROAD TO PEACE

In 1998 a peace accord called the Good Friday Agreement was approved by both governments, by all the main factions and political parties. It received the support of the voters, too. The Irish Republic agreed to drop its claim to the six counties of the north. The treaty provided for a return to regional government, the release of prisoners, the handing in of weapons, the scaling down of the military presence and reform of the Royal Ulster Constabulary (RUC). Each one of these presented huge difficulties, but the agreement did offer the first hope of peace in 30 years.

Would the Good Friday Agreement bring peace? A wall painting displays a note of caution.

232

✝ **1964**
Harold Wilson ends 13 years of Conservative government

✝ **1979**
Margaret Thatcher becomes first woman Prime Minister of UK

✝ **1979**
New Conservative government plans large-scale privatization

✝ **1981**
Social Democratic Party (SDP) formed after split with Labour

✝ **1984**
Coal miners strike against pit closures, led by Arthur Scargill

LEFT, RIGHT ⊙ OR CENTRE?

AFTER THE Second World War, the three chief political parties within the United Kingdom were the Conservative Party, the Labour Party and the Liberal Party, although the Liberals never achieved government during this period. It is common to talk about parties as 'right-wing' (following conservative policies) or 'left-wing' (inclined to more liberal or socialist policies). Which course would British politics follow, left or right?

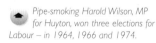
Pipe-smoking Harold Wilson, MP for Huyton, won three elections for Labour – in 1964, 1966 and 1974.

'YOU'VE NEVER HAD IT SO GOOD'

In 1951 Sir Winston Churchill regained power for the Conservative Party. They kept it for 13 years. Sir Anthony Eden lost votes over the Suez Crisis. Harold Macmillan was nicknamed 'Supermac' by the press. His slogan was 'You've Never Had It So Good' – which in economic terms was probably true. Sir Alec Douglas Home, like his predecessors, came from the upper classes and lacked the common touch. By contrast Harold Wilson, who brought Labour back to power in 1964, prided himself on being a man of the people. Between 1951 and 1979 both Labour and Conservative parties moved towards the centre ground, rejecting policies of the far right or left. Edward Heath, the Conservative who took Britain into Europe in 1973, was a centrist, as was Labour leader James Callaghan.

PRIME MINISTERS OF THE UNITED KINGDOM

♣ Clement Attlee (Labour)	1945-1951
♣ Sir Winston Churchill (Conservative)	1951-1955
♣ Sir Anthony Eden (Conservative)	1955-1957
♣ Harold Macmillan (Conservative)	1957-1963
♣ Sir Alec Douglas Home (Conservative)	1963-1964
♣ Harold Wilson (Labour)	1964-1970
♣ Edward Heath (Conservative)	1970-1974
♣ Harold Wilson (Labour)	1974-1976
♣ James Callaghan (Labour)	1976-1979
♣ Margaret Thatcher (Conservative)	1979-1990
♣ John Major (Conservative)	1990-1997
♣ Tony Blair (Labour)	1997-

✝ **1988**
SDP unites with Liberal Party
to form Liberal Democrats

✝ **1989**
'Poll Tax' introduced in
Scotland (England and
Wales 1990)

✝ **1989**
Over three million people
unemployed in the UK

✝ **1989**
Environmentalist Green Party
wins 15 percent of UK vote in
Euro-election

✝ **1997**
John Major's government falls
to Tony Blair

233

THE THATCHER YEARS

During the 1970s, unemployment rose. Both Heath and
Callaghan came under pressure from striking trade unionists.
Conservative Margaret Thatcher who came to power in 1979,
was Britain's first woman Prime Minister. She moved her party
to the right, attacking trade union rights and defeating a
national miners' strike in 1984. Nationalized industries were
now privatized – sold back into private ownership.
Unemployment rose still further, but Thatcher believed that the
forces of the 'free market' would improve society more than
reliance on a welfare state. She was an ardent supporter of the
United States in the Cold War.

BACK TO THE CENTRE

Margaret Thatcher won popular support in three general
elections, but her government ran into economic problems.
Social policies such as a community charge (the 'poll tax') were
widely resisted. Her own party ousted her as leader in 1990. She
was replaced by the more moderate John Major.

Labour had suffered long years of division whilst in
opposition. There had been battles between the left and right
and some members had left to form another party, the Social
Democratic Party (SDP) in 1981. Labour abandoned its socialist
policies and returned to power under Tony Blair in 1997.

The Houses of Parliament were still
organized into two chambers or
Houses. The 1997 Labour government
began to reform the House of Lords. Lords
who had inherited their title through their
families could no longer be members.

The miners' strike of 1984 was long
and bitter. Its effects were felt
throughout Britain. The miners failed to prevent
widespread closures in the coal industry.

234

✝ 1920
The Church of England is
disestablished (no longer
official) in Wales

✝ 1946
Founding of the Edinburgh
International Festival

✝ 1966
Wales elects Gwynfor Evans as
first *Plaid Cymru* MP

✝ 1966
Coal tip collapses over
school, Aberfan, South Wales

✝ 1967
Scotland elects Winifred Ewing
as first SNP MP

WALES, SCOTLAND, ENGLAND

I N THE 1920s and 30s more and
more people in Scotland and Wales
were looking at ways of reforming
or abolishing the union of nations within
the United Kingdom. By the 1960s they
were beginning to make their mark at
general elections. Devolution of power
from the parliament at Westminster
became an important issue. Across
Europe, regional cultures were gaining
more political recognition.

The Welsh Language Society was formed in
1962. The Society often used dramatic methods
of protest to campaign for Welsh language rights in
education, broadcasting and other fields.

A WELSH ASSEMBLY

Wales went through great social
changes in the twentieth
century. The upheaval of the
two world wars disrupted towns
and rural communities. The
coalmining industry of the south
and northeast was closed down
after 1984. The Welsh Nationalist
Party (later, *Plaid Cymru*) was
founded in 1925, and after the 1960s
moved leftwards in its politics. The flooding
of the Tryweryn valley to make a reservoir,
pushed through the Westminster Parliament
against the wishes of Welsh MPs, increased
support for nationalists. The unionist policies
of the Conservative governments in the
1980s and 90s were also opposed by Liberals
and by many Labour supporters. A Welsh
Assembly, based in Cardiff, was voted into
existence in 1997.

THREE POETS

The Scottish poet Hugh MacDiarmid (1892–
1978) was a founder member of the SNP and a
communist. His poems championed the language
of the Scottish Lowlands. The Welsh poet Dylan
Thomas (1914–1953) wrote in English. In the
play *Under Milk Wood* he recreates a day in the
life of a small town in South Wales. English
poet Ted Hughes
(1930–98) was
born in
Yorkshire and
was inspired by
wildlife and the
forces of nature.

◀ Hugh
MacDiarmid

◀ Dylan
Thomas

✝ **1975**
Discovery of oil in North Sea off Scotland, boom for Aberdeen

✝ **1982**
Launch of Welsh-language TV channel, *Sianel Pedwar Cymru*

✝ **1986**
Local government reform in Britain, Greater London Council abolished

✝ **1997**
Scottish Parliament and Welsh Assembly established

✝ **2000**
Ken Livingstone becomes first elected mayor of London

235

A SCOTTISH PARLIAMENT

In Scotland as in Wales there was wide-scale emigration, a decline in heavy industry and a rural population which struggled to make a living. The 1990s saw extensive clearance of poor housing from cities such as Glasgow.

Scotland too was a Labour party stronghold. It was not until the 1960s that the Scottish Nationalist Party (SNP, founded in 1928) began to make inroads. In 1975 oil was discovered off the Scottish coast. Many Scots wanted to control this vital resource themselves, rather than the Westminster Parliament. Scotland already had its own separate legal and education system, and in 1997 it voted in its own Parliament too.

In 1999 Scotland had its own Parliament again for the first time since the reign of Queen Anne. The state opening in Edinburgh was a grand affair.

Independent Ken Livingstone became London's first elected mayor in 2000. He was the former Leader of the Greater London Council, which had been abolished by Margaret Thatcher in 1986.

ENGLISH REGIONS AND CITIES

Where did the devolution of power to Wales and Scotland leave England? Some politicians proposed regional assemblies for England. Regions such as the Northeast or Cornwall certainly saw themselves as culturally different from the Southeast. Some people believed that the real problem was economic, a North-South divide based on prosperity. Some wanted to bring life back to local government, which had become increasingly under the thumb of national government since the 1980s. The 1997 Labour government proposed directly elected mayors for big cities.

236

✝ 1983
Flood barrier completed across
the River Thames, London

✝ 1985
Live Aid concerts for African
famine victims raise £48
million

✝ 1986
Nuclear fallout from
Chernobyl, Ukraine, reaches
British Isles

✝ 1987
Hurricane devastates
southern England, 15 million
trees destroyed

✝ 1992
First Earth Summit held by
UN in Brazil, global
warming treaty

CHILDREN OF
THE MILLENNIUM

WHEN THE first millennium ended in AD 1000, many people in the British Isles thought that the world would come to an end. At the end of the second millennium in 2000 there were still many grave concerns about the future – but also expectations undreamed of by our ancestors.

CHANGING WORK PATTERNS

In the later years of the twentieth century, the way in which people worked changed greatly. By 1996, only 2 percent of the UK labour force worked on the land, and 27 percent in industry. Seventy-one percent now work providing services, such as banking, insurance, education or tourism. Ireland was more agricultural, but still had 62 percent providing services.

GOING GLOBAL

The economy had gone global. Companies were now operating worldwide. They were transnational, no longer tied to the economy of a single nation state. Manufacturing moved to wherever the workforce was cheapest – to Asia, for example, or Central America. Some transnational corporations were richer and more powerful than governments, yet they did not answer directly to the democratic process.

By the year 2000 it was clear that mobile telephones, the internet and television were all linking up. Telecommunications had become a major British industry.

Globalization meant that a factory in the United Kingdom or Ireland might be owned by a firm based in Japan or Korea. Likewise, a British company might own factories in Germany or the United States.

✝ 1994
Completion of the Channel Tunnel, England-France

✝ 1997
Dolly the Sheep, world's first cloned animal, is bred in Scotland

✝ 1997
Death of Princess Diana, popular ex-wife of the Prince of Wales

✝ 1999
Irish Republic adopts common European currency, the Euro

✝ 2000
Millennium celebrations throughout the British Isles

237

LIFE IN THE 1990S

The communications revolution of the 1980s and 90s aided globalization. Computers, smaller and more powerful than ever, were in the home and workplace and linked to a worldwide web.

However people were now realizing that many of the advances in technology since the industrial revolution had been bought at a price. Industrial chemicals and exhaust fumes had poisoned the environment and warmed up the Earth's atmosphere, changing climate patterns. Scientists could now clone animals and change the genes in crops – but what kind of world were they creating? Wonderful new medicines had been invented, but then dreadful new diseases were appearing. Would AIDS devastate the world in the way the Black Death had in the Middle Ages?

NEW DIRECTIONS?

The peoples of the British Isles had clung to their ancient customs and ceremonies through the industrial revolution and a century of wars. Would this change in the new century? Might the United Kingdom even become a republic? One thing was certain. The British Isles might be islands, but they were not isolated. Their future, for better or for worse, would be tied in with that of the whole world.

Transport in Britain had reached a crisis point by 2000. The rail network was failing and the motorways were often jammed with traffic.

This barrier across the River Thames was built in 1983, to protect London against flooding. Global warming would make the climate of the British Isles more stormy, and sea levels would rise again.

SEE FOR YOURSELF

ENGLAND

British Museum
Museum Street, London
A dazzling array of treasures may be seen at the United Kingdom's leading national museum. They include the Roman treasure from Mildenhall, the Saxon helmet from Sutton Hoo and an ornate Celtic shield recovered from the River Thames.

Canterbury Cathedral
Canterbury, Kent
This ancient cathedral, a centre of pilgrimage, includes the the site where Archbishop Thomas Becket was murdered in 1170 and tomb of Edward, the 'Black Prince'.

Fishbourne Roman Palace and Gardens
Salthill Road, Fishbourne, near Chichester, Sussex
Fishbourne started its life as a Roman army base but was soon transformed into a luxurious palace with fine mosaic floors.

Hadrian's Wall
Start exploring the Roman wall from Newcastle upon Tyne or from Carlisle
At Vindolanda you can see Roman jewellery or the armour worn by Roman soldiers as they marched off to war. At the Roman Army Museum you can sign up to join the legions for a taste of army life.

Hampton Court Palace
near Kingston, Surrey
Visit a Tudor palace by the River Thames, with splendid rooms, furnishings and paintings – and a famous maze to get lost in.

HMS Victory
Portsmouth docks, Hampshire
Experience life below decks in England's most famous wooden warship and see where Nelson was fatally wounded at the Battle of Trafalgar, in 1805.

Imperial War Museum
Lambeth, South London
Warfare and weapons since the outbreak of the First World War in 1914 are the chief themes of this museum. It also tells the story of civilians in the war years, of the London Blitz and food rationing.

Jorvik Centre
Coppergate, York
This attraction recreates the sounds, sights – and smells – of York in the time of the Vikings.

Merseyside Maritime Museum
Liverpool
This tells the story of Liverpool's merchant shipping over the last 200 years, with a remarkable collection of model boats and ships.

Museum of London
London Wall, London
A fascinating look at life in London through the ages, with many of the latest archaeological finds on display.

Royal Armouries Museum
The Waterfront, Leeds, Yorkshire
This is the national collection of arms and armour, with exhibitions on warfare, hunting and tournaments. You might even get the chance to fire a crossbow...

Royal Cornwall Museum
River Street, Truro, Cornwall
Bronze Age archaeology is on display here, also minerals from this region with a long history of mining.

Explore history through a single city. Oxford, in England, was a university town in the Middle Ages and an industrial centre in the twentieth century.

Stonehenge
near Amesbury, Wiltshire
These massive pillars of stone, set in a great circle, still tower above the grasslands of Salisbury Plain after 4,000 years of wind and rain.

Tower of London
Tower Hill, London
Started by William the Conqueror, the Tower became a palace and then a dreadful prison for the likes of Sir Thomas More, Anne Boleyn and Lady Jane Grey.

Victoria and Albert Museum
Cromwell Road, South Kensington, London
A museum of decorative arts and crafts through the ages, with a spectacular collection of historical costumes and dresses.

Warwick Castle
Warwickshire
This impressive medieval castle houses a collection of armour, weapons and works of art.

WALES

The Big Pit
Blaenafon, Torfaen, Gwent
Descend 90 metres to the coalface and see what it was like to work underground. The days when coal was king have ended in South Wales, but are movingly recalled at this museum of mining.

Caernarfon Castle and fort
Caernarfon, Gwynedd
Caernarfon, in northwest Wales, was chosen by invaders as a site from which to control North Wales. The Romans built the fort of Segontium here, and a massive castle, started in 1283, was part of King Edward I's conquest. Both can be visited today.

England likes to preserve many of its historical ceremonies, such as the Changing of the Guard at royal palaces.

National Library of Wales
Aberystwyth, Ceredigion
The library stages public exhibitions of historical documents, paintings and photographs.

National Museum of Wales
Central Cardiff
Here you can see gold from the Bronze Age and Celtic iron-work, as well as stone crosses and monuments from the early days of Christianity in Wales.

St Fagans
Glamorgan
This open-air folk museum shows rural life in Wales from the days of the ancient Celts to the Victorian era. Old farmhouses, chapels, schoolhouses and cottages have been reassembled. You can see bread being baked and blacksmiths hammering iron.

Slate Museum
Llanberis, Gwynedd
This museum is located in the old slate-cutting sheds below the Dinorwig quarry in North Wales. It includes the mighty water wheel which once powered the whole works and the foundry where parts were made for machinery and drains.

Valle Crucis Abbey was founded in 1âl, mid-Wales, by Madog ap Gruffudd, Prince of Powys. It dates back to 1201.

Welsh Highland Railway
Porthmadog, Gwynedd
One of several narrow-gauge tracks through the mountains of Snowdonia, which recall the days of steam railways.

A visitor discovers North Wales industrial past at a Power of Wales exhibition in Llanberis, Gwynedd.

SCOTLAND

Discovery Point
Dundee, Tayside
Visit RRS (Royal Research Ship) *Discovery*, which took explorer Robert Falcon Scott to Antarctica in 1901-04. Visit also the working jute mill at Verdant Works, a museum of the jute industry which brought wealth to Dundee.

Edinburgh Castle
Castle Hill, Edinburgh
On its rock high above the Scottish capital, the castle houses the Scottish crown jewels and the Stone of Destiny. A gun is fired daily from the castle, at 1pm.

Falkland Palace
Falkland, Fife
This impressive royal palace of the Stewarts was built between 1501 and 1541. It contains rich tapestries and a royal tennis court dating from 1539.

Hill House
Upper Colquhoun Street, Helensburgh
This elegant home dates from 1905. It was designed by Scotland's most famous architect, Charles Rennie Mackintosh.

Melrose Abbey
Roxburghshire
Founded in AD 660, this religious foundation was relocated to it present site in 1131-46. It was attacked and burned by King Richard II of England. Look for the fine gargoyles (decorated gutter ends to be seen on medieval cathedrals).

New Lanark Mills
Clyde valley, Lanarkshire
This village was rebuilt during the Industrial Revolution by idealistic social reformer Robert Owen. It housed workers in the cotton mills which Owen purchased in 1799 and has been restored to its original condition.

Scottish Fisheries Museum
Anstruther, Fife
This small museum tells the fascinating story of Scotland's fisheries, from the earliest times to the present day.

Stirling Castle
Forth valley, Stirlingshire
Commanding routes to north, south, east and west, Stirling castle was the scene of many sieges and dire murders. Visit the medieval Great Hall and the later palace apartments and Chapel Royal.

Weaver's Cottage
Shuttle Street, The Cross, Kilbarchan near Glasgow
This small weaver's house was once part of a thriving cottage industry in the area. Today it houses the last working loom and an exhibition of weaving equipment.

CHANNEL ISLANDS

Cornet Castle
Guernsey
This harbour fortress contains displays about the castle's history, about a Roman shipwreck discovered offshore and about the local militia.

La Hougue Bie
Grouville, Jersey
Visit a massive burial mound dating back to 3800 BC, as well as a Neolithic passage grave and medieval chapels.

ISLE OF MAN

Laxey Wheel
Laxey
The largest waterwheel in the British Isles is the Lady Isabella wheel, which may be seen at Laxey. It has a circumference of 69.5 metres and was built in 1854, when this valley was a centre of lead mining.

A visit to the Highland Games provides another insight into Scotland's history and culture.

Stone is a rich source of study for archaeologists and historians, because it survives when wood or cloth rots away.

NORTHERN IRELAND

Ulster Folk and Transport Museum
Holywood, County Armagh
Historical buildings including churches, factories and farms complete with livestock have been reassembled here, along with exhibitions of historical vehicles.

Ulster Museum
Botanic Gardens, Belfast
This collection includes everything from dinosaurs to early Irish jewellery, from waterwheels to steam engines.

REPUBLIC OF IRELAND

Glendalough
County Wicklow
Founded by St Kevin over 1,400 years ago, this historical religious site includes a famous round tower, set amidst forests, lakes and hills.

Irish National Heritage Centre
Ferrycarrig, County Wexford
Beside the River Slaney, make a tour of Irish history, taking in Stone Age hunters, Celts, Vikings and Normans.

King John's Castle
Limerick, County Limerick
Five stone towers and high walls rise from the banks of the River Shannon. This castle was built in 1200, shortly after the Norman invasion.

National Museum of Ireland
Dublin
This is the place to see the products of Celtic art's golden age. They include the Tara brooch, the Ardagh chalice and the Cross of Cong. Another section covers the history of the period 1916-1921.

Newgrange
Slane, near Drogheda, County Meath
Travel back in time over 5,000 years to see one of the world's most imposing Stone Age burial chambers, and its neighbours in the Boyne valley.

Old Library, Trinity College
Dublin
The tall, book-lined shelves are impressive enough in themselves, but the real treasure on display here is the masterpiece of early Christian art and design, the *Book of Kells*.

SEARCH FOR YOURSELF

www.angelfire.com/folk/jacobites2
History through song – learn the words of songs associated with the Jacobites and the rebellion of 1745.

www.archaeology.co.uk
This is the website for *Current Archaeology* magazine. It includes information on the latest digs and finds, archaeological cyber-tours, timelines and education.

www.bbc.co.uk/history
A gateway to a wide range of historical topics, events and people, the best starting point for your queries about British history.

www.blackpresence.co.uk
This website includes links to articles about the history of Black people in the United Kingdom.

www.britannia.com/celtic/scotland/history
A brief history of Scotland, with links to related websites.

www.britannia.com/celtic/wales
A brief history of Wales, with links to related websites.

www.castlesontheweb.com/glossary
If you are fascinated by castles, you need to know your battlements from your belvederes. This glossary lists all the correct terms for castles and their architecture.

www.castlewales.com
List of important medieval sites in Wales, with maps, photographs and all kinds of interesting information.

www.discovery.com/stories/history/blackdeath
See how the Black Death swept across the medieval world, trace its route and hear the words of people from plague-stricken communiites.

englishhistory.net/tudor/relative/maryquos
This tells the life story of Mary, Queen of Scots and tells of her execution.

www.esg.ndirect.co.uk
The Ermine Street Guard researches and stages battles of Roman Britain. The site contains all sorts of useful information and photographs.

www.fortunecity.com/bally/kilkenny
A history of Ireland in maps.

www.hinchbk.cambs.sch.uk/original/pepys
This site has been put together by a school class interested in the diarist Samuel Pepys. It tells the story of his life, offers links to his diaries with reports of the Great Plague and the Fire of London.

www.historyplace.com/worldwar2/
timeline/london-blitz
Photographs of London taken during the bombing of the Second World War – the so-called 'Blitz'.

Electronic mail and the internet can help people all over the world find out more about British and Irish history.

An internet search engine will connect you to many websites or pages about the Rock of Cashel, one of the most spectacular historical sites in Ireland. Some of the websites may be very useful, but some may be irrelevant or innacurate. Try www. historic.irishcastles.com/ rockofcashel.htm for views of the site, a brief history and a video.

www.museumofcostume.co.uk
If you are interested in costume through the ages, check out this website of the Museum of Costume, Bath, England.

www.royal.gov.uk
Have you ever wondered what Queen Victoria wrote in her diary? This official website offers a history of Britain's monarchs, their family trees, their palaces and royal traditions.

www.sealedknot.org
The Sealed Knot organization researches the Civil War and stages reconstructions of battles around Britain. The website includes details of regiments, pictures and other Civil War information.

www.spartacus.schoolnet.co.uk
An online encyclopedia of historical subjects from Alfred of Wessex to farming in the Middle Ages.

tbls.hypermart.net/ history/1588armada
This website tells the story of the Spanish Armada, life on board ship, invasion plans and ways of fighting at sea.

www.thinkquest.libraryorg
Welcome to 'Shakey's Place in 3D' – that is, the Globe Theatre. This hi-tech interactive site introduces you to Shakespeare's theatre, his life and works.

www.iqc.org/ddickerson/ cliffords-tower
This website tells the shocking story of anti-Jewish prejudice in medieval England, with an account of the massacre and suicide of Jews in York in 1190.

www.industrial-archaeology.org.uk
Check the official website of the Association for Industrial Archaeology for links dealing with the history of Britain's industries.

www.isle-of-man.com/ information/history
The history of the Isle of Man

www.morgue.demon.co.uk/ britannia
Britannia offers detailed information on Britain and the Roman legions, with ancient sites, maps, reconstructions and photographs.

www.tower-of-london.com
Take a virtual journey around the Tower of London, discovering all about the English Crown Jewels, the Yeoman Warders and the Tower's ravens.

www.tudorhistory.org
This website, assembled by a private enthusiast, offers all kinds of information about the Tudor kings and queens.

WORDS WE USE

abbey
A religious site such as a Roman Catholic monastery or convent, whose head is called an abbot or abbess.

abdicate
To resign as king or queen, giving up the throne.

AD
Anno Domini, Latin for 'in the year of Our Lord'. The calendar used in the British Isles today is centred on the birth date of Jesus Christ, although the date chosen is probably inaccurate. Non-Christians may prefer to use the term CE (Current Era)

Anglo-Saxon
1 A member of the various Germanic peoples that conquered England after the fall of the Roman Empire.
2 The language that eventually developed into English.

apprentice
A young person who is taken on to learn a trade.

archery
Shooting with bows and arrows, or crossbows and bolts.

aristocrat
Someone belonging to a powerful upper class or nobility.

armada
A fleet of warships, especially that sent by Spain to invade England in 1588.

asylum
Refuge, or a place where refuge can be found.

auxiliary
A member of a military unit which offers assistance to the main force.

In the Roman army, for example, cavalry units or foreign troops conscripted in the empire could both be described as auxiliaries.

BC
Before Christ. The calendar used in the Britsh Isles today is centred on the birth date of Jesus Christ, although the date chosen is probably inaccurate. Non-Christians may prefer to use the term BCE (Before Current Era).

Briton
1 A member of the Celtic people inhabiting Great Britain during the Iron Age.
2 Anyone living in Great Britain today.

broch
A type of round, fortified tower built by the ancient Picts in northern Scotland.

burgess
In early meetings of the British parliament, the burgess was a leading citizen chosen to represent a borough, a town or a university.

c
Short for the Latin *circa*, meaning 'about'. So *c*1100 means 'in about 1100'.

capitalist
1 A private individual or business person who profits from the interest made on the capital, or wealth, that they hold.
2 Someone who supports an economic system based on capital and profit.

cartographer
Someone who designs and draws maps.

cathedral
Within the Roman Catholic or the

printing press c1490

Anglican Church, the chief building within a diocese, or district governed by a bishop.

Celt
1 Any of the peoples of Iron Age Europe who spoke a Celtic language, or followed the Celtic way of life. They included Iberian Celts, Galatians, Gauls, Gaels and Britons.
2 Any of the peoples descended from the ancient Celts, such as the Bretons, Cornish, Welsh, Irish, Manx or Scots.

century
A period of 100 years. Because the first century lasted from AD1-100, the 100s are called the second century, the 1700s are called the eighteenth century, the 1900s are called the twentieth century and so on.

chivalry
A code of honour which developed amongst European knights in the later Middle Ages. Knights were expected to to treat their enemies with mercy and respect women. The ideals were written about more often than put into practice.

civil war
A war fought between rival factions within the same nation. Examples include the Wars of the Roses (1455-1485) and the wars between Parliamentarians and Royalists (1642-52).

civilian
Someone who is not a member of the armed forces, an ordinary citizen.

clan
A group of families or households claiming descent from a common ancestor, an important social unit in the Gaelic culture.

colony
1 A group of people who have settled overseas, or the place where they have settled.
2 A country ruled by another nation.

Commonwealth
1 The government of England and Wales during the period of rule by Parliament, from 1649 until the declaration of the Protectorate in 1653.
2 A federation of states or provinces, as the Commonwealth of Australia.
3 The Commonwealth of Nations, an international forum, most of whose members were formerly part of the British empire.

communism
1 A social theory or system, by which all property is commonly owned by the community or the state.
2 A social system in which economic activity is controlled or directed by a state which represents workers through the communist party.

conscription
The calling up of civilians to serve in the armed forces.

conservative
Tending to preserve the existing state of affairs, cautious, traditional.

Conservative
A member of the party formerly known as Tories, supporting capitalism, free trade and minimal state control.

Covenanter
A supporter of various documents drawn up by the Presbyterians in Scotland, such as the National Covenant of 1638 or the Solemn League and Covenant of 1643.

crannog
A type of settlement built by the Gaels, based on an artificial island in a lake in order to prevent attack.

Crusade
One of the holy wars approved by the Pope in the Middle Ages. In many of these, Christian armies attacked Moslems in the Near East. The Islamic word for a holy war is Jihad.

Danelaw
1 The laws enforced by the Vikings or Northmen in the part of England they occupied in the ninth century.
2 The lands ruledby these invaders.

democracy
This Greek word means 'rule by the people' and has been taken to mean many different things. It is normally used to describe a social system in which power lies with the people, through an assembly or parliament with elected representatives.

devolution
The passing of power from central government to regional assemblies or parliaments.

diplomat
An official who represents the interests of his or her country to another nation. Diplomatic behaviour means action which does not offend or aggravate.

dun
A citadel or fortified settlement of the Celtic Iron Age. The word appears in many place names, such as Dunfermline.

economy
The way in which resources, labour, industries and money are organized within society.

eisteddfod
1 One of the gatherings of Welsh poets held in the Middle Ages, to consider the forms of verse that they used.
2 Since the 1800s, a local, national or international competition in poetry, music and the arts held in Wales.

emigrate
To leave one's country to make a home overseas.

empire
1 A large number of lands or peoples ruled over by a single government or monarch.
2 A nation in which the monarch is titled emperor or empress.

evict
To force someone to leave their home.

fascism
A political system in which central government holds complete power over its citizens and operates strict social controls. Fascists are extremely nationalistic, anti-communist and anti-democratic.

feminism
The belief that women should be empowered within society, politically and socially.

feud
A long-standing and bitter quarrel between individuals, families or clans, where one side swears to take revenge on the other.

flying boat 1938

feudal system
An economic and political system in which land is held in return for services, guaranteed by oaths of loyalty. The feudal system operated in Europe during the Middle Ages.

Gael
A member of the people occupying Ireland during the Celtic Iron Age, or their descendants, who include the Scots of the Highlands and islands.

galleon
A large wooden sailing vessel of the sixteenth century, first developed by the Spanish.

galley
A large wooden sailing vessel which uses oars as well as sails.

general election
An election for national government, as opposed to local or regional government.

global warming
The raising of temperature in the gases that surround the Earth, as has happened in recent years as a result of air pollution by humans.

antiseptic spray 1867

globalization
The move away from national economies to a single world economy, in which businesses operate in many different countries using modern telecommunications.

guild
One of the associations formed in the Middle Ages to protect and regulate crafts and trades.

heir
Someone designated to inherit a property or title from another. For example, during the reign of George VI, his eldest daughter Princess Elizabeth was heir to the throne.

henges
Circle of large pillars, made from stone or wood, erected in the British Isles between 5,500 and 4,000 years ago, as ritual sites.

heraldry
A system of coloured patterns and emblems first used to identify noble families in the Middle Ages.

independent
Of a nation, recognized as not beng ruled by any other.

inherit
To receive property or a title as the heir of the previous owner.

Jacobite
A supporter of King James VII of Scotland, II of England, after he lost the throne in 1688 – or of his descendants such as the Old Pretender and the Young Pretender.

jingoist
A nationalist who is keen for his or her country to go to war. The term dates from the 1870s, when a popular pro-British song included the words 'by jingo!'.

jury
A group of citizens sworn in to consider a case before a law court and to give a verdict of guilt or innocence.

knight
1 A horse soldier of the Middle Ages, who gained high social status.
2 A rank in the system of nobility in the British Isles, with the title 'Sir'.

labour
1 The act of working for a wage.
2 The workforce itself.

Labour
The name of a political party formed by various trade unions and political groups in 1900. At that time its policies included representing the interests of the working class, nationalization and the provision of social welfare.

legion
The major unit within the Roman army, numbering (at various periods in Roman history) anything from 3,000 to 6,000 troops.

liberal
1 Progressive, sympathetic to reform.
2 Reluctant to interfere with the activities or rights of the individual.

Liberal
The name of a political party which, in the nineteenth century developed from that of the Whigs. It supported democratic reform.

mail
A type of armour made from closely interlinking rings of iron.

medieval
Dating from, or to do with, the Middle Ages.

megalith
Any giant stone, like those used in the construction of Neolithic and Bronze Age monuments, such as burial chambers and henges.

mercenary
Somone who hires out his services as a soldier for a fee.

Mesolithic
The middle period of the Stone Age, following the Palaeolithic or Old Stone Age. It started in about 8500BC and was marked by a warming of the climate and new hunting technology.

Middle Ages
The thousand year period that
followed the fall of the Roman
empire in western Europe, in AD
476. The first half (known as the
Early Middle or 'Dark' Ages) were
marked by invasions and the spread
of Christianity. The second half was
the age of knights and castles.

millennium
A period of 1,000 years. We have
just entered the third millennium
AD.

missionary
Someone who is sent to teach their
religion to others or to work
helping people of a different faith.

mosaic
A picture, on a floor, wall or
ceiling, made up of many small
fragments of coloured stone, glass or
pottery.

musket
A long-barrelled firearm, used from
the sixteenth century onwards. It
was the ancestor of the modern
rifle.

mutiny
A revolt by sailors or soldiers
against their officers, a refusal to
obey orders.

nationalization
Bringing privately owned industries
under state control.

nationalism
1 A belief that one's country should
  be united, self-governing or
  independent.
2 A belief in the superiority of
  one's own nation.

nemeton
A sacred enclosure or sanctuary
used for religious rituals by the
ancient Celts.

Neolithic
Belonging to the New Stone Age,
when farming first came to Europe.

In the British Isles, this period
begins in about 4500BC.

neutral
Taking neither side in a conflict or
war.

nomadic
Moving from one place to another,
rather than living in a permanent
settlement.

non-conformist
Not conforming to the forms of
worship ordered by the official or
established Christian Church.
Baptists and Methodists were nonconformists, because they did not
accept the teachings of the Church
of England.

Pale
An area of eastern Ireland
surrounding Dublin, where English
rule was enforced from the reign of
Henry II onwards.

paramilitary
Unofficial or private armies, such as
those formed by republican and
unionist terrorists in Northern
Ireland during the 1970s.

parliament
The word parliament means
'speaking place' and is the law-
making assembly of a country. The
Parliament at Westminster began as
a meeting place for the Church, the
nobility and the common people. It
gradually developed into a
democratic institution.

partition
The division of a country into
separate nations. Both Ireland and
India were partitioned under
British rule.

Pict
One of the ancient peoples of
Scotland. Their origins are uncertain,
but they may have been a pre-Celtic
group which adopted the Celtic way
of life. Their name comes from the
Latin for 'painted people'.

seed drill 1701

pilgrimage
A journey to a religious site or
shrine as an act of faith.

plague
Any very infectious or deadly
disease, such as the Black Death of
the Middle Ages or the Great
Plague of 1664-65.

plantation
1 The enforced settlement of
  Ireland by Protestants from
  Scotland or England, and the
  creation of fortified colonies.
2 An estate given over to the
  cultivation of sugar cane, cotton
  or other crops. During the British
  colonization of the Caribbean
  region, these were worked by
  slave labour.

politics
The way in which society is
organized and governed, or methods
by which it may be changed.

poll tax
A tax which applies alike to all
citizens, regardless of their income
or status. They therefore place a
greater burden on poor people than
on the rich. Poll taxes caused the
Peasants' Revolt in southern
England in 1381, and riots when
they were reintroduced to the
United Kingdom in the 1980s.

Pope
The leader of the Roman Catholic
Church. Popes were normally based
in Rome, but from 1309-77 there
were rival popes based at Avignon,
in southern France.

press gang
A group of sailors sent out to force young men to join the Royal Navy. They would often beat them up and then carry them on board ship before it sailed.

pretender
A claimant, especially to the the throne. It refers most famously to two Jacobites, James Edward Stuart (the 'Old Pretender') who rebelled in 1715, and Charles Edward Stuart (the 'Young Pretender') who rebelled in 1745. Other pretenders to the English throne included impostors called Lambert Simnel (1487) and Perkin Warbeck (1497).

privatization
The selling off of state-owned industries to private companies.

prospector
Someone who searches for deposits of minerals which are worth mining.

Protestant
Someone who rejects Roman Catholic forms of worship, following instead the simpler forms taught by Martin Luther, John Calvin or John Knox.

public schools
Despite the name, these are private, fee-paying schools. Many of them grew out of the old grammar schools founded in Tudor England. In Victorian times they aimed to educate boys to go on to run the British empire.

Puritan
An extreme Protestant, who rejected the forms of worship laid out by the Church of England.

racism
The belief that human beings can be classified in groups called 'races', and that some races are superior to others.

radical
1 Going to the root of things, basic.
2 Calling for thorough or extreme political reform.

ragged schools
Schools set up by volunteers in the Victorian period to educate the poorest children in society, many of them employed as child labour.

ransom
A fee paid for the return of a prisoner, goods or land captured by the enemy. Ransoms often were paid to liberate captured knights after battles in the Middle Ages.

rath
A royal citadel or enclosure, or a chieftain's hillfort, amongst the Gaels.

rationing
To share out limited supplies of food or other items, with a fixed allowance for each citizen. Official rationing was brought in during the hardships of the Second World War.

Reformation
The movement that spread across northern Europe in the 1500s, calling for radical reforms to the Roman Catholic Church.

regent
Someone who rules on behalf of a king or queen. This might be because the ruler is still a child, or because he or she is suffering from mental or physical illness and cannot perform the full duties of a monarch.

Renaissance
The great rebirth of learning, arts and science that swept across southern Europe in the late 1400s and 1500s.

republic
A state or nation that is not ruled by a monarch, but by public representation.

Restoration
The return to power of the Stuart monarchs after the period of the Commonwealth and the Protectorate.

Roman Catholic
Catholic means 'universal' and the Church based in Rome claimed to be the only true representative of the Christian faith in the world. Although Henry VIII broke with Rome, he was not a true Protestant and the English Church still claimed to be 'catholic'.

satirical
Mocking, making fun of social or political vices or follies.

scabbard
A protective casing for a sword blade, a sheath.

seal
An emblem pressed in wax, attached to an official document to show that it is genuine.

segregate
To keep apart. Black and white citizens were officially segregated in South Africa from 1948 until 1991. This policy was called *apartheid*.

sepoy
An Indian soldier in the service of the British East India Company, between 1600 and 1874.

serf
Someone who had to work the land for his lord, and was not allowed to move or seek employment elsewhere. He could be bought or sold along with the land on which he worked.

shares
The capital or wealth of a company may be divided into parts called shares and sold to the public. If the company prospers, they share in its profits. If it fails, they lose their investment.

skirmish
A fight between small groups of soldiers, aside from the main action between two armies.

slum
A run-down, poverty-stricken building or district of a town.

smelt
To heat ore (mineral-bearing rock) so that metal can be melted down and extracted.

socialism
A political theory or system based on social justice and the public ownership of resources and manufacture.

sovereignty
The power to rule or govern. For example, people might ask to what extent joining an international alliance affects the sovereignty of each member state.

standard
A flag, pole or emblem used as a rallying point in battle, or to indicate the presence of a monarch.

stage coach
A horse-drawn passenger coach which travelled across the country using relays of horses stabled at inns on the route. Some stage coaches were later used to carry mail.

statute
A law that is passed and written out in an official document.

strike
The withdrawal of labour by a workforce as an act of protest against wages or conditions.

suburb
Areas surrounding cities. The growth of railways in the late 1800s and early 1900s meant that many people could now live away from the city centres but travel in to work there each day.

suffrage
The right to vote in elections. Women demanding this right were known as suffragettes.

synod
An assembly called by a Church to discuss religious affairs.

taxation
A demand for money imposed on citizens by governments, in order to pay for defence, public services and so on. It may be charged on income, property or goods purchased.

tenant
Someone who rents buildings or land from a landlord.

tithe
'Tithe' means one-tenth, the traditional proportion of produce or income demanded as a tax by the Church. The term later came to mean any tax imposed by the established Church.

trade union
An association of workers formed to protect their rights and further their interests.

treason
A crime carried out against the monarch or the state. Examples would include assassination of the king, blowing up parliament or spying for an enemy.

trench
A ditch cut in the ground to shelter troops from enemy fire. During the First World War, a great network of trenches was dug by both armies along the Western Front.

Tory
1 In seventeenth century Ireland, a dispossessed Royalist who became an outlaw.
2 A nickname given to those in England who supported the Roman Catholic James, Duke of York, succeeding to the throne in 1681.
3 A member of one of Britain's first great political parties, in the 1700s.
4 A nickname for a Conservative, still in use today.

tournament
A festival of mock battles and feats of arms, held in medieval Europe.

unemployment
Being out of work, having no job.

Unionist
1 Supporting the Union of England, Scotland, Wales and Northern Ireland in a single nation.
2 Someone belonging to a political party opposed to a united Ireland.

vaccination
The prevention of disease by introducing a milder form of the virus into the human body, which then builds up resistance against it.

Viking
A raider, trader or settler from Denmark, Norway or Sweden, after the end of the eighth century. Vikings attacked many parts of Europe.

villein
A person within the feudal system of the Middle Ages who was bound to serve his master like a serf, but who enjoyed some of the rights of a free man.

welfare state
A state which aims to care for its citizen's welfare by providing old age pensions, health care, disablement allowances, unemployment pay and other benefits.

Whig
1 In seventeenth century Scotland, a supporter of the Presbyterians.
2 Someone opposed to the Roman Catholic James, Duke of York, succeeding to the throne in 1681.
3 A member of one of Britain's first great political parties, in the 1700s. It later became the Liberal Party.

Witan
The *Witan* or *Witenagemot* was a national council made up of Anglo-Saxon nobles.

INDEX

Look up subjects to be found in this book.
Illustrations are shown in *italic* print.

ACKNOWLEDGEMENTS

The publishers would like to thank the following sources for the use of their photographs:
Page 7 (B/R) Eyewire; 16 (B/C) Adam Woolfitt/Corbis; 18 (B/C) Mick Sharp Photography; 25 (B/L) Courtesy Vale of White Horse District Council; 30 (B/L) British Museum;38 (B/L) Courtesy Fishbourne Roman Palace; 50 (B/L) Mick Sharp Photography; 54 (B/C) Robert Estall/Corbis; 55 (B/C) Jean Williamson/Mick Sharp Photography; 57 (B/C) Ted Spiegel/Corbis; 59 (B/R) Werner Forman/Corbis; 71 (B/R) Pawel Libera/Corbis; 86 (T/R) Archivo Iconografico/Corbis; 88 (B/C) Adam Woolfitt/Corbis; 94 (T/L) Courtesy Lincolnshire County Council; 95 (T/R) Private Collection/Bridgeman Art Library; 97 (B/L) Bettmann/Corbis; 100 (T/R) Dean Conger/Corbis;107 (T/R) Edifice/Corbis; 108 (B/C) Eye Ubiquitous/Corbis; 109 (T/L) Historical Picture Archive/Corbis, (B/L) Michael Nicholson/Corbis; 111 (B/R) Michael Nicholson/Corbis; 112 (T/L) Robert Williams(Magma), (B/R) Robert Williams(Magma); 113 (T/C) Robert Williams(Magma); 114 (B/R) Adam Woolfitt/Corbis; 115 (B/C) Bettmann/Corbis; 116 (T/R) National Portrait Gallery, London, UK/Bridgeman Art Library, (B/L) Corbis; 117 (B/R) The Art Archive; 119 (B/C) Buddy Mays/Corbis; 125 (B/L) Mary Evans Picture Library; 128 (B/R) Bettmann/Corbis; 131 (B/C) Kit Houghton Photography/Corbis; 137 (T/L) The Royal Collection 2000 Her Majesty Queen Elizabeth 11; 137 (B/C) Historical Picture Archive/Corbis;139 (B/R) Scheufler Collection/Corbis;143 (T/L) AFP/Corbis; 147 (C/R) Bob Krist/Corbis, (B) Phillips, The International Fine Art Auctioneers/Private Collection/Bridgeman Art Library; 151 (T/R) Private Collection/Bridgeman Art Library; (B/R) Archivo Iconografico/Corbis; 152 (B/L) Philip Mould Historical Portraits Ltd. London/Private Collection/Bridgeman Art Library; 154 (B/L) McMaster University Library, Ontario; 157 (T/R) Bettmann/Corbis; 158 (B/L) Bob Krist/Corbis; 160 (T/R) Historical Picture Archive/Corbis; 164 (C/R) Bettmann/Corbis; 165 (B/L) Mary Evans Picture Library, (T/R) Corbis; 167 (C/R) Ferens Art Gallery, Hull City Museums and Art Galleries, UK Bridgeman Art Library, (B/C) Archivo Iconografico/Corbis; 171 (T/R) Hulton-Deutsch Collection/Corbis, (C/L) Hulton-Deutsch Collection/Corbis; 172 (T/C) Historical Picture Archive/Corbis; 173 (T/L) Philip Steele; 174 (T/R) Mary Evans Picture Library; 177 (C/L) Topham Picturepoint, (B/L) Mary Evans Picture Library, (T/R) Private Collection/Bridgeman Art Library; 179 (B/C) Camera Press; 180 (C/R) Mary Evans Picture Library, (B/R) Topham Picturepoint; 181 (T/R) Topham Picturepoint, (C/L) Topham Picturepoint;183 (B/R) The Art Archive/Eileen Tweedy; 185 (C/R) Topham Picturepoint; 186 (T/R) Brace Private Collection; 187 (T/L) Topham Picturepoint, (B/L) Hulton-Deutsch Collection/Corbis; 189 (B/L) Mary Evans Picture Library; 192 (C/L) Topham Picturepoint; 195 (C/L) Museum of Mankind, London, UK/Bridgeman Art Library; 197 (B/L) Barnabas Bosshart/Corbis; 201 (T/R) Topham Picturepoint; 202 (T/L) Mary Evans Picture Library, (C) Courtesy Castrol, (B/R) Camera Press Ltd; 203 (T/L) Topham Picturepoint, (B/C) Courtesy Castrol; 204 (B/L) Bettmann/Corbis; 206 (B) Hulton-Deutsch Collection/Corbis; 207 (C/L) Crawford Municipal Art Gallery, Cork, Ireland/Bridgeman Art Library, (T/R) Hulton-Deutsch Collection/Corbis; 208 (B/R) Hulton-Deutsch Collection/Corbis; 209 (C/R) & (B/L) Hulton-Deutsch Collection/Corbis; 210 (C) Bettmann/Corbis, (R) Topham Picturepoint; 211 (B/L) Bettmann/Corbis, (T/R) Courtesy John D.Jenkins; 212 (B) Hulton-Deutsch Collection/Corbis, (T/R) Ken Lambert/Camera Press, London; 214 (B/R) Michael Nicholson/Corbis; 215 (T/R) Bettmann/Corbis;217 (B) Topham Picturepoint; 218 (B/L) Topham Picturepoint, (C/R) Hulton-Deutsch Collection/Corbis; 219 (T/L) & (C/R) Hulton-Deutsch Collection/Corbis; 220 (B/L) Bettmann/Corbis; 221 (B/L) David Beal/Camera Press, (T/R) Topham Picturepoint, (C) Ray Green/Camera Press; 222 (B/R) Topham Picturepoint; 223 (T/R) Topham Picturepoint, (B) Michael Nicholson/Corbis; 224 (C/R) Topham Picturepoint; 225 (C/L) Topham Picturepoint, (T/R) Kobal Collection/Paramount ; 226 (T/R) Bettmann/Corbis, (B/R) Corbis; 227 (T/R) Topham Picturepoint, (B/R) Pawel Libera/Corbis; 228 (T/L) Courtesy VSO/Liba Taylor; 229 (C) Topham Picturepoint; 230 (B/R) Reuters Newmedia Inc./Corbis; 231 (T/L) & (B/R) Press Association/Topham; 232 (B/L) Topham Picturepoint; 233 (B) Chris Nevard/Camera Press; 234 (T/R) Jeff Morgan/Photolibrary, Wales, (C) & (B/R) Hulton-Deutsch Collection/Corbis; 235 (B/L) Press Association/Topham, (C/R) Press Association/Topham, 236 (B/C) Courtesy Nissan Motor Manufacturing (UK) Ltd. (T/R) Courtesy Red Consultancy.

All other images from MKP archives.

The publishers would like to thank the following artists whose work appears in this book:
Julie Banyard; Mike Bell/Specs Art; Richard Berridge/Specs Art;Vanessa Card; Peter Dennis/Linda Rogers Associates; Nicholas Forder; Terry Gabbey /AFA; Studio Galante; Peter Gregory; Alan Hancocks; Ron Hayward; Sally Holmes; Richard Hook/Linden Artists; John James/Temple Rogers; Stewart Johnson; Andy Lloyd Jones/Allied Artists; Kevin Maddison; Janos Marffy; Terry Riley; Pete Roberts/Allied Artists; Martin Sanders; Peter Sarson; Rob Sheffield; Guy Smith/Mainline; Graham Sumner/Specs Art; Rudi Vizi; Mike White/Temple Rogers.

Maps created by John Christopher/White Design and Martin Sanders.